Sustainability Management for Industries

Herausgegeben von

Univ.-Prof. Dipl.-Ing. Dr. mont. Wolfgang Posch
Univ.-Prof. Dipl.-Ing. Dr. techn. Stefan Vorbach
Univ.-Prof. Dr. Helmut Zsifkovits
Dr. Gerald Feichtinger

Band 11

Wolfgang Posch | Stefan Vorbach
Helmut Zsifkovits | Gerald Feichtinger [Hrsg.]

Nachhaltige Transformation in Krisenzeiten

Nomos

Gefördert durch

Bundesministerium
Innovation, Mobilität
und Infrastruktur

klima energie fonds+

Mit Unterstützung der Stadt
Leoben

Die Deutsche Nationalbibliothek verzeichnet diese Publikation in der Deutschen Nationalbibliografie; detaillierte bibliografische Daten sind im Internet über http://dnb.d-nb.de abrufbar.

ISBN 978-3-7560-1990-8 (Print)
ISBN 978-3-7489-5529-0 (ePDF)

Onlineversion
Nomos eLibrary

1. Auflage 2025

Vorwort

Tiefgreifender Wandel auf mehreren Ebenen – von geopolitischen Umbrüchen über wirtschaftlich-ökologische Transformationen bis hin zu häufig daraus resultierenden gesellschaftspolitischen Neuausrichtungen – prägt unsere Zeit. Die vor allem aus dem wirtschaftlich-ökologischen Kontext heraus konstatierte sog. „Twin Transition", die neben dem ökologischen Wandel hin zur Nachhaltigkeit auch die Digitalisierung als wesentlichen Veränderungsmotor der Wirtschaft thematisiert, erweitert sich damit zunehmend zur „Triple Transition", die die soziale Dimension stärker in den Fokus rückt.

Der daraus resultierende Transformationsbedarf manifestiert sich auch auf regulatorischer Ebene. Im EU-Bereich wird auf diese Anforderung ausgehend vom 2019 vorgestellten European Green Deal mit vielfältigen Regularien wie beispielsweise der EU-Taxonomie, der Richtlinie zur Nachhaltigkeitsberichterstattung von Unternehmen (CSRD) oder auch dem geplanten Kreislaufwirtschaft-Gesetz (CEA) reagiert. Diese Regularien sind allerdings nicht ausschließlich als zu erfüllende Pflichten zu verstehen. Vielmehr stellen sie einen strategischen Handlungsrahmen dar, der es Unternehmen und Gesellschaft ermöglicht, Transformationen nicht nur zu bewältigen, sondern die Zukunft aktiv und erfolgreich zu gestalten.

In diesem Sinne sollte der mitunter als mehrdimensionale Krise empfundene Umbruch als positiv besetzter Wendepunkt und Chance verstanden werden, der die Möglichkeit zu einer Neuorientierung und Schaffung nachhaltiger Wertschöpfung im Rahmen eines Wertewandels bietet.

Der vorliegende Herausgeberband greift zentrale Dimensionen des erforderlichen Wandels auf. Er analysiert die industrielle Transformation im Spannungsfeld von Innovation und Resilienz, beleuchtet die Pfade zur Klimaneutralität und zeigt Perspektiven für eine funktionierende Kreislaufwirtschaft auf.

Wir wünschen den sich damit auseinandersetzenden Beiträgen eine interessierte und breite Leserschaft und hoffen, dass der Band ganz im Sinne des Winston Churchill zugeschriebenen Ausspruchs „Never let a good crisis go to waste“ sowohl Orientierung aber vor allem auch die Impulse für eine konkrete Umsetzung in Politik, Wirtschaft und Gesellschaft bietet.

Leoben, Graz
September 2025

Die Herausgeber
Wolfgang Posch
Stefan Vorbach
Helmut Zsifkovits
Gerald Feichtinger

Danksagung

Wir danken dem Team des Lehrstuhls für Wirtschafts- und Betriebswissenschaften für nützliche Diskussionen, deren großartige Unterstützung und Hilfe bei der Fertigstellung dieses Kongressbuches.

Inhaltsverzeichnis

Klimaneutralität

Josef Baumüller, Walter S. A. Schwaiger

Activity-Based GHG-Management

Compliance with 'Clean Industrial Deal' Requirements

Summary: The Clean Industrial Deal focuses on the decarbonisation of the European economy in order to create growth drivers and competitive advantages in international markets. The creation of climate-friendly production processes is thus (increasingly) moving to the center of attention of politicians and companies. This paper identifies links between the regulatory focus of the Clean Industrial Deal and operational GHG management. 'Activity-based GHG Management' is a way in which companies can fulfil the requirements arising out of the Clean Industrial Deal in an effective and efficient manner. Due to its activity-based GHG accounting foundation it completely integrates with financial accounting in existing ERP systems and the employed GHG assessment metrics provide a fundament for external assurance. Beyond mere regulatory GHG emission reporting compliance, the GHG accounting's five levers of control form the basis for the activity-based GHG management of GHG emissions by formulating and implementing strategies for GHG reduction.

Keywords: Clean Industrial Deal, CSRD, GHG Management Control System, 3 Levers of Emission Control, Emission Liability.

1. Introduction

The EU Green Deal set forth the ambition to make Europe the first climate-neutral continent in the world. This ambition is driven by both the need for a change in the prevailing economic systems in Europe and beyond – but also by the vision that decarbonization can act as source of innovation and thus for new competitive advantage in a time of global changes (European Commission, 2019). Of course, similar programs have been initiated around the world eversince, as climate change is a global crisis. However, the EU strived to be at the forefront of these global actions to set their pace and to reap their benefits for its economy accordingly.

In the years that have passed since the publication of the Green Deal, the momentum on sustainability in general and fighting climate change especially, has changed. Critics argue that the level of ambition was too high, and that the means for achieving the aims of the Green Deal ultimately have proven to be inadequate; the increasing number of incoherent and too complex regulations confronted European companies with a level of bureaucracy that impair the competitiveness of the economy and leave too little time to focus on innovation for more sustainability. This problem is aggravated by the severe economic downturn that Europe has been experiencing since 2022 (Draghi et al., 2024).

The European Commission had to react to that; and after the elections of the year 2024, a new political agenda was announced. The Clean Industrial Deal. Often referred to as "Competitiveness Deal", a clearer focus on decarbonization and the cutting of red-tape should be achieved. To achieve this aim, existing regulations should be overhauled in order to reduce bureaucracy: "What is agreed is too much today. [...] So it's our task to reduce this bureaucratic burden without changing the correct content of the law that we all want." (von der Leyen, 2024).

As a result, Europe is currently experiencing a time of regulatory uncertainty. Since early 2025, the European Commission has proposed substantial changes to core elements of the regulatory framework on sustainability. Especially requirements on reporting (e.g. CSRD, Taxonomy) and due diligence (CSDDD) are under revision. This has consequences for a considerable part of the European economy, raising the question about which priorities companies face for their management and the expectations directed towards them with regard to sustainability. Amongst other, the necessary level of ambition regarding their decarbonization efforts is also put to question. This has also consequences for the necessary investments in tools and systems in order to manage their sustainability aims, in a time where many companies struggle economically.

The following chapters outline that even though the political agenda is changing, the need for decarbonization and thus both effective and efficient GHG management remains unchanged. Chapter 2 discusses the role of decarbonization in the Clean Industrial Deal and the various elements of European regulation that will continue to put pressure on companies to establish mechanisms for GHG emission reduction. Chapter 3 introduces a tool for companies to tackle this challenge: 'Activity-based GHG Management' which accounts for GHG emissions on the product level via five levers of control and that also provide the key mitigation measures for reducing the products' GHG emissions in the future. Finally, chapter 4 adds final considerations on the challenges that companies might face and the benefits that activity-based GHG management promise in that respect.

2. The Clean Industrial Deal and GHG Management

The ambivalent role of sustainability – and more specifically, decarbonization – in the context of the current political debate is best illustrated in the words of Mario Draghi. In his report on European competitiveness, he advises streamlining the regulatory framework whilst maintaining the level of ambition: "If Europe's ambitious climate targets are matched by a coherent plan to achieve them, decarbonisation will be an opportunity for Europe. But if we fail to coordinate our policies, there is a risk that decarbonisation could run contrary to competitiveness and growth." (Draghi et al., 2024, p. 6)

"The Clean Industrial Deal confirms the EU's dedication to its climate goals by offering clear business incentives for industry to decarbonise within Europe." (European Commission, 2025, p. 2). As a consequence, the European Commission aims at supporting the business case of decarbonized products. Both supply- and demand-sided actions will be considered, covering aspects such as improved access to clean energy by European companies or revising the Public Procurement Framework.

As part of the Clean Industrial Deal, an Industrial Decarbonisation Accelerator Act is announced. It shall contribute to developing comprehensive as well as harmonized life-cycle assessments and introduce a voluntary label on the carbon intensity of industrial products. This new label will be aligned with existing labels introduced with the Green Deal, on which the Industrial Decarbonisation Accelerator Act builds: most notably, the Ecodesign for Sustainable Products Regulation, the Construction Products Regulation as well sectoral legislation such as batteries or buildings (European Commission, 2025, p. 8).

The actions of the Clean Industrial Deals also build on the EU Emissions Trading System (ETS). By putting a price on GHG emissions, further incentives for decarbonization shall be given – which is considered to be amongst the most effective measures for achieving reductions (e.g. Döbbeling-Hildebrandt et al., 2024). Already under the existing rules, the scope of application of the ETS will be extended on further sectors and a market-price mechanism introduced. The Clean Industrial Deal announces the establishment of an Industrial Decarbonisation Bank that provides additional support with decarbonization: "It will use ETS allowances reserved for this purpose as part of the architecture of the EU ETS to support projects with carbon emission reduction as a metric [...]. It will complement the ETS price signal and help bridge the funding gap in both capital and operational expenditures." (European Commission, 2025a, p. 11)

In turn, general-purpose reporting requirements such as the CSRD or Taxonomy shall be considerably reduced. In parallel to the presentation of the Clean Industrial Deal, the EU Commission proposed its "omnibus-package on sustainability" (European Commission, 2025b). Fewer companies will be subjected to mandatory sustainability reporting requirements and existing standards on sustainability reporting will be simplified (Baumüller, 2025). Additionally, voluntary standards will be introduced. Again, it is implied that the reporting requirements on a company level shall also focus more on GHG emissions and the way these are managed by companies, in turn reducing the broader topical scope of existing rules and extensive narrative reporting contents (e.g. Albuquerque, 2025).

It shall be noted that one fundamental principle will not be changed: the principle of double materiality, the cornerstone of existing reporting requirements which can be traced well as to the EU Commission's approach towards sustainability in general. Both how the economy impacts society and environment ("inside-out") as well as how it is impacted by society and environment ("outside-in") shall be considered. Only by considering these two perspectives, the full benefits of a sustainable economy can be reaped. This, however, requires companies to adjust their management control systems according to these perspectives (Baumüller/Sopp, 2022).

Finally, it can be summarized that with its Clean Industrial Deal, the European Commission shows a shift in priorities – with competitiveness of the European economy becoming a new political priority. At the same time, the ambitions of the Green Deal shall be preserved; here, a more focused approach towards decarbonization can be observed. In any case, clear (financial) incentives shall be given to companies to manage and reduce their GHG emissions. Which, in turn, shall serve as a source for future competitiveness.

3. Activity-Based GHG Management: Working and Application

3.1. Activity-Based GHG Accounting and Management

The "activity-based GHG accounting" introduced by Baumüller/Schwaiger (2024) provides the GHG accounting metrics applied in the GHG management for assessing the carbon footprints of the company's finished products. In essence, it covers the product's cradle-to-gate carbon footprint (PCF) by incorporating the "internal" scope 1 and 2 emissions related to the company's internal activities that are attributable to the acquisition of resources as well as the manufacturing and distribution of their products and the "external" scope 3 emissions resulting from the materials and equipment applied in the internal activities.

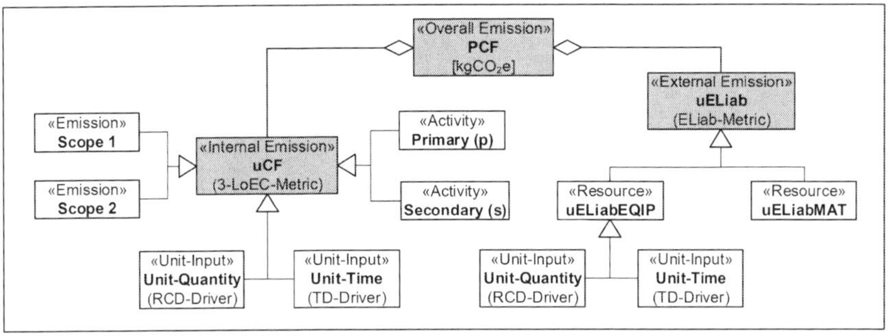

Figure 1: Activity-Based GHG Accounting – Conceptualization (own illustration)

Fig. 1 shows the conceptual model of the activity-based GHG accounting where for the assessment of the internal and the external emissions the 3-Levers-of-Emission-Control (3-LoEC)-metric and the Emission Liability (ELiab)-metric are applied. With the 3-LoEC-metric the internal GHG emission (unit Carbon Footprint ‚uCF‘) for the product (finished Product ‚fP‘) manufactured in the activity (‚acty‘) is accounted for by combining the unit-input (production coefficient ‚a‘), the power level (‚p‘) and the emission factor (emission coefficient ‚e‘) individually over all resources (‚res‘) applied in the activity.

$$\underbrace{uCF_{acty,fP}}_{[kgCO_2e]} = \sum_{res} \underbrace{Unit\_Input}_{\substack{\text{Production Coefficient} \\ a_{acty,res,fP} \\ [res.unit/outp.unit]}} * \underbrace{Power\ Level}_{\substack{\text{Power Coefficient} \\ p_{acty,res,fP} \\ [kW/res.unit \text{ or } kWh/res.unit]}} * \underbrace{Emission\ Factor}_{\substack{\text{Emission Coefficient} \\ e_{res,scope} \\ [kgCO_2e/kWh]}}$$

Figure 2: Internal GHG-Emission – Activity-based Assignment via 3-LoEC-Metric (own illustration).

The 3-LoEC-model – as mathematically expressed in Fig. 2 – relates to direct scope 1 and indirect 2 emissions depending on the energy consumed in the activity. The usage of the production coefficient (unit-input) is important for connecting the activity-based GHG accounting directly to the activity-based cost accounting as there these coefficients also are used for assessing the unit-consumptions of the resources applied in the activities.

Over the life cycle of a product, most often indirect emissions outside of a company are prevailing. These indirect emissions are distinguished among emissions from value chain upstream activities and value chain downstream activities. For avoiding multiple counting over different enterprises and for a precise measurement of the indirect emissions Kaplan/Ramanna (2021) developed the "Environmental-Liability" accounting. In this accounting system the "value added" concept is applied to assess in each stage of the product life cycle the correspondingly prevailing environmental impacts and to add them to the impacts accumulated over the previous stages. Applied to the GHG emission context Kaplan/Ramanna's accounting relates to an "Emission-Liability (E-Liability)" accounting system, where the product specific GHG emissions are successively accumulated over the product's life cycle stages.

A) $$\underbrace{uELiabMAT_{acty,MAT,fP}}_{[kgCO_2e]} = \underbrace{a_{acty,MAT,fP}}_{\left[\frac{res.input}{outp.unit}\right]} * \underbrace{ELiabMAT_{MAT,scope3}}_{\left[\frac{kgCO_2e}{res.input}\right]}$$

B) $$\underbrace{uELiabEQIP_{acty,EQIP,fP}}_{[kgCO_2e]} = \underbrace{a_{acty,EQIP,fP}}_{\left[\frac{time}{outp.unit}(h)\right]} * \underbrace{cuELiabEQIP_{EQIP,scope3}}_{\left[\frac{kgCO_2e}{h}\right]}$$

$$\underbrace{cuELiabEQIP_{EQIP,scope3}}_{\left[\frac{kgCO_2e}{h}\right]} = \underbrace{ELiabEQIP_{EQIP,scope3}}_{[kgCO_2e]} / \underbrace{LifetimeCapacity_{EQIP}}_{[h]}$$

Figure 3: External GHG-Emission – Activity-based Allocation via E-Liability-Metric (own illustration).

Fig. 3 shows the two ELiab-metrics that relate to the materials ("MAT") as well as the equipment ("EQIP") that are consumed as well as used in the company's internal activities. With these metrics the emission liabilities coming from the production of the materials and equipment in the company's external upstream activities are allocated to the finished products. The materials' emission liabilities are completely allocated to the finished products whereas the emission liabilities from the equipment are allocated in proportion to their usage in the sense of a "units-of-production depreciation". The unit-inputs in both metrics are the production coefficients so that all GHG accounting metrics have the same resource-based unit-input view like in the resource consumption driven activity-based cost accounting.

3.2. Activity-Based GHG Accounting: Demonstration

For demonstrating the working of the activity-based GHG accounting it is applied in the "Food-Bowl" use case (Baumüller/Schwaiger, 2024). In Tab. 1 it can be seen that producing one food-bowl lot – consisting of 100 units of food-bowls – gives a carbon footprint of 42.87 kgCO_2e that is composed of internal emissions amounting to 25.77 and external emissions of 17.10 kgCO_2e.

Activity	Production Coefficient (Unit-Input)	Internal GHG Emission (3-LoEC-Metric)	External GHG Emission (E-Liability-Metric)	Abbreviation
Manufacturing	3.333 (h/Lot)	18.73		up2CF
Manufacturing (EQIP)	3.333 (h/Lot)		1.10	uELiabEQIP
Manufacturing (MAT)	32.00 (kg/Lot)		16.00	uELiabMAT
Transport	0.072 (l/Lot)	0.19		up1CF
Heating	3.333 (h/Lot)	6.85		us1CF
Total	**42.87**	**25.77**	**17.10**	**kgCO_2e/Lot**

Table 1: Activity-Based GHG Accounting – Food-Bowl demonstration case (own results).

The manufacturing activity, which is a primary (p) activity where an electricity driven injection molder is used, has a scope 2 unit-carbon footprint (up2CF) of 18.73 kgCO_2e. In this activity the emission liability of the used injection molder equipment (EQIP) and the consumed PLA plastics material (MAT) amounts to 1.10 and 16 kgCO_2e. For demonstrating the GHG accounting's broad applicability the use case also covers the support (secondary) heating activity operated with a gas driven heater and a primary transport activity operated with a diesel driven vehicle which have scope 1 unit-carbon footprints of 6.85 (us1CF) and 0.19 (up1CF). The transport activity distinguishes from the manufacturing activity by the applied emission driver, the manufacturing has a time-driven metric (in hours) for the resource's unit-input, i.e. production coefficient whereas transport has a quantity-driven (in litres) metric.

The activity-based GHG accounting is constructed as a CSRD and ESRS compliant framework that extends the 3-LoEC-metric (Baumüller/Schwaiger 2023) with the ELiab-metric (Kaplan/Ramanna 2021) for covering not only the company's internal emissions but also external emissions resulting from the company's external upstream activities. Furthermore, it anchors the GHG emission assessment for the first time in the language of the financial and cost accounting domain and as such it becomes understood and acknowledged in the company's C-level. Its close connection to the activity-based cost accounting makes it ready for immediate implementations. Finally, the activity-based GHG accounting provides the metrics needed for assessing cisions are made and planning and control systems are established. The activity-based GHG management provides the essential concepts for improving traditional management concepts that are urgently needed in the currently changing regulatory framework and the always changing business environment. Having reliable and understandable metrics for assessing the products' GHG emissions also allows the view into the future by planning and budgeting next to the revenues and costs of future sales volumes also their related future GHG emissions. Additionally, having the five levers of emission control allows reasoning about setting and achieving GHG emission reduction targets and corresponding GHG-related risk mitigations within both views of the double materiality perspective.

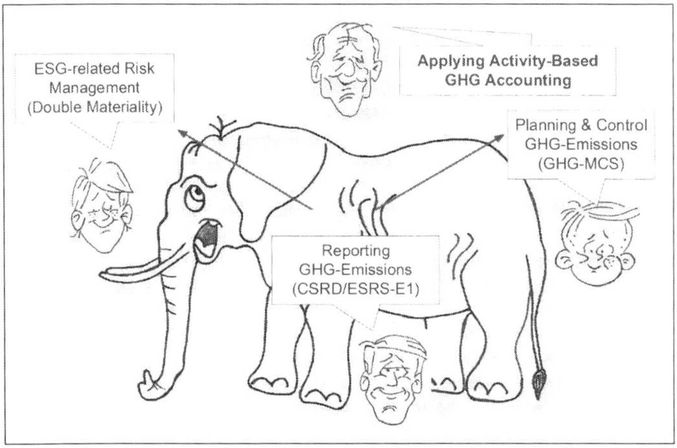

Figure 4: Activity-Based GHG Accounting & Management (John Godfrey Saxe).

In Fig. 4 the interplay between the activity-based GHG accounting and (risk) management is summarized according to John Godfrey Saxe's metaphor "The Blind Men and the Elephant". The activity-based GHG accounting is the conceptual foundation that aligns the often separated perspectives taken in the GHG reporting, the GHG management and the GHG-related risk management with the double materiality perspectives. Having this overarching perspective, a more holistic approach towards managing organizations can be taken. This is especially important in the current time of the changing regulatory framework concerning GHG emissions and decarbonisation as announced in the Clean Industrial Deal. This is relevant for companies but it also establishes new perspectives on how the success of companies is to be understood by regulators and society at large.

Abbreviations

3-LoEC	3-Levers-of-Emission-Control
ABB	Activity-Based Budgeting
COSO	Committee of Sponsoring Organizations of the Treadway Commission
CSRD	Corporate Sustainability Reporting Directive
Eliab	E(mission)-Liability
EQIP	Equipment
ERM	Enterprise Risk Management
ESG	Environmental, Social and Governance
ESRS	European Sustainability Reporting Standards
et al.	et alii (and others)
ETS	Emissions Trading System
EU	European Union
GHG	Greenhouse Gas
GRI	Global Reporting Initiative
LoC	Levers of Control
MAT	Materials
MCS	Management Control System
PCF	Product Carbon Footprint
PDCA	Plan-Do-Check-Act

References

Albuquerque, M. L. (2025): Letter to EFRAG, available at: https://www.efrag.org/sites/default/files/media/document/2025-03/Commissioner%20Albuquerque%20Letter%20to%20EFRAG%20March%202025.pdf.

Baumüller, J. (2025): EU omnibus package on sustainability – something we don't want to ride (yet)? "Omnibus I", CSRD (new) and the revised future of sustainability reporting in the EU: Evidence from Austria (March 20, 2025), available at SSRN: https://ssrn.com/abstract=5195189

Baumüller J. / Schwaiger, W. (2024): Aktivitätsbasierte Standard-Kosten- & Treihausgas-Rechnung – Integration der CSRD-Treibhausgas-Rechnung in die Standard-Kostenrechnung. Austrian Management Review 14, 106–115

Baumüller, J. / Schwaiger, W. (2023): Activity-Based Product Carbon Footprint Measurement with the 3-Levers of Emission Control (3-LoEC)-Metrics, in: Posch, W. / Vorbach, S. / Zsifkovits, H. / Feichtinger, G. (eds.), 10. Congress – Sustainability Management for Industries, Leoben, 135–151

Baumüller, J. / Sopp, K. (2022): Double materiality and the shift from non-financial to European sustainability reporting: review, outlook and implications. In: Journal of Applied Accounting Research 23 (1), 8–28

COSO-ERM (2017): Enterprise Risk Management – Aligning Risk with Strategy and Performance, Committee of Sponsoring Organizations of the Treadway Commission, June 2017

COSO-ESG (2018): Enterprise Risk Management – Applying enterprise risk management to environmental, social and governance-related risks, COSO & WBCSD, October 2018

Döbbeling-Hildebrandt et al. (2024): Systematic review and meta-analysis of ex-post evaluations on the effectiveness of carbon pricing, Nature Communications 15, 4147

Draghi, M. et al. (2024): The future of European Competitiveness, Part A: A Competitiveness Strategy for Europe, available at: https://commission.europa.eu/document/download/97e481fd-2dc3-412d-be4c-f152a8232961_en?filename=The%20future%20of%20European%20competitiveness%20_%20A%20competitiveness%20strategy%20for%20Europe.pdf

European Commission (2019): The European Green Deal, COM(2019) 640 final

European Commission (2025a): The Clean Industrial Deal: A joint roadmap for competitiveness and decarbonization, COM(2025) 85 final

European Commission (2025a): Omnibus I, available at: https://commission.europa.eu/publications/omnibus-i_en

Kaplan, R. S. / Ramanna, K. (2021): Accounting for Climate Change, Harvard Business Review 99, 120–131

Simons, R. (1995): Levers of Control – How Managers Use Innovative Control Systems to Drive Strategic Renewal, Boston MA, Harvard Business School Press

von der Leyen, U. (2024): Informal meeting of Heads of State and Government in Budapest, Hungary, available at: https://www.youtube.com/watch?v=wZUzRlsyDr8

Gerald Feichtinger, David Koller, Wolfgang Posch

Environmental Performance Analysis using the LCA-based Environmental Decision Matrix

A Novel Model Framework for Analysing the Entire Chain of Activities

Abstract: Due to increasingly stringent environmental requirements and regulations, companies are facing the challenge of continuously analysing and improving their individual environmental performance. In this context, simple yet flexible tools are required to analyse environmental performance not only at the site, but also along the upstream and downstream process chains. This article presents a novel model framework in which a dynamic environmental decision matrix (EDM) is linked with the results of an environmental life cycle assessment (LCA). The model framework can be used by companies for further decision-making, particularly regarding the development of environmental strategies for optimising the environmental performance of companies along the entire activity chains. An exemplary implementation of the EDM-LCA coupling is shown and, finally, future research aspects are highlighted.

Keywords: Environmental Decision Matrix (EDM), Life Cycle Assessment (LCA), Environmental Performance Optimisation, Decision Making, Strategy Development.

1. Introduction

The European Green Deal is a cornerstone policy package to turn the economies of the European Union member states into climate neutral by 2050 with the explicit goal of transforming the economies through sustainable growth. Several sustainability related initiatives are included in this initiative that will cause a significant effect on companies. Among many the most relevant are the European Climate Law, the EU Taxonomy Regulation, the Fit for 55 Package, reforms of the EU Emissions Trading Scheme (EU-ETS), the Carbon Boarder Adjustment Mechanism (CBAM), the Circular Economy Action Plan (CEAP), the EU Industrial Strategy, the Net-Zero Industry Act, the Critical Raw Materials Act (CRMA), the Biodiversity Strategy, the Ecodesign for Sustainable Products Regulation (ESPR), the Corporate Sustainability Reporting Directive (CSRD) including the European Sustainability Reporting Standards (ESRS) and the Corporate Sustainability Due Diligence Directive (CSDDD). With this already shortened list of EU regulations it will be crystal clear, that the demands on corporate environmental responsibilities will significantly increase in the medium and long term. (European Commission, 2019; Kettner-Marx and Feichtinger, 2021; Vis and Delbeke, 2020)

A result of that, the demand for establishing more effective environmental management systems (EMS) grows to assess sustainability related activities across all operations and supply chains. Regulatory frameworks such as the CSRD and the EU Taxonomy require transparent reporting on environmental impacts within operational activity chains at the site, but also along upstream and downstream value chains. In this context, companies must adapt product design, energy consumption and corporate strategies to EU standards and EU targets (including the Paris Agreement targets). For this reason, companies often establish management systems such as ISO standards (including 14001 or 50001) or the Eco-Management and Audit Scheme (EMAS) or adapt science-based targets (SBT) to ensure compliance with regulations and maintain competitiveness. (ISO, 2025a; EMAS, 2025; Science Based Targets Initiative, 2024)

A key challenge in this context is the recording and subsequent analysis of all operational activities affected by these regulations and, in turn, cause various impacts on the environment along the entire chain of operational activities. These environmental impacts are generally divided into direct and indirect effects, which differ in terms of the direct influence exerted by the company. Direct effects are subject to the organisation's direct operational control and include, among others, emissions into the atmosphere, discharges into water, waste (inclusive recycling, reuse, transport and disposal), land use and contamination, but also the usage of energy, natural resources and raw materials, and pre-finished, auxiliary and semi-finished-products. Local phenomena such as noise, vibrations, odours, dust or aesthetic impairment are also subject to direct control by the company. Indirect effects, on the other hand, arise from an interrelationship between the company with third parties such as suppliers or customers, that the company may not be able to fully control. Examples for indirect impacts include, among others, all aspects of the life cycle of products and services, capital investments, lending and insurance services, services but also the environmental impacts of contractors, subcontractors, suppliers and sub-suppliers.

Life cycle assessments (LCAs) are a widely recognised tool for systematically analysing all direct and indirect environmental impacts along the entire chain of operational activities, either at product level or, if necessary, at organisational level. However, the latter is a much more complex undertaking and therefore more time-consuming. LCA-based analyses can be very extensive depending on the scope of the analysis (e.g., gate-to-gate, cradle-to-grave or cradle-to-cradle representing a circular economic system) and the objective of the study, and require a detailed data basis. The result of an LCA is usually a representation of the environmental effects of the object under investigation, which can then be used to improve the environmental footprint of the object under investigation.

This paper presents a novel environmental decision matrix (EDM), which is linked to the results of a life cycle assessment (LCA), that can subsequently be flexibly used to assess and further optimise the environmental performance of products or entire companies.

2. Methodological approach

This article presents a multi-stage modelling framework. It introduces a novel EDM that can be customised to suit individual requirements. This matrix is linked to the results of an LCA, which requires a few additional adjustment steps. The result of this combination is a flexible tool which integrates LCA-based results with relative flexibility and enables assessments of environmental impacts at both the product and company level.

2.1. Environmental Decision Matrix (EDM)

The environmental performance of an object under investigation (e.g., a product) is usually measured by using various process-based environmental indicators. These indicators can be taken from an existing EMS or environmental reports which have been published, for example, and then analysed further. In a so-called EDM, all direct and indirect environmental impacts of the investigation are analysed and evaluated in terms of their significance and the existing process-based optimisation potential to subsequently optimise the environmental performance of individual products or entire companies. An EDM based assessment involves all processes to be analysed – if required throughout the entire life cycle – and is created in a multi-stage process. The structure of the EDM and its general functioning is explained in detail below.

Structure of the EDM

For the EDM, all process steps to be investigated and all the environmental assessment categories of interest for this investigation must be collected. The processes can be taken from a previous LCA or extracted separately from other documents and reports. The environmental assessment categories can include various environmental aspects (e.g., emissions to air of different sources), for example from an already existing LCA and its associated life cycle inventory (LCI) or the life cycle impact assessment (LCIA). But also, other aspects such as health, safety and environmental (HSE), legal and regulatory aspects, or opinions of interested parties (e.g., employees) can be considered in the assessment. A schematic illustration of an EDM is shown in Figure 1.

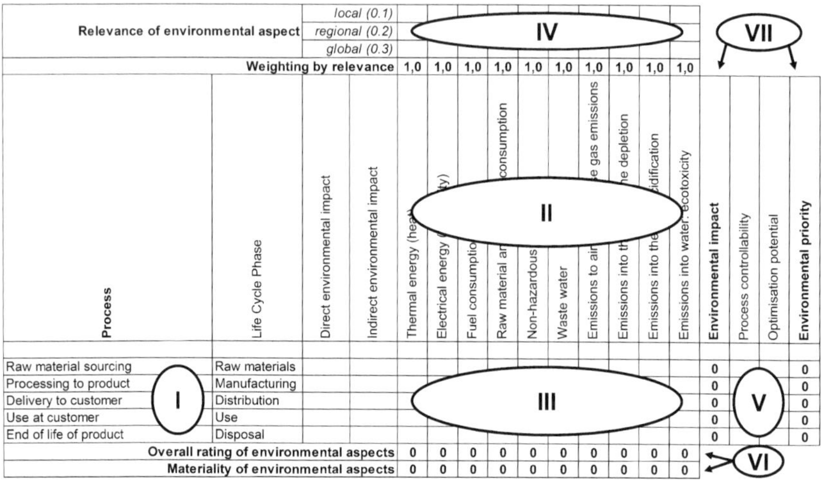

Figure 1: Schematic illustration of the EDM indicating all input and output areas (based on (Egger, 2025); own supplements).

In the EDM, the processes are listed in the rows and the environmental assessment categories (or environmental aspects) in the columns. As indicated in Figure 1, an EDM[1] includes seven important areas, five of which are input based and two of them are automatically calculated results by the model:

1 The number of processes and environmental aspects can be changed as desired. There is no upper or lower limit on the number of components.

- Area (I) includes all considered processes and the associated life cycle phases of the investigation, which could cover processes from the entire life cycle.
- Area (II) includes all environmental aspects under consideration.
- Area (III) relates to the environmental relevance of each process with respect to the environmental aspect being considered.
- Area (IV) indicates the environmental impact of the environmental aspects which results in automatically derived weighting factors of each environmental aspect.
- Area (V) relates to inputs regarding the controllability of the process and its optimisation potential with regard to environmental impacts.
- Area (VI) consists of the environemental aspect related output figures: the overall rating and the materialy of all environmental impacts.
- Area (VII) consists of the process-related output figures: the environmental impact and the environmental priority of all processes.

All environmental aspects are weighted using associated factors[2] which are related to the impact of the environmental aspect on the environment (local, regional and global), the influenceability of the process and the process-related optimisation potential. This results in the final environmental priority for all processes taken into account (horizontal product totals). In addition, all environmental aspects taken into account are evaluated and compared in terms of their significance. The higher the sum, the higher the priority or significance. The columns "direct environmental impacts" and "indirect environmental impacts" are of purely informative nature to show whether the process under consideration causes direct and/or indirect environmental effects.

Creation of the EDM

Each environmental aspect is considered and evaluated separately for each individual process. For each process, the respective environmental aspects are assessed on a 4-point standardised rating scale[3] that indicates the environmental relevance (invdivdual environmental priority) as follows (region III): 0 (not relevant), 1 (low priority), 2 (medium priority), and 3 (high priority). This assessment will be carried out for all processes and all environmental aspects which are investiged in the EDM.

---

2 The weighting factors are also a result of the matrix and are determined endogenously after entering the environmental impacts into the model.

3 Based on the idea of the sensitivity model (Vester and von Hesler (1980)).

As mentioned before, the environmental aspects (columns) are assessed in terms of the state of the environment and environmental pollution and damage at spatial scales[4] (at local, regional and global level). The weighting factor of an environmental aspect (area IV) is calculated from four sub-factors: a base factor with a value of 1, a local weighting factor (with a weighting of 0.1), a regional weighting factor (with a weighting of 0.2) and a global weighting factor (with a weighting of 0.3). These three impact categories (local, regional and global) are also rated on a 4-level scale according to the already mentioned environmental relevance: 'n.r.' (not relevant, or 0), 'l' (low priority, or 1), 'm' (medium priority, or 2) or 'h' (high priority, or 3).[5] More formally, the weighting factor is defined as follows

$$w_i = BASE + LOC_i + REG_i + GLOB_i \quad , \quad \forall i$$

with the weighting factor w of an environmental aspect i, a base weighting factor $BASE$, a weighted local impact factor LOC, a weighted regional impact factor REG, and a weighted global impact factor $GLOB$. The base weighting factor is usually set to 1 to consider all environmental aspects in further calculations.

The overall rating of the environmental aspects is calculated as the (column) sum of the environmental relevances across all processes. Based on this, the materiality of an environmental aspect is derived as the product of the overall rating and the weighting factor of the environmental aspect. More formally this can be defined as

$$M_i = w_{ij} \times \sum_j R_{ij} \quad , \quad \forall i$$

with the materialy M of an environmental aspect i, the environmental relevance R, the weighting fator for each environmental aspect w, and all processes j being investigated. The result is, in simplified form, the materiality of each environmental aspect for the object under investigation. The higher the materiality of an environmental aspect, the more critical the respective

4 Based on the idea of pollution management and geographical distribution (K and Kumar (2022)).

5 For example: for local, a rating of mid priority would result in an overall weighting of '2 * 0.1 = 0.2'; for regional, the same would result in '2 * 0.2 = 0.4'' and for global in '2 * 0.3 = 0.6'.

environmental aspect is to be classified. All environmental aspects could then be sorted in descending order to obtain a prioritised list.

In a further step, the environmental priority is determined for all processes. First, the environmental impact of a process (line) is calculated as the sum product of the relevance of the environmental aspect in the process multiplied by the respective weighting factor of the environmental aspect. Based on this, the environmental priority for each process can be derived. This is the product of the environmental impact of a process, its influenceability and its optimisation potential. More formally this is defined as

$$EP_j = \left(\sum_i w_{ij} \times R_{ij} \right) \times I_{ij} \times O_{ij} \quad , \quad \forall j$$

with the environmental priority EP of a process j, the weighting factor of an environmental aspect w, the environmental relevance R, the influencability of a process I, the optimisation potential of a process O, and all environmental aspects i being investigated.

To sum up: all environmental aspects of all process are weighted using associated factors related to the environmental relevance of the environmental aspect (local, regional and global), the influenceability of the process itself and the process-related optimisation potential. This results in the final environmental priority for all process steps taken into account (horizontal product totals). In addition, all environmental aspects taken into account are evaluated and compared in terms of their materiality. The higher the sum, the higher the environmental priority of the process or the materiality of the environmental aspect.

2.2. Life Cycle Assessment (LCA)

This methodological approach links the EDM already shown with the results of an underlying LCA. LCAs are generally used to examine the environmental impact of an object under investigation (e.g., a product or an organisation) throughout its entire life cycle. The applicant is free to choose which analysis scope to use, i.e., which life cycle phases are to be taken into account in the LCA. However, it should always be kept in mind that LCAs are standardised in accordance with ISO 14040/44 and must be implemented on the basis of four LCA phases (ISO, 2025b): (i) the definition of the objective and scope of the study, (ii) the preparation of a life cycle inventory (LCI), (iii) the calculation of a life cycle impact assessment (LCIA), and (iv) the evaluation and interpretation of the derived results. Modern software tools facilitate the ISO-compliant implementation of LCA, as they automatically perform the necessary calculations and subsequently deliver LCA-based results. This makes it easier to calculate LCIA results, which require the input of underlying impact assessment methods. These impact assessment methods have been and are continuously revised, are highly complex, and are regularly updated by LCA software providers. (Frischknecht, 2020)

However, as already explained above, both results from the LCI (e.g., thermal/electrical energy consumption, fuel, materials, waste) and the LCIA (e.g., global warming potential, acidification, water scarcity) can be used in the model approach presented in this contribution. An LCI usually comprises a compact list of environmental impacts, such as resource consumption, energy demands, wastes or other emissions. Special characterisation methods are used to calculate the impact indicator results in the form of an LCIA. This weighs and evaluates all substances considered in the LCA model according to their environmental impact. In all effect categories, so-called reference substances are used to illustrate the individual effectiveness of the substances. For example, the effectiveness of greenhouse gas (GHG) emissions[6] (such as CO2 or methane) is determined on the basis of GHG potentials in CO2 equivalents (e.g., in kg CO2eq). (Huijbregts *et al.*, 2017)

A particular challenge in conducting LCAs is choosing the assessment method for preparing the LCIA. Over time, various assessment methods have been developed, which differ in terms of various criteria, but in particular in terms of the number of environmental impact indicators taken into account. The most important and best-known environmental impact categories include (among others): global warming potential (or climate change: total, fossil, biogenic and land use), ozone depletion, acidification, eutrophication (freshwater, marine, terrestrial), photochemical ozone formation, depletion of abiotic resources (minerals, metals), human toxicity (cancer, non-cancer), freshwater toxicity, water use, land use, ionising ration, and particulate matter formation. All of the categories mentioned differ in terms of the reference substance.

6 The main GHGs are: carbon dioxide (CO2), methane (CH4), nitrous oxide (N2O), hydrofluorocarbons (HFCs), perfluorocarbons (PFCs), sulfur hexafluoride (SF6), and nitrogen trifluoride (NF3).

Table 1: Overview of number of environmental impact categories by environmental assessment method at midpoint level and endpoint level available for LCA (based on: (Frischknecht, 2020; Hauschild et al., 2018); own supplements and illustration)

Category Method	**Year**	**Midpoint oriented**	**Endpoint oriented**
AWARE	2024	1	-
BEES +	2021	13	-
Carbon Footprint	2021	1	-
CML-IA baseline	2016	11	-
CML-IA non-baseline	2016	14	-
Cumulative Energy Demand	1970s	1	-
Eco-Indicator 99	1999	11	3
Ecological Scarcity 2021	2021	20	-
EDIP	2003	9	-
Environmental Footprint 3.1	2023	19	-
EN 15804+A2	2019	19	-
EPD	2018	8	-
GLAM[1)]	2024	~20	2+
ILCD	2011	16-18	-
IMPACT 2002+	2002	14	4
IMPACT World+[1)]	2023	24	2
LC-IMPACT[1)]	2013	-[2)]	3
LUCAS	2000s	10	-
ReCiPe 2016	2016	18	3
TRACI 2.1	2012	10	-
USEtox	2023	3	-

[1)] Still under development; [2)] Currently not available.

The existing assessment methods comprise various environmental impact indicators, which are also calculated using midpoint and endpoint indicators.[7] Table 1 provides an overview of the most important environmental impact methods, its year of implementation and the number of midpoint and endpoint-indicators. The table shows that the number of these indicators varies considerably with a trend towards an increasing number of environmental

7 Midpoint indicators focus on individual environmental problems (e.g., climate change, acidification), while endpoint indicators show the environmental impact at a higher level of aggregation (e.g., effects on human health, biodiversity or resource scarcity) (Huijbregts *et al.* (2017)).

indicators in more recent methods such as ReCiPe, Environmental Footprint, Impact World+ or GLAM.

2.3. Integration of LCA results into EDM

The approach presented in this article can basically be used for both midpoint and endpoint indicators. In order to integrate results from both, the LCI and the LCIA results, into the EDM, the respective indicators must be normalised using the 4-step prioritisation scale between 0 (not relevant) and 3 (highly relevant). A three-phase process is used for this: first, the number of steps must be determined, which must correspond to the number of priorities. Then, the step height is calculated for each environmental indicator (that is the environmental aspect) to be analysed based on its maximum value[8] across all processes being considered. In the final phase, the normalized environmental relevance of the environmental aspect is determined for all processes based on the step height.

The first phase is quickly done and is based on the prioritisation scale mentioned several times above, meaning that three steps[9] are required. In the second phase, the step height is determined as follows

$$STEP_i = \frac{\max_j(IND_{i,j})}{n} \quad , \quad \forall i$$

with the step height $STEP$ for an environmental indicator i, processes j and number of priorities n (which is also usually three), and an LCA-based indicator IND (which could originate from LCI or LCIA). Based on this information, the third and final phase of determining the normalized environmental relevance, again for each environmental aspect, can take place. This is done as follows

8 Alternatively, the sum can also be used to calculate the step height. However, the maximum value (rather than the sum) achieves a better distribution of relevance between the processes, whereas the sum would only highlight the absolute maximums in the processes.

9 The 4-step prioritisation scale prioritisation scale ranges between 0 (not relevant) and 3 (highly relevant).

$$R_i = \begin{cases} 0 & 0 \\ 1 & 0 < IND_{i,j} \leq STEP_i \\ 2 & STEP_i < IND_{i,j} \leq 2 * STEP_i \\ 3 & 2 * STEP_i < IND_{i,j} \end{cases}$$

with the (normalised) environmental relevance R of an environmental aspect i, the process j, the LCA-based indicator IND, and the step height $STEP$. The key result of this procedure is the normalized environmental relevance for every environmental aspect and every process step considered, which is directly integrated (inserted) into the EDM.

3. Results

The results presented below describe an example of the integration of an LCA with the novel type of EDM described above. All results shown are sample data and are intended solely to illustrate the procedure for integrating the two modelling approaches. First, the LCA results will be normalised, which will be integrated into an EDM as a further step.

3.1. *Normalization of LCA-results*

As previously explained, an LCA can provide very comprehensive results. In the case presented below, a simplified "cradle-to-grave" analysis across the five important product life cycle stages[10] was carried out. Indicators from both the LCI (thermal energy, electrical energy, fuel, raw materials and resources, non-hazardous waste, waste water) and the LCIA (GHG emissions, ozone depletion, acidification, ecotoxicity) were extracted from the LCA to cover different categories and factors with different units. Figure 2 shows the selected data set and the normalised data.

10 Alternatively, a "gate-to-gate" analysis with various processes at one location could also be carried out.

Process	Life Cycle Phase	Thermal energy (heat)	Electrical energy (electricity)	Fuel consumption	Raw material and resource consumption	Non-hazardous waste	Waste water	Emissions to air: greenhouse gas emissions	Emissions into the air: ozone depletion	Emissions into the soil: acidification	Emissions into water: ecotoxicity
	Unit	kWh	kWh	kWh	kg	kg	m3	kg CO2-Eq	kg CFC-11-Eq	mol H+-Eq	CTUe
Input from LCA											
Raw material sourcing	Raw materials	4 289,30	1 523,29	28,84	720,18	33,38	5,51	1 649,12	6,83533E-05	2,42	2 869,88
Processing to product	Manufacturing	-	-	63,34	-	-	-	319,60	6,95213E-06	0,70	2 242,52
Delivery to customer	Distribution	-	645,00	-	-	106,00	-	266,33	5,55568E-06	0,69	1 136,87
Use at customer	Use	-	-	21,21	-	-	-	106,99	2,32743E-06	0,23	750,75
End of life of product	Disposal	-	2 000,00	-	66,33	-	-	947,99	2,15079E-05	3,96	9 677,13
	Max	*4 289,30*	*2 000,00*	*63,34*	*720,18*	*106,00*	*5,51*	*1 649,12*	*6,83533E-05*	*3,96*	*9 677,13*
	Step	*1 429,77*	*666,67*	*21,11*	*240,06*	*35,33*	*1,84*	*549,71*	*2,27844E-05*	*1,32*	*3 225,71*
Normalized results											
Raw material sourcing	Raw materials	3	3	2	3	1	3	3	3	2	1
Processing to product	Manufacturing	-	-	3	-	-	-	1	1	1	1
Delivery to customer	Distribution	-	1	-	-	3	-	1	1	1	1
Use at customer	Use	-	-	2	-	-	-	1	1	1	1
End of life of product	Disposal	-	3	-	1	-	-	2	1	3	3

Figure 2: Exemplary application of the normalization procedure for LCA-based results (own calculations).

In a first step, the maximum value[11] based on the given LCA results is determined for each indicator in order to determine the step height for normalisation (upper part of Figure 2). Depending on the indicator, the characteristics vary across the processes: thermal energy is required in only one process (raw material sourcing), while all considered processes cause GHG emissions.

The step height is then determined in a second step based on the maximum value of the respective indicator, which was calculated previously, and serves as the basis for the normalisation. Normalisation converts all values to a 4-point scale, eliminating any differences between the indicators (e.g., units, upper/lower limits). The normalised results show differences between the indicators (lower part of Figure 2): while the results for some indicators are spread across several processes (e.g., emissions to air/soil/water), other indicators focus on just a few processes (e.g., thermal energy, raw materials, waste, waste water). The latter may enable a clear focus when implementing measures to reduce environmental impacts.

11 In this analysis, the maximum value (and not the sum) was used.

3.2. Completion of the EDM

Based on the normalisation of the LCA results per indicator shown above, an EDM can then be calculated using the method presented in this contribution. Not only must the standardised LCA results be entered into the EDM itself, but the weightings for the individual environmental aspects must also be added. In addition, two columns with direct and indirect effects are added for the individual processes, solely for information purposes. The company's view of the process is important here: if, from the company's point of view, the processes under consideration have indirect effects in addition to direct environmental effects, this should (or can) be noted in the matrix. Figure 3 shows an example of an EDM incorporating the LCA results shown above and weightings for the environmental aspects.

Relevance of environmental aspect			*local (0,1)*	h	m	h	l	h	m	h	m	h	h				
			regional (0,2)	h	h	h	m	m	l	h	m	m	m				
			global (0,3)	h	h	h	h	n.r.	n.r.	h	h	m	m				
			Weighting by relevance	**2,8**	**2,7**	**2,8**	**2,4**	**1,7**	**1,4**	**2,8**	**2,5**	**2,3**	**2,3**				
Process	Life Cycle Phase	Direct environmental impact	Indirect environmental impact	Thermal energy (heat)	Electrical energy (electricity)	Fuel consumption	Raw material and resource consumption	Non-hazardous waste	Waste water	Emissions to air: greenhouse gas emissions	Emissions into the air: ozone depletion	Emissions into the soil: acidification	Emissions into water: ecotoxicity	**Environmental impact**	Process controllability	Optimisation potential	**Environmental priority**
Raw material sourcing	Raw materials	x	x	3	3	2	3	1	3	3	3	2	1	**58**	2	2	**232**
Processing to product	Manufacturing	x	x			3				1	1	1	1	**18**	2	3	**110**
Delivery to customer	Distribution	x			1			3		1	1	1	1	**18**	1	2	**35**
Use at customer	Use	x	x			2				1	1	1	1	**16**	3	1	**47**
End of life of product	Disposal		x		3		1			2	1	3	3	**32**	2	3	**194**
			Overall rating of environmental aspects	**3**	**7**	**7**	**4**	**4**	**3**	**8**	**7**	**8**	**7**				
			Materiality of environmental aspects	**8**	**19**	**20**	**10**	**7**	**4**	**22**	**18**	**18**	**16**				

Figure 3: Exemplary EDM using the LCA-based results shown above supplemented by weightings (own calculations).

The weightings can have a significant impact on the final results. Extreme caution should be exercised here and a mix of expert opinions should be obtained to avoid individual bias. The resulting outcomes vary significantly. Some environmental aspects are emerging as material, e.g., GHG emissions, fuel consumption, electrical energy, ozone depletion or acidification. In order to reduce environmental impacts in these areas, a quite comprehensive sustainability strategy would most likely be necessary.

From a process perspective, a significantly greater variation in the results is becoming visible. According to the environmental priority, the following priority-based ranking would result: raw material sourcing, end of life of product, processing to product, use at customer, and finally the delivery to customer. A strategic consequence here would probably focus on raw material sourcing (or procurement strategies, if applicable) and disposal (end of life strategies) of the examined object.

4. Discussion

The modelling framework presented in this article describes a novel combination of a dynamic EDM with the results of LCAs for optimising the environmental performance under consideration. This powerful tool assesses the materiality of the environmental aspects of the target object, the environmental priority of the investigated processes and thus enables priority-based ranking of environmental aspects and processes for proper decision-making in companies. The integration of an LCA also gives EDM a much more analytical and objective character.

One of the weaknesses of this approach is that the determination of geographical impact in the form of weightings (local, regional, global) can be entirely subjective, and assessment by a single individual should be avoided. In this context, a collegial body of experts should always be consulted to agree on the weightings. If no LCA is to be included, this also applies to the assessment of the relevance of environmental aspects for the individual processes. Here, too, an individual appraisal could be rather subjective and would therefore be subject to assessment bias. When incorporating additional topics, such as HSE or legal aspects, a uniform assessment methodology must also be used to avoid unnecessary bias.

Various challenges can also arise when integrating LCA results. In the LCA, it is important to select an appropriate number of processes. If, for example, too many processes are aggregated, the LCA results may suddenly show dominant aggregates, which could have a significant impact on the normalisation of the results. Dominant individual aggregates (e.g., the purchase of materials) could also arise. If necessary, a workaround would have to be used here, for example by removing such an outlier from the normalisation and evaluating it separately.

In any case, sensitivity analyses would be advisable in order to identify the key levers of the model. The one-at-a-time method,[12] in which individual

12 Alternatively, Monte Carlo simulations would be advisable.

parameters are changed in a targeted manner, would be suitable for this purpose. In the case shown, the weighting factors for geographical environmental impact (at local, regional or global level) are of course significant. A change in these factors can alter the overall result, for example the ranking. A change in these factors can alter the overall result, for example the ranking of the processes by environmental priority or of the environmental aspects by materiality. The sensitivity analysis should also examine two further parameters: the influenceability of the process and the optimisation potential within the process. These two factors also have a direct and, above all, very high effect on the environmental priority of the processes.

5. Conclusion

In conclusion, the novel modelling procedure presented in this contribution ensures that significant environmental aspects are identified in time and that measures can be taken in a timely manner at both product and organisational level. Moreover, this approach can be used in a variety of ways for decision-making and strategy development in companies. An important advantage of the EDM shown is that it can be expanded relatively flexibly to include relevant aspects in companies, such as HSE or legal aspects to comply with specific environmental standards in various processes. With regard to the integration of LCA results, the model framework shown is also extremely flexible: assessment categories can be exchanged flexibly, e.g., by using alternative LCIA methods.

The EDM itself can in any way be taken into account in companies' environmental statements (including EMAS, ISO 14001). This highlights hotspots, particularly during audits, and enables companies to take targeted action to improve their environmental performance and to promote transformation through innovation.[13]

In future, research is particularly needed on the integration of other LCA-based categories such as the inclusion of economic aspects in the form of a Life Cycle Costing (LCC), the analysis of LCA-based external environmental costs (Feichtinger and Posch, 2025b), the consideration of social aspects in the form of a social LCA (S-LCA), or also the consumption and reduction of critical raw materials (Feichtinger and Posch, 2025a). This would enable a more holistic life cycle sustainability assessment (LCSA) within this modelling framework.

13 For inspiration, see: Sinabell *et al.* (2022).

Abbreviations

CBAM	Carbon Boarder Adjustment Mechanism
CEAP	Circular Economy Action Plan
CRMA	Critical Raw Materials Act
CSDDD	Corporate Sustainability Due Diligence Directive
CSRD	Corporate Sustainability Reporting Directive
EDM	Environmental Decision Matrix
EMAS	Eco-Management and Audit Scheme
EMS	Environmental Management System
ESPR	Ecodesign for Sustainable Products Regulation
ESRS	European Sustainability Reporting Standards
EU-ETS	EU Emission Trading Scheme
GHG	Greenhouse Gas
HSE	Health, Safety and Environment
ISO	International Standardisation Organisation
LCA	Life Cycle Assessment
LCI	Life Cycle Inventory
LCIA	Life Cycle Impact Assessment
LCC	Life Cycle Costing
LCSA	Life Cycle Sustainability Assessment
S-LCA	Social Life Cycle Assessment
SBT	Science based Targets

References

Egger (2025), "Sustainability", available at: https://www.egger.com/en/about-us/sustainability/?country=GB (accessed 23 May 2025).

EMAS (2025), "Eco-Management and Audit Scheme (EMAS)", available at: https://green-forum.ec.europa.eu/emas_en (accessed 23 May 2025).

European Commission (2019), "The European Green Deal", available at: https://commission.europa.eu/strategy-and-policy/priorities-2019-2024/european-green-deal_en (accessed 23 May 2025).

Feichtinger, G. and Posch, W. (2025a), "Evaluation of European Critical Raw Material Assessments under Energy Transition Considerations. Applications and Prospects", *Circ.Econ.Sust.*, pp. 1–75. 10.1007/s43615-024-00493-0.

Feichtinger, G. and Posch, W. (2025b), "Monetization of Life-Cycle based Environmental Impacts. A Case Study on External Environmental Costs of Steel-based Wear Parts for Biogas Plants", *Energy Storage and Saving*, in press.

Frischknecht, R. (2020), *Lehrbuch der Ökobilanzierung, Lehrbuch*, Springer Spektrum, Berlin, Heidelberg.

Hauschild, M.Z., Rosenbaum, R.K. and Olsen, S.I. (2018), *Life cycle assessment: Theory and practice*, Springer, Cham.

Huijbregts, M.A.J., Steinmann, Z.J.N., Elshout, P.M.F., Stam, G., Verones, F., Vieira, M., Zijp, M., Hollander, A. and van Zelm, R. (2017), "ReCiPe2016: a harmonised life cycle impact assessment method at midpoint and endpoint level", *Int J Life Cycle Assess*, Vol. 22 No. 2, pp. 138–147. 10.1007/s11367-016-1246-y.

ISO (2025a), "ISO 14001:2015", available at: https://www.iso.org/standard/60857.html (accessed 23 May 2025).

ISO (2025b), "ISO 14040:2006", available at: https://www.iso.org/standard/37456.html (accessed 30 May 2025).

K, P. and Kumar, P. (2022), "A critical evaluation of air quality index models (1960-2021)", *Environ Monit Assess*, Vol. 194 No. 4, p. 324. 10.1007/s10661-022-09896-8.

Kettner-Marx, C. and Feichtinger, G. (2021), "Fit for 55? The EU's New Climate and Energy Package", *WIFO-Monatsberichte*, Vol. 94 No. 9, pp. 665–677.

Science Based Targets Initiative (2024), "The Corporate Net-Zero Standard", available at: https://files.sciencebasedtargets.org/production/files/Net-Zero-Standard-Criteria.pdf?dm=1734357634 (accessed 23 May 2025).

Sinabell, F., Bärenthaler-Sieber, S., Böheim, M., Christen, E., Feichtinger, G. and Sommer, M. (2022), "Green Deal and Transformation by Innovation. An Economic Analysis of the Chemical Industry in Austria", *Green Deal and Transformation by Innovation. An Economic Analysis of the Chemical Industry in Austria*.

Vester, F. and von Hesler, A. (1980), *Sensitivity model.*

Vis, P. and Delbeke, J. (Eds.) (2020), *Towards a Climate-Neutral Europe: Curbing the Trend*, Verlag nicht ermittelbar, Erscheinungsort nicht ermittelbar.

Gerald Feichtinger, Wolfgang Posch

The Scientific Spectrum of Life Cycle Assessments

A Modular Morphological Box Approach to Classify LCA-oriented Analyses

Abstract: This article provides an overview of the basic idea behind life cycle assessments (LCAs) in general. It briefly summarizes the history of LCAs and provides an overview of various standards and regulations that take the concept of LCAs into account. The most important characteristics of LCAs are then summarised and presented using a novel morphological box for LCAs. Its application is illustrated using two helpful exemplary profiles.

Keywords: Life cycle assessment (LCA), ISO, Regulations, Classification, Morphological box (Zwicky box).

1. Introduction

Originally, the idea of life cycle assessments (LCAs) dates back to the 1960s and 1970s in which serious concerns regarding environmental pollution, energy consumption and the depletion of natural resources emerged. As a collaboration between industries and university, initial life cycle-oriented methods and tools such as Ecobalances or the Resource and Environmental Profile Analysis (REPA) were developed and published. These initial methodological approaches, which originated mainly in the USA and in Europe, focused more on accounting for material and energy consumption and use, as well as emissions and waste management over the life cycle (from raw material extraction to the end of life) of products. Over time, the requirements for the inventories became more complex, leading to the development of initial functions for calculating environmental impact potentials. At this time, first software-based assessment tools (e.g., Gabi, SimaPro) as well as new impact methods emerged (e.g., critical volumes, Swiss Ecopoints, CML), and the term 'Life Cycle Assessment' was first mentioned by the SETAC[1] organisation in the beginning of the 1990s. Subsequently, the LCA methodology was defined and normalised on the basis of an ISO standard (1997) in the form of the follow-

1 Society of Environmental Toxicology and Chemistry

ing four phases: goal and scope definition, life cycle inventory (LCI), life cycle impact assessment (LCIA) and interpretation. From this point onwards, the LCA methodology developed into a very powerful and, above all, publicly accepted tool for analysing the environmental impacts of products, industrial processes and even entire organisations. (Bjørn *et al.*, 2018)

A further development of the basic idea behind LCAs describes the concept of life cycle thinking (LCT). This approach expands the basic idea of a life cycle-based environmental analysis to include two important dimensions: the economic perspective and the social aspects within the entire life cycle chain (respectively activity or value chain). The LCT approach thus describes a holistic analytical approach in which all three dimensions of sustainability are addressed together leading to a life cycle sustainability assessment (LCSA). While a life cycle costing (LCC) analysis is carried out to catch the economic dimension, social aspects are analysed using a social LCA (S-LCA). The basic idea of LCT is also attracting steadily growing interest at the level of political strategy (or decision) making. Within European Union (EU) legislation in particular, the concept of LCT and LCA has been increasingly taken into account across industrial sectors since 1990, especially in communications, decisions, regulations and directives (Sala *et al.*, 2021). Due to these legal requirements, but also due to new dynamics arising from the digital transformation towards a new type of data economy, the development of LCA methodology has experienced an enormous boost in recent years, resulting in the emergence and development of new methodological approaches and tools being developed or currently being under development.

This broad spectrum of LCA-based approaches has become somewhat confusing and requires a systematic approach to capture and classify the methodological range of LCA. Based on that, this contribution provides an attempt of a classification of several LCA-related sub-disciplines to better understand the existing full scientific spectrum of this research field. Therefore, a morphological box approach was chosen to analyse the LCA methodology using its main features, characteristics and its associated manifestations. All considerations presented here can be taken into account in future analyses to classify the relevant dimensions of chosen LCA-based assessment approach.

2. Standards and regulations for LCAs

After LCA was established as an analytical method in the 1990s, various activities were undertaken to standardise (through ISO) and harmonise[2] the

2 For example, through the International Life Cycle Data (ILCD) system introduced by the European Commission (EC) in the 2010s.

conduct of LCA-based studies internationally. Since then, a large number of standards but also regulations have been adopted that use the general principles of the LCA methodology.

2.1. ISO standardization

In principle, the ISO 14040/44 standards serve as the foundation for conducting LCA studies, which have been gradually adopted by ISO since 1997: ISO 14040 defines some basic principles for conducting LCAs (published in 1997), ISO 14041 defines objectives/scope and the life cycle inventory (LCI, in 1998), ISO 14042 defines the life cycle impact assessment (LCIA, in 2000), and ISO 14043 provides principles for the interpretation of LCAs (also in 2000). In 2006, these ISO norms have been consolidated and republished in the ISO 14040 which provides now the general framework for LCAs and the ISO 14044 which defines all technical requirements for conducting LCAs.

The ISO 14040/44 standards define the four LCA phases: definition of objectives and scope, the LCI, the LCIA, and interpretation of the results. Important to note is that the LCIA comprises three key steps: selection of impact categories, classification through assigning the LCI results to the impact categories, and characterisation through quantifying the environmental impacts. In the final evaluation of the results, hotspots are identified and, if necessary, an uncertainty and sensitivity analysis is carried out to draw conclusions and derive recommendations for further action.

Since then, various other LCA-oriented ISO standards have been adopted, which include (selection): eco labels (ISO 14021/24/25), water footprint (ISO 14046), carbon footprint (ISO 14064/67), organisations (ISO 14072) or carbon neutrality (ISO 14068). Table 1 provides a summary of the most commonly known LCA-related ISO standards.

Eco-labels have recently become increasingly important. In principle, there exist three types of ISO-based eco-labels: type I labels (ISO 14024) consist of voluntary but third-party verified certifications of products, type II labels (ISO 14021) consist of self-declarations of manufacturers without any third-party verification, and type III labels (ISO 14025) consist of verified environmental product declarations (EPDs) which are steadily gaining in importance. While type I and II labels use LCAs on a voluntary basis, LCAs are mandatory for type III labels based on so-called product category rules (PCRs). Of importance are LCA-based calculations for greenhouse gas (GHG) stock-taking (ISO 14064) and for assessing the carbon footprint of products (ISO 14067) and companies (ISO 14064 and ISO 14072).

An ISO standard exists for conducting LCCs, although with a specific focus on buildings (ISO 15686). Interestingly, currently no ISO standard for conducting an S-LCA exists. However, the assessment of an S-LCA is generally also based on the four familiar LCA phases.

2.2. Other standards and regulations

As also indicated in Table 1, several other LCA-oriented standards, guidelines and legislations exist, which vary considerably between sectors, countries and regions. The most important contributors include (among others): United Nations Environment Programme (UNEP) in cooperation with the Life Cycle Initiative (LCI), World Resource Institute (WRI) with its GHG protocol, the EPD international including the international EPD system, and the European Union (EU) with various important contributions.

Table 1. Overview of applicable standards and norms for LCA creation (selection; based on: (ISO, 2025)).

Standard	Level			Scope of application
	Product	*Organization*	*Country*	
ISO 14000 series		X		Requirements for EMS for organisations
ISO 14020	X			Lays down the principles for all environmental labelling programmes
ISO 14021	X			Type II eco-label: Self-declarations by manufacturer/ distributor
ISO 14024	X			Type I eco-label: For products with good performance
ISO 14025	X			Type III eco-label: Environmental Product Declaration (EPD)
ISO 14026	X			Eco-labels: Principles/procedures on environmental information
ISO 14027	X			Eco-labels: Development of product category rules (PCR)
ISO/TS 14029	X			Mutual recognition of EPDs and footprint communication programmes
ISO 14040	X	X		Framework and principles of LCA
ISO 14044	X	X		Requirements and guidelines for conducting LCA
ISO 14045	X			Eco-efficiency assessment of product systems
ISO 14046	X	X		Assessment of the water footprint based on LCA principles
ISO 14047	X			Examples: ISO 14044 to impact assessment
ISO 14048	X	X		Requirements for transparent/consistent documentation of LCI
ISO 14049	X			Examples: ISO 14044, scope definition and baseline analysis
ISO 14051/52	X			General framework for material flow cost accounting (MFCA)

Standard	Level			Scope of application
	Product	*Organiza-tion*	*Country*	
ISO 14063		X		Guidelines relating to internal/external environmental communication
ISO 14064-1		X		Greenhouse gases and their removal: organisational level, CCF
ISO 14064-2		X		Greenhouse gases and their removal: project level
ISO 14064-3		X		Guidelines for the verification/validation of greenhouse gas statements
ISO 14067	X			Carbon footprint of products (product carbon footprint, PCF)
ISO 14068 (*)		X		Main focus is on greenhouse gas management and carbon neutrality
ISO 14069		X		Quantifying/Reporting direct/indirect GHG emissions of organisation
ISO 14071	X	X		Requirements and guidelines for the critical review process
ISO 14072		X		Technical specification of LCA at organisational level
ISO 14074 (*)	X	X		Guidelines for normalisation/weighting/interpretation of LCIA
ISO 14080		X		Guidelines for methods for climate change mitigation measures
ISO 14097 (*)		X		Principles for climate change-related financing activities/ investments
ISO 15686-5	X	X		Life cycle costing (LCC) of buildings
ISO 20915	X			Guidelines for the preparation of LCA inventories for steel products
ISO 21930	X			Core rules for EPDs of construction products and ser-vices
ISO 22526	X			Principles for carbon/environmental footprint of bio-based plastics
ISO 24758-1	X			Guidelines/principles for life cycle management (LCM)
ISO 59000 series (*)	X	X		Guidelines/principles for CE, BM and value chains
Bilans GES		X	France	Guidelines for organisations to report GHG emissions (Scope 1, 2, 3)
BP X30-323	X		France	Method for environmental impact of products & labelling
BS 8001		X	UK	Guidelines for organisations wishing to apply CE
Catena-X (CX-PCF-rules)	X			Rulebook for conducting PCF in the automotive industry
CFP	X		Korea	Guidelines for the carbon footprint of products (CFP)
CSDDD			EU	Debits companies for exercising due diligence along supply chains
CSR		X		Concept for companies to take responsibility for socio-ecol. impacts

Standard	Level			Scope of application
	Product	*Organiza-tion*	*Country*	
CSRD			EU	Directive requiring companies to prepare sustainability reports
DEFRA		X	UK	Guidelines for measuring and reporting greenhouse gas emissions
EcoLeaf	X		Japan	Methodology for assessing the environmental impact of products
EN 15804+A1	X			EPDs for construction products (according to the CML method)
EN 15804+A2	X			EPDs for construction products (according to EF 3.1)
ESPR	X		EU	Legislative proposal to promote eco-design of products (DPP)
Global Water Foot-print Standard		X		Methodology for quantifying/assessing water consump-tion
GHG Protocol	X	X		Measurement of GHG emissions at product and organi-sational level
ILCD	X	X	EU	Technical guidance for conducting detailed LCA studies
UNEP/SETAC	X	X		Promotes development/application of LCA (globally)
OEF		X	EU	EU standard on the environmental performance of organisations
OEFCR		X	EU	Organisation-specification for OEF creation
PAS 2050	X		UK	Specification for GHG emissions over the life cycle of products
PAS 2060	X	X	EU	Requirements for achieving and demonstrating carbon neutrality
PCR	X			Product-specification for EPD creation
PEF	X		EU	EU standard on the environmental performance of products
PEFCR	X			Product-specification for PEF creation
S-LCA	X	X		Guidelines for S-LCA of products and organisations (by UNEP)
S-PCR	X			Product-specification for SPD creation
SPD incl. SPD-PCR	X			Transparency of social impacts of products (social label)

(*) Under development

First and foremost, the UNEP/LCI cooperation contributes to the publication of guidelines and specifications, particularly for the comparable implementation of LCAs. These include, among other things, non-binding guidelines for dealing with LCA, S-LCA and LCSA, with its most recent publication of the GLAM[3] method in 2024. EPD international manages and develops the

3 Global Guidance for Life Cycle Impact Assessment Indicators and Methods.

most important platform for handling EPDs and recently published (in 2023) a novel type of social product declaration (SPD). However, ISO 21930 and standards EN 15804+A1 (based on the CML methodology) and EN 15804+A2 (based on the PEF methodology) are of central importance for the preparation of EPDs.

From a global perspective, the EU's contribution in the field of LCAs is also extremely valuable. The EU began harmonising LCA studies at a very early stage, in particular by publishing the ILCD handbook (in 2010). Subsequently in 2012, the EU began developing a uniform method for assessing the ecological footprint of products and organisations, which was finally published in 2021 with accompanying product/organisation environmental footprint (PEF/OEF) category rules (PEFCR/OEFCR). The steadily increasing importance of LCA in recent EU legislation is shown by (Sala *et al.*, 2021). The most important initiatives include (among others): European Green Deal in general, Clean Industrial Deal, circular economy action plan, public procurement, sustainable investments, single use plastics, packaging waste, renewable energy directives (RED), or the ecodesign for sustainable products regulation (ESPR). However, LCAs can and will also be important for the corporate sustainability reporting directive (CSRD) and the corporate sustainability due diligence directive (CSDDD) in the future, as LCAs provide helpful information for the assessment of sustainability-related information along the entire activity chain of a company.

3. Methodological classification of LCAs

The historical development of LCA methodology shows a continuous progression towards an integrated analytical approach such as LCSA or LCT. In particular, ongoing digitalisation and the associated technological advances (e.g., software tools, databases for real-time applications, automation) created completely new opportunities for the application and further development of the LCA methodology. Due to today´s large number of available characteristics that can be taken into account when conducting an LCA, a systematic classification would in any case be helpful for LCA practitioners.

3.1. Morphological analysis of LCAs

A morphological analysis is a systematic method for breaking down complex problems into individual components and examining all possible combinations of solutions. This method was developed by Fritz Zwicky back in the

1960s and is still used today for developing ideas and innovative solutions. The result of the morphological analysis is a so-called "morphological box",[4] which represents in general a two- or multi-dimensional decision matrix in which all independent characteristics[5] and all possible manifestations of the respective characteristic are presented. Each combination of characteristics in the morphological box thus represents a theoretically possible solution. Based on the objective basis of the morphological box, new combinations of characteristics that may not have been intuitively apparent can become visible as potential new solutions for the further decision-making process (Zwicky, 1967).

This article uses a morphological analysis to provide a general classification of various characteristics in relation to LCA-based assessments. Based on a comprehensive literature review, various characteristics of the LCA methodology were identified and possible manifestations for each characteristic were defined. Some characteristics shown may not seem intuitive at first glance, but the overview demonstrates the theoretical potential of the LCA methodology today. All identified characteristics and the respective manifestations of each characteristic are then merged into a, from the authors' perspective to date, novel morphological box for LCA-oriented assessments. This novel morphological box offers various, potentially novel, problem-solving approaches for the application of LCA-oriented assessments. The results achieved with this analysis also highlight the complexity of applying LCA-based assessments which are possible nowadays.

The identified characteristics[6] for LCA-oriented assessments include: approach, impact, model coupling, object, scope, system model, spatial (geography), technology readiness (past-oriented vs. future-oriented), time (temporality), model integration and sources (for data). Figure 1 depicts and summarizes the novel morphological box for LCA-oriented assessments by combining all identified characteristics and the associated manifestations.

4 Also known as "Zwicky box".

5 Also referred to as attributes, factors, parameters or dimensions.

6 There even may be further characteristics that have not been taken into account here.

Super-class	Characteristic	Manifestation					
Framework	Approach	Assessment (LCA)		Optimisation (LCO)		Management (LCM)	
	Impact	Environmental (E-LCA, LCA)		Life Cycle Costing (LCC)	Social (S-LCA)	Integrated LCA (LCSA)	
	Model design	Bottom-Up		Top-Down		Hybrid LCA (HLCA)	
	Object	Business Model (BM-LCA)	Product / Process (P-LCA)	Organisation LCA (O-LCA)	Territory (Te-LCA)	Transition (Tr-LCA)	Input-Output (IO-LCA)
Boundary	Scope	Gate-to-Gate	Cradle-to-Gate	Cradle-to-Grave		Cradle-to-Cradle (CE)	Well-to-Wheel
	System model	Attributional (ALCA)			Consequential (CLCA)		
	Spatial (geography)	Regionalized		Partially spatially explicit		Spatially explicit	
Time	State	Static		Partially dynamic		Dynamic	
	Temporal	Lab-scale LCA		Retrospective LCA	Ex-post LCA	Historical LCA	
				Prospective LCA	Ex-ante LCA	Anticipatory LCA	
Network	Coupling	Stand-alone		Partially integrated		Fully-integrated	
	Integration	Manual		Semi-automated		Fully-automated	
	Sources	Internal		External		Mixed	
Supplementary	Extensions	Parametric LCA (PLCA)		Real-time		Model linking	

Figure 1. Classification of LCA-oriented assessments using a novel morphological box (own illustration[7]).

7 Based on: Frischknecht (2020); Hauschild *et al.* (2018); Huijbregts *et al.* (2017); Valdivia and Sonnemann (2024); Arvidsson *et al.* (2024); Hagenaars *et al.* (2025); Ventura (2022);

3.2. Terminology for the morphological analysis of LCAs

All identified characteristics of the morphological box comprise various manifestations, which are briefly explained for the sake of comprehensible application. Some combinations are purely theoretical in nature and do not necessarily have to be applied in practice. Below follows a brief explanation of the relevant terminology used in the morphological box.

Approach: Describes the underlying concept for the sustainability and/or business assessment. A distinction is made here between classical life cycle assessment (LCA) to evaluate different impacts (e.g., ecological, social, economic), life cycle optimisation (LCO) to find the best-possible solution and life cycle management (LCM) to integrate LCT into in a broader management process.

Impact: Describes the key impacts to be analysed by the LCA-based investigation. A distinction is made between six identified characteristics: the classic ecological LCA (E-LCA or LCA), the social LCA (S-LCA), the economic life cycle costing (LCC), and a fully integrated life cycle sustainability assessment (LCSA) which combines all three pillars of sustainability.

Model design: The basic design is essential in techno-economic modelling and defines the underlying model structure, which must be determined in advance. A basic distinction is made between the following options: bottom-up (or "from the bottom up") is a step-by-step model development starting with individual components and progressing to more complex systems, top-down (or "from the top down") is a step-by-step breakdown of a complex system into its subsystems, and hybrid systems, such as hybrid LCA (HLCA), are a combination of the two approaches.

Object: Describes the defined target object of the LCA-based investigation. A distinction is made between the following objects: an existing business model (BM-LCA), a product or entire process (P-LCA), an entire organisation (O-LCA), a higher-level territory (Te-LCA), an analysis of profound structural changes (transition) in interconnected economic sectors (Tr-LCA), and an input-output LCA (IO-LCA) examines all direct and indirect environmental impacts of a product based by using the economic flow data of goods and services of an entire economy (based on an economic input-output table).

Scope: The scope describes the boundary or boundary line of an LCA-based investigation. A distinction is generally made between the following

Loiseau *et al.* (2018); Böckin *et al.* (2022); Kamalakkannan and Kulatunga (2021); Basic *et al.* (2019); Shi and Yan (2024); Ma *et al.* (2024); Potrč Obrecht *et al.* (2020); Mastrucci *et al.* (2015); Sonnemann and Margni (2015); Beloin-Saint-Pierre *et al.* (2020); Lueddeckens *et al.* (2020); Azapagic and Clift (1999).

boundaries: Gate-to-Gate for investigations of operational activities at the site; Cradle-to-Gate supplements all upstream processing steps including raw material extraction; Cradle-to-Grave also takes all downstream process steps into account up to the disposal; Cradle-to-Cradle describes the concept of circular economy (CE) in which all products are recycled; describes an independent concept for analysing energy resources from their origin ('well') to their usage in cars ('wheel').

System model: The system model of an LCA describes which impacts are analysed by the LCA. An attributional LCA (ALCA) estimates the environmental burden associated with a product's specific life cycle, and a consequential LCA (CLCA) assesses the environmental impact of a change in demand for that product.

Spatial (geography): The inclusion of spatial information or geo-referenced data (e.g., Ecoinvent) in LCA-based analyses is becoming increasingly important. The following categories can be distinguished here: regionalised LCA uses higher level average values (e.g., at country or global level), spatially explicit LCA takes spatial information into account to increase the accuracy of the calculation, and a partially spatially explicit LCA is a hybrid form of the two aforementioned in which spatial information is taken into account where available and regionalised values are used otherwise.

State: The state of a model is a key aspect of LCA-based analyses since certain parameter (e.g., data-inputs, used technologies) change over time, but it is often neglected, leading to temporal distortions in the results. However, in relation to temporality and LCAs, the following characteristics can be distinguished: a static LCA considers a rigid and therefore time-fixed system, a partially dynamic LCA includes temporality in at least one modelling phase,[8] and a dynamic LCA (DLCA) includes temporality in all of the modelling phases mentioned before.

Temporal (past-oriented): Past-oriented LCAs are usually more robust assessments since existing historical (real) data can be included in the analyses. Depending on the maturity of the technologies considered, a distinction is made as follows: lab scale LCA takes into account technologies at a very low technology readiness level (TRL) to identify hotspots at very early stages of technology development, retrospective LCA is a study at a recent past time which considers technologies which are not yet fully mature, an ex-post LCA denotes an LCA of technologies that have already become mature at a past point in time, and a historical LCA is a study at a more distant time in the past to assess historical impacts.

---

8 Including: goal and scope definition, LCI, LCIA, and evaluation, but also normalisation and weighting

Temporal (future-oriented): Future-oriented LCA studies are becoming increasingly important and widely used. However, due to uncertainties in the data and technology assumptions, caution is advised when interpreting the results. As with the past-oriented LCA, future-oriented LCA are divided using the TRL: lab-scale LCA focus on LCA studies at a future point in time with a relatively low TRL level (e.g., to identify potential hotspots), a prospective LCA is a study at a future point in time relative to the time at which the study is conducted, an ex-ante LCA is a study at a future point in time which considers technologies that have become more mature at this future point in time (a future state of the technologies is being modelled), and an anticipatory LCA additionally considers a strong focus in terms of a stakeholder engagement process to further consider methodological choices (for, e.g., system boundaries, functional unit, impact category selection, weighting) which is done by an increased social engagement to avoid privileging selected stakeholders.

Coupling: Describes how LCA-based models can be set up and operated in a digitalised environment. A distinction is made between the following environments: Stand-alone as an isolated model, partially integrated (i.e., in unidirectional exchange with another model), fully integrated (i.e., in bidirectional exchange with another model), or as fundamentally hybrid LCA (H-LCA) in which different LCA approaches are coupled (e.g., product-based with a macroeconomic input-output model).

Integration: Describes the integration of the LCA model into a more comprehensive and uniform information framework. A key aspect of this integration is the form of data exchange between the LCA model and surrounding information framework. The following approaches are distinguished: manual data transfer involves a data exchange process through human interaction, semi-automated data transfer refers to a data exchange process in which some aspects require human intervention, and fully-automated data transfer refers to a fully automated data exchange (especially via interfaces) to minimise error rates and increase efficiency.

Sources: In LCA studies, data sources are particularly important to better assess the significance and robustness of the study. In this context, the following data sources can be distinguished: internal[9] data describe the ideal state in the form of proprietary real-time data, external data (e.g., open-source or proprietary material flow databases such as Ecoinvent) is required if no appropriate internal data is available, and mixed data is a combination of the first two options (which is usually the norm).

---

9 However, some of this data may be confidential/sensitive and therefore not available.

Supplementary (extensions): Recently, new variants of LCA-based analyses have been developed. These include, for example, parametric LCA (PLCA) which enables the generation of different design variants in a simple manner or real-time LCA which allows the creation of studies by using real-time data. Other options are model extensions to expand the scope of application of LCA-oriented analyses trough linking LCAs with other approaches such as agent-based, emergy,[10] exergy or Building Information Modelling (BIM).

3.3. Super-classes for the morphological analysis of LCAs

To simplify the analysis somewhat, all of the characteristics mentioned above can be grouped into higher-level 'super-classes'. Such 'super-classes' should summarise the fundamental characteristics and facilitate the classification of the LCA analysis to be carried out. In total four 'super-classes' have been identified, which are:

Framework: A general framework is essential for an LCA-based assessment and includes several fundamental characteristics of LCA analysis. These are approach, impact, model design and object.

Boundary: For each LCA model, various boundaries must be defined in advance in order to narrow down the scope of the analysis somewhat. These include the scope, system model and spatial (or geographical) restrictions with regard to the input parameters.

Time: The time factor must be taken into account in every LCA analysis and includes the state of the model and the temporality (past- and future-oriented) under consideration.

Network: The integration of an LCA-based model is playing an increasingly important role in the age of digitalisation and enables significantly more efficient analyses. The categories identified for this purpose include (model) coupling, (data) integration and (data) sources.

Supplementary (optional): New fields of application and corresponding specialisations or linked modelling approaches are constantly emerging within the spectrum of LCA applications. These include parametric LCAs (PLCA), real-time LCAs and, in general, a linking of LCAs to complementary modelling approaches from other disciplines.

---

10 A systems-based approach to highlight complex internal energy flows and material conversion processes within systems.

3.4. Exemplary application of the morphological box

Figure 2 depicts an exemplary illustration of the newly developed morphological box by deriving two possible application profiles for LCA-based analyses: a traditional approach to determine the product carbon footprint using an LCA and a novel concept of a Green Digital Twin (GDT).[11] Both application examples have different characterisation profiles.

The traditional LCA approach shown in the figure has the following characteristics: a classic environmental assessment based on a bottom-up principle for determining the carbon footprint for a product (attributional), a cradle-to-grave approach with partially spatially explicit information (e.g., for electricity), a static but retrospective approach with uncertainties, without a connection to other models and with manual data entry.

On the other hand, the GDT approach is somewhat more comprehensive and dynamic due to its complete integration into a DT-based system. In principle, a GDT-based model offers various implementation options, ranging from past-oriented assessments to future-oriented scenario analyses. The GDT profile shown here focuses rather on the strategy development (management) using an integrated LCA approach in which all three dimensions of sustainability (environment, economy and social) can be mapped. In this ideal situation, the mapping of a CE with spatially explicit data and complete integration is planned as part of a higher-level information management system. Moreover, the chosen GDT profile takes into account fully automated data exchange via pre-defined and implemented interfaces (or pipelines) and enables real-time assessments.

11 A GDT is a digital twin (DT) based concept for performing LCAs in real-time (Feichtinger *et al.* (2024)).

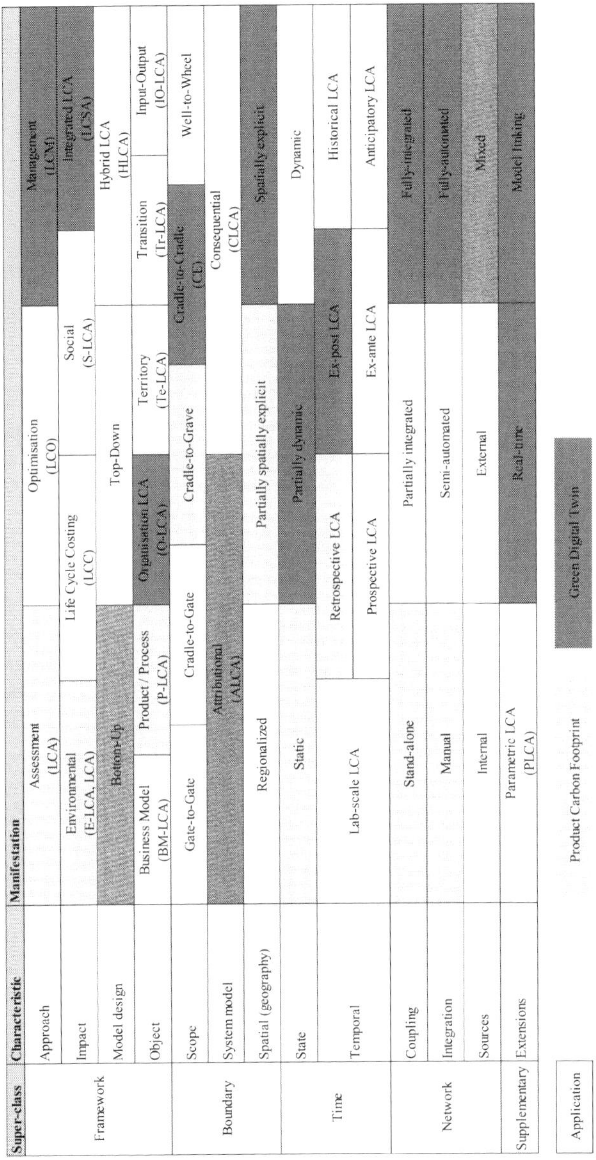

Figure 2. Comparative application of the developed morphological box (own assumptions).

Both illustrated profiles demonstrate the simple and flexible applicability of the morphological box for LCA-oriented analyses. In addition to proven approaches (e.g., traditional E-LCA), this modular system can also be used to map future applications (e.g., GDT).

4. Discussion and Outlook

The aim of this paper was to develop a simple modular assessment tool for LCA-oriented analyses based on a morphological box. This modular-based analysis tool should map all important characteristics for LCAs to be able to define a profile of requirements for LCA-based applications in advance, to compare different profiles of LCA-based applications and to explore new, initially perhaps counterintuitive, application possibilities for LCAs.

The development of the modular morphological box presented here is still in its early stages and will be adapted and/or expanded where necessary in the future in the course of critical discussion within the scientific community. All manifestations shown were taken from scientific literature, but may well be new to individual LCA practitioners. When deriving new or alternative application profiles, overlaps are certainly conceivable, but these should not cause any further confusion. Rather, this modular representation of the morphological box serves to generate ideas to identify further possible applications of LCA-oriented analyses, which could create new applications for LCAs in the future.

Some characteristics for LCAs were not yet included in this first version of the morphological box for LCA analyses. The reasons are manifold, but the integration of additional aspects require further discussion due to the involved complexity matrix. Potential candidate characteristics for the morphological box include an option for an application-oriented benchmarking[12] to determine whether the analysis is being carried out for internal or external purposes (e.g., to compare the environmental performance of a product with competitors within or outside the industry/sector). Another option could be to integrate the results directly into follow-up applications such as the creation of an EPD, a digital product passport (DPP), an environmental decision matrix (EDM)[13] or to estimate external costs (Feichtinger and Posch, 2025). The aspect of multifunctionality in terms of the production of co-products in the system under consideration and its consequences (including problems with allocation and expansion of system boundaries) as well as the consider-

12 This also includes the aspect of performing comparative LCAs.

13 For a detailed definition, see Feichtinger *et al.* (2025).

ation of recycling aspects (including cut-off issues and closed-loop scenarios) should also be taken into account. A comparatively simple addition would be to specify the planned impact assessment method (for E-LCA, e.g., CF according to IPCC, ReCiPe, EF 3.1, GLAM). With regard to scope, classification could be based on the nomenclature in accordance with EN 15804: A1-A3 production, A4-A5 installation, B1-B7 use, C1-C4 disposal and D supplementary (e.g., measures for CE). The discussion regarding the definition of functional unit (including inherent vs. explicit) and its characteristics is much more complex (Frigerio *et al.*, 2023). When considering new characteristics in the morphological box, it is generally important to determine whether the considered characteristic is generally applicable (i.e. relevant for all LCAs) or specific to a particular area of application of LCAs.

The 'super-classes' also shown in this article serve to structure and thus simplify the application of the morphological box presented here. Changes and further developments are still being considered.

Furthermore, due to the larger quantity of manifestations considered in the morphological box, it would make sense to create a simplified influence matrix (Vester matrix)[14] to analyse the mutual influence of the individual manifestations (of the characteristics). It is important to note again that not all theoretical combinations are feasible or make sense in practice.

Abbreviations

ALCA	Attributional Life Cycle Assessment
BIM	Building Information Modelling
BM-LCA	Business Model Life Cycle Assessment
CCF	Corporate Carbon Footprint
CE	Circular Economy
CFP	Carbon Footprint of Products
CLCA	Consequential Life Cycle Assessment
CSDDD	Corporate Sustainability Due Diligence Directive
CSR	Corporate Social Responsibility
CSRD	Corporate Sustainability Reporting Directive

14 For example, using a simplified scale: '-1' negative impact, '0' no impact, and '+1' positive impact.

DEFRA	Department for Environment, Food&Rural Affairs
DPP	Digital Product Passport
DT	Digital Twin
E-LCA	Environmental Life Cycle Assessment
EDM	Environmental Decision Matrix
EMS	Environmental Management System
EPD	Environmental Product Declaration
ESPR	Ecodesign for Sustainable Products Regulation
EU	European Union
GDT	Green Digital Twin
GHG	Greenhouse Gas
GLAM	Global Guidance for LCIA Indicators and Methods
HLCA	Hybrid Life Cycle Assessment
ILCD	International Life Cycle Data
IO-LCA	Input-Output Life Cycle Assessment
ISO	International Organization for Standardization
LCA	Life Cycle Assessment
LCC	Life Cycle Costing
LCI	Life Cycle Inventory (but also: Life Cycle Initiative)
LCIA	Life Cycle Impact Assessment
LCM	Life Cycle Management
LCO	Life Cycle Optimisation
LCSA	Life Cycle Sustainability Assessment
LCT	Life Cycle Thinking
MOO	Multi-Objective Optimisation
O-LCA	Organisation Life Cycle Assessment
OEF	Organisation Environment Footprint
P-LCA	Product/Process Life Cycle Assessment
PCF	Product Carbon Footprint
PCR	Product Category Rules
PEF	Product Environment Footprint

PLCA	Parametric Life Cycle Assessment
RED	Renewable Energy Directive
REPA	Resource and Environmental Profile Analysis
S-LCA	Social Life Cycle Assessment
SC	Supply Chain
SETAC	Society of Environmental Toxicology and Chemistry
SPD	Social Product Declaration
Te-LCA	Territory Life Cycle Assessment
Tr-LCA	Transition Life Cycle Assessment
TRL	Technology Readiness Level
UNEP	United Nation Environmental Programme
WRI	World Resource Institute

References

Arvidsson, R., Svanström, M., Sandén, B.A., Thonemann, N., Steubing, B. and Cucurachi, S. (2024), "Terminology for future-oriented life cycle assessment: review and recommendations", *Int J Life Cycle Assess*, Vol. 29 No. 4, pp. 607–613. 10.1007/s11367-023-02265-8.

Azapagic, A. and Clift, R. (1999), "Life cycle assessment and multiobjective optimisation", *Journal of Cleaner Production*, Vol. 7 No. 2, pp. 135–143. 10.1016/S0959-6526(98)00051-1.

Basic, S., Hollberg, A., Galimshina, A. and Habert, G. (2019), "A design integrated parametric tool for real-time Life Cycle Assessment – Bombyx project", *IOP Conf. Ser.: Earth Environ. Sci.*, Vol. 323 No. 1, p. 12112. 10.1088/1755-1315/323/1/012112.

Beloin-Saint-Pierre, D., Albers, A., Hélias, A., Tiruta-Barna, L., Fantke, P., Levasseur, A., Benetto, E., Benoist, A. and Collet, P. (2020), "Addressing temporal considerations in life cycle assessment", *The Science of the total environment*, Vol. 743, p. 140700. 10.1016/j.scitotenv.2020.140700.

Bjørn, A., Owsianiak, M., Molin, C. and Hauschild, M.Z. (2018), "LCA History", in Hauschild, M.Z., Rosenbaum, R.K. and Olsen, S.I. (Eds.), *Life Cycle Assessment*, Springer International Publishing, Cham, pp. 17–30.

Böckin, D., Goffetti, G., Baumann, H., Tillman, A.-M. and Zobel, T. (2022), "Business model life cycle assessment: A method for analysing the environmental performance of business", *Sustainable Production and Consumption*, Vol. 32, pp. 112–124. 10.1016/j.spc.2022.04.014.

Feichtinger, G., Koller, D. and Posch, W. (2025), "Analysis of Environmental Performance using a flexible Environmental Decision Matrix based on Life Cycle Assessment. A Novel Model Framework for Analysing the Entire Chain of Activities", in Posch, W., Vorbach, S., Zsifkovits, H.E. and Feichtinger, G. (Eds.), *Nachhaltige Transformation in Krisenzeiten*, *Sustainability Management for Industries*, 1. Auflage, Nomos Verlagsgesellschaft mbH & Co. KG, Baden-Baden.

Feichtinger, G., Mark, D., Schlar, D. and Posch, W. (2024), *Green Digital Twin for Organizations as Enabler for Carbon Management*, 19th Conference on Sustainable Development of Energy, Water and Environment Systems, Rome, Italy.

Feichtinger, G. and Posch, W. (2025), "Monetization of Life-Cycle based Environmental Impacts. A Case Study on External Environmental Costs of Steel-based Wear Parts for Biogas Plants", *Energy Storage and Saving*, in press.

Frigerio, V., Casson, A. and Limbo, S. (2023), "Comparison of different methodological choices in functional unit selection and results implication when assessing food-packaging environmental impact", *Journal of Cleaner Production*, Vol. 396, p. 136527. 10.1016/j.jclepro.2023.136527.

Frischknecht, R. (2020), *Lehrbuch der Ökobilanzierung, Lehrbuch*, Springer Spektrum, Berlin, Heidelberg.

Hagenaars, R.H., Heijungs, R., Tukker, A. and Wang, R. (2025), "Hybrid LCA for sustainable transitions: principles, applications, and prospects", *Renewable and Sustainable Energy Reviews*, Vol. 212, p. 115443. 10.1016/j.rser.2025.115443.

Hauschild, M.Z., Rosenbaum, R.K. and Olsen, S.I. (2018), *Life cycle assessment: Theory and practice*, Springer, Cham.

Huijbregts, M.A.J., Steinmann, Z.J.N., Elshout, P.M.F., Stam, G., Verones, F., Vieira, M., Zijp, M., Hollander, A. and van Zelm, R. (2017), "ReCiPe2016: a harmonised life cycle impact assessment method at midpoint and endpoint level", *Int J Life Cycle Assess*, Vol. 22 No. 2, pp. 138–147. 10.1007/s11367-016-1246-y.

ISO (2025), "ISO - Standards", available at: https://www.iso.org/standards.html (accessed 4 June 2025).

Kamalakkannan, S. and Kulatunga, A.K. (2021), "Optimization of eco-design decisions using a parametric life cycle assessment", *Sustainable Production and Consumption*, Vol. 27, pp. 1297–1316. 10.1016/j.spc.2021.03.006.

Loiseau, E., Aissani, L., Le Féon, S., Laurent, F., Cerceau, J., Sala, S. and Roux, P. (2018), "Territorial Life Cycle Assessment (LCA): What exactly is it about? A proposal towards using a common terminology and a research agenda", *Journal of Cleaner Production*, Vol. 176, pp. 474–485. 10.1016/j.jclepro.2017.12.169.

Lueddeckens, S., Saling, P. and Guenther, E. (2020), "Temporal issues in life cycle assessment—a systematic review", *Int J Life Cycle Assess*, Vol. 25 No. 8, pp. 1385–1401. 10.1007/s11367-020-01757-1.

Ma, L., Azari, R. and Elnimeiri, M. (2024), "A Building Information Modeling-Based Life Cycle Assessment of the Embodied Carbon and Environmental Impacts of High-Rise Building Structures: A Case Study", *Sustainability*, Vol. 16 No. 2, p. 569. 10.3390/su16020569.

Mastrucci, A., Popovici, E., Marvuglia, A., Sousa, L. de, Benetto, E. and Leopold, U. (Eds.) (2015), *GIS-based Life Cycle Assessment of urban building stocks retrofitting- a bottom-up framework applied to Luxembourg*.

Potrč Obrecht, T., Röck, M., Hoxha, E. and Passer, A. (2020), "BIM and LCA Integration: A Systematic Literature Review", *Sustainability*, Vol. 12 No. 14, p. 5534. 10.3390/su12145534.

Sala, S., Amadei, A.M., Beylot, A. and Ardente, F. (2021), "The evolution of life cycle assessment in European policies over three decades", *Int J Life Cycle Assess*, Vol. 26 No. 12, pp. 2295–2314. 10.1007/s11367-021-01893-2.

Shi, S. and Yan, X. (2024), "A critical review on spatially explicit life cycle assessment methodologies and applications", *Sustainable Production and Consumption*, Vol. 52, pp. 566–579. 10.1016/j.spc.2024.11.015.

Sonnemann, G. and Margni, M. (2015), *Life cycle management, LCA compendium - The complete world of life cycle assessment*, Springer Open, Dordrecht, Heidelberg, New York, London.

Valdivia, S. and Sonnemann, G. (2024), *Handbook on life cycle sustainability assessment, Elgar handbooks in development*, Edward Elgar Publishing, Cheltenham, Northampton.

Ventura, A. (2022), "Transition life cycle assessment: A new method to face ecological transition", *Front. Sustain.*, Vol. 3. 10.3389/frsus.2022.801668.

Zwicky, F. (1967), "The Morphological Approach to Discovery, Invention, Research and Construction", in Zwicky, F. and Wilson, A.G. (Eds.), *New Methods of Thought and Procedure: Contributions to the Symposium on Methodologies*, Springer Berlin Heidelberg, Berlin, Heidelberg, pp. 273–297.

Bernhard Freiseisen, David Schönmayr, Anna Fölser

Life Cycle Assessment of Gas Metal Arc Welding

Results and implications for the decarbonization of an industrial process

Summary: Gas metal arc welding (GMAW) is a widely used technology in the metalworking industry. Considering the efforts of many industrial companies to drive a transformation toward sustainable production processes, this paper examines how and to what extent the process under investigation causes environmental impacts. Based on the results, possible courses of action for reducing CO_2 emissions of the gas metal arc welding process itself are discussed.

Keywords: Electric Arc Welding, Life Cycle Assessment (LCA), System Sciences, Decarbonization, Green Electric Arc.

1. Introduction

In the industrial sector, it is becoming increasingly important to know about the sustainability of the manufactured products. Electric arc welding technology is a common process in manufacturing of metal-based products.

Several studies on the environmental impact of welding processes are available (Mierzwa, et al., 2025). Despite the available results for the welding processes, there is so far no evidence about the environmental impact of the arc welding equipment itself. Knowledge about this is of vital interest for manufacturers of arc welding equipment.

Mainly responding to existing and future customer requirements regarding detailed information about the environmental impact of arc welding machines, the afterwards explained Life Cycle Assessment (LCA) has been performed. Additionally, the results obtained will also be used as an information source for innovation to improve the overall sustainability of the next product generation as well as the welding process itself.

2. Methodology

This study follows the guidelines and requirements outlined in EN ISO 14040 (Europäisches Komitee für Normung, 2021) and specified EN ISO 14044 (Europäisches Komitee für Normung, 2021), which provide a framework for conducting a comprehensive life cycle assessment. As shown in Figure 1, the methodology includes goal and scope definition, life cycle inventory analysis, life cycle impact assessment, and evaluation. The LCA carried out has been reviewed by an external expert from the Fraunhofer IZM Institute based on EN ISO 14044:2006 6.2.

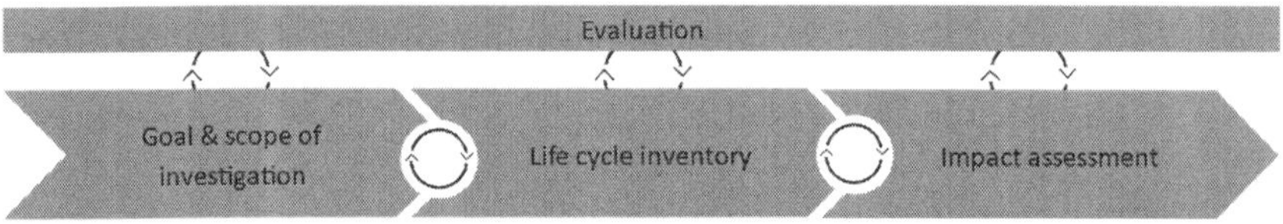

Figure 1: LCA structure according to EN ISO 14040 (own illustration).

Data for this LCA is sourced from the Ecoinvent database 3.9.1. (Wernet, et al., 2016) and is evaluated based on criteria such as temporal, geographical, and technological representativeness. Direct measurements from production and usage data from a real customer scenario is used for the evaluation. The inventory includes all inputs (e.g. materials, energy) and outputs (e.g. emissions, waste) associated with each life cycle phase. The collected data is analysed and processed in Excel to quantify the environmental impact associated with the individual phases of the product life cycle.

3. Scope

In this LCA, a Fronius TPS 400i welding system (Figure 2) including additional components is considered in a typical robotic configuration for a Tier 1 and Tier 2 supplier in the automotive industry. This customised configuration for steel welding serves as the starting point for the creation of the bill of materials (BOM). Some minor adjustments are made to this customer specific BOM to consider deviation from common customer configurations.

Figure 2: Illustration of a robotic application with the TPS 400i welding system (own illustration).

3.1. Functional Unit

The functional unit describes a defined product quantity or performance to which all environmental impacts are related in the results. In this LCA, the purpose is the production of a weld seam (see Figure 3 and Figure 4). The functional unit is one meter of weld seam (fillet weld) with a cross-sectional area of 9 mm^2. Each meter of weld seam produced by the welding application is considered in the functional unit of this study. Scrap from welded components is not considered.

Figure 3: Sketch of a fillet weld in cross-sectional view (own illustration).

Figure 4: Exemplary workpiece with two steel sheets connected by a fillet weld (own illustration).

3.2. System boundaries

The *system boundaries* define the extent of the study, including all relevant life cycle phases. The phases considered are the procurement of raw materials, production, distribution, the use phase including repair and end-of-life treatment.

The *geographical system boundary* is defined by the countries for the production and use of the welding equipment. The countries in which the upstream production chains are located are also included. It is assumed, that the welding equipment is operated in Germany.

The *temporal system boundaries* for the data collection relate to the years 2022 and 2023. A service life of 8 years is defined for the welding equipment, which corresponds to an average service life in the automotive and supplier industry.

The EN ISO 14044 standard proposes three different *cut-off criteria*: energy, mass and environmental relevance. According to this standard, inputs that contribute less than a defined proportion to these criteria can be disregarded (Europäisches Komitee für Normung, 2021). For this purpose, a percentage of 1% has proven to be appropriate for an individual process flow. However, the sum of all unconsidered shares should not exceed 5% (Frischknecht, 2020).

There is a specific situation in this LCA because it is expected that most of the carbon footprint occurs in the use-phase. Therefore, the use-phase is analysed as accurately as possible. However, as one aim of the LCA is to identify potential improvements in product development, and a considerable amount of data on the components is already available from previous Life Cycle Assessments (Pilz, 2023), extrapolations are only made for 0.12% of the component mass. In waste utilisation, the percentage of cut-off amounts to 2.5%.

3.3. Life Cycle Phases

In the *production phase*, the product development and the management of the production company of the welding equipment are not included. During the use phase only the welding application on which the welding machine has an influence is considered. The following factors are excluded: welding cell including gate and extraction system and the associated energy consumption, the welding robot including operating energy, the platform for the power source, and pre- and postprocessing of the weld seam.

For the *use phase*, framework conditions for Germany are assumed in the model.

The *repair* of the welding equipment is defined by the replacement of the most frequently replaced print circuit board and the most frequently replaced mechanical component.

A scenario with metal recycling and thermal waste utilization was selected for the *end-of-life-phase*. Metals like aluminium, copper, steel and stainless steel are separated for recycling from the total quantity of wear parts and replaced components and from the TPS 400i at the end of the service life. Packaging cartons are recycled. The remaining residues are thermally utilized in waste incineration plants.

3.4. Impact categories

This model calculates 16 different environmental impacts (Table 1, No. 1-16) based on the Environmental Footprint 3.1/ILCD 2022 method. Additionally, further impact categories are calculated as shown in Table 1 (No. 17-21).

Using the three single-score methods listed above (Table 1, No. 22a-22c), the results of the environmental impacts analysed (Table 1, No. 1-21) are summarised into a single overall value (single score). These single-score methods are used to identify the five environmental impacts that are most significant in this system:

- Climate change (GWP 100 according to IPCC 2021)
- Particulate matter formation (2 methods: EF 3.1 and ReCiPe 2016)
- Material resources: metals/minerals (2 methods: EF 3.1 and ReCiPe 2016)
- Human toxicity: carcinogenic (EF 3.1)
- Energy consumption (2 methods: Energy resources: non-renewable according to EF 3.1 and Cumulative energy demand: total)

Table 1: Calculated impact categories (own illustration).

No.	Impact category	Unit
1	Climate change, GWP 100	kg CO_2-eq
2	Acidification	mol H^+-eq
3	Ecotoxicity: freshwater	CTUe
4	Energy resources: non-renewable	MJ, net calorific value
5	Eutrophication: freshwater	kg P-eq
6	Eutrophication: marine	kg N-eq
7	Eutrophication: terrestrial	mol N-eq
8	Human toxicity: carcinogenic	CTUh
9	Human toxicity: non-carcinogenic	CTUh
10	Ionising radiation: human health	kBq U235-eq
11	Land use	dimensionless
12	Material resources: metals/minerals	kg Sb-eq
13	Ozone depletion	kg CFC-11-eq
14	Particulate matter formation	disease incidence
15	Photochemical oxidant formation: human health	kg NMVOC-eq
16	Water use	m^3 world eq. deprived
17	Climate impact according to IPCC 2021, GWP 100	kg CO_2-eq
18	Cumulative energy consumption fossil and nuclear	MJ
19	Cumulative energy consumption renewable	MJ
20	Particulate matter formation, according to ReCiPe 2016 v1.03	kg PM2.5-eq
21	Material resources: metals/minerals, according to ReCiPe 2016 v1.03	kg Cu-eq
Single score methods:		
22a	Normalisation and weighting, PEF-Method (Sala, et al., 2018; Crenna, et al., 2019; Damiani, et al., 2022)	UPT
22b	Ecological scarcity**Es ist eine ungültige Quelle angegeben.**	UBP
22c	Monetarisation (Bruyn, et al., 2018; Huijbregts, et al., 2016; Sala, et al., 2015)	EUR

4. Life Cycle Inventory

For the life cycle inventory, all relevant inputs and outputs were collected and quantified throughout the entire life cycle. The effort involved in the areas of data collection on the one hand, and the creation of specific data sets for environmental impacts on the other hand can vary widely for all life cycle phases. This effort was iteratively adapted to the respective relevance of the life cycle phases or to the relevance of material groups within the components. As Table 3 shows, the use phase is dominant with a contribution of over 99% to the carbon footprint. For this reason, a correspondingly large amount of effort was invested in this study in defining the parameters for the use phase and in modelling the environmental impact of the use phase.

4.1. Components for welding equipment

The environmental impact of the components purchased by Fronius was determined in this study based on complete component parts lists. A total of 1.585 different components were assessed. The material composition of components above 200 g which are made up of several materials was determined by disassembly and weighing.

Table 2: Contributions of the material groups to the carbon footprint of the components for the welding equipment (own results).

Material group	Share of component CO_2-eq
Semiconductor parts	17.39%
Cables	15.44%
Aluminium	15.03%
Plastics	12.02%
Capacitors	8.21%
Other	6.93%
Circuit board	5.42%
Diode	5.21%
Copper	4.23%
Complex	3.75%
Steel	3.45%
Inductors	2.92%
Total	100.00%

4.2. Transportation to the manufacturer

Due to the minor influence of transporting the components to Fronius (0.015% of the carbon footprint over the entire life cycle of the welding equipment), the environmental impact of these transports is only calculated on an approximate basis. Smaller truck classes are chosen to consider that the net load weight on the truck can be low, especially when transporting small components. 20% is added to the transported product weight to take packaging and pallets into account.

4.3. Production

The data for the production was collected at the Sattledt (AT) and Krumlov (CZ) sites, specifically for the production of TPS 400i welding equipment including assembly lines and driverless transport systems as well as required process cooling and processing of sheet metal components.

4.4. Transportation to customer

Transporting the manufactured welding equipment to the end customer generally only accounts for 0.003% of the carbon footprint over the entire life cycle of the welding equipment, depending on the country of destination. The transport distances from Sattledt in Austria to the end customers in the destination country are combined with the regarding Ecoinvent data sets.

4.5. Use phase of welding equipment

The welding application of an existing customer example serves as the basis for the CO_2 footprint of the use phase. This is a robotic series production of an automotive supplier using the TPS 400i in its robotic configuration for steel welding. A typical service lifetime of eight years is assumed for the welding machine.

The following parameters are considered according to the customer example: welding speed, duty cycle, operating days, total weld seam length produced, welding current, shielding gas consumption, filler material (= welding wire), welding fume emissions, supply energy and losses. Furthermore, operating materials, wear parts, replacement components, compressed air and the production of the cleaning station are included in the calculation.

4.6. Repair

The potential effects of repair activities are conservatively estimated with an assumed failure rate of 30%. It is assumed that an electronic component is replaced in 90% of cases and a mechanical component in 10% of cases during the defined lifetime of 8 years. The replacement of the most frequently replaced electronic component and most frequently replaced mechanical component is considered as a proxy for other small repair processes.

4.7. End-of-Life

For the end of the product life, a scenario with metal recycling in combination with waste incineration is defined. Therefore metals (aluminium, copper, steel, stainless steel) are separated for recycling with an assumed separation efficiency of 90%. Packaging cartons are recycled too, and the remaining quantity is thermally utilised in waste incineration plants.

5. Life Cycle Impact Assessment Results

The results of the LCA indicate that the most significant impact occurs during the use-phase. As shown in Table 3, the use-phase accounts for over 99% of the overall impact in all calculated impact categories. Due to the importance of climate change in current political, economic and social developments, the climate impact of products is of particular interest. Therefore, the focus in the following is on climate change. The production of the welding equipment itself plays a minor role in the overall climate impact, contributing around 0.01% to the carbon footprint over the entire life cycle of the welding equipment.

Table 3: LCA results in percentages, according to life cycle phases (own results).

Impact category	Climate change GWP 100 IPCC 2021	Particulate matter formation EF 3.1	Particulate matter formation ReCiPe 2016	Material resources: metals/ minerals EF 3.1	Material resources: metals/ minerals ReCiPe 2016	Human toxicity: carcinogenic EF 3.1	Energy resources: non-renewable EF 3.1	Cumulative energy demand: total
Unit	kg CO_2-eq	disease incidence	kg PM2.5-eq	kg Sb-eq	kg Cu-eq	CTUh	MJ	MJ-eq
Components	0.348%	0.574%	1.187%	9.424%	0.142%	0.245%	0.344%	0.330%
Transport to Fronius	0.015%	0.019%	0.009%	0.006%	0.002%	0.001%	0.016%	0.014%
Production at Fronius	0.014%	0.021%	0.016%	0.116%	0.003%	0.003%	0.017%	0.020%
Transport to customer	0.003%	0.007%	0.002%	0.001%	0.0003%	0.0003%	0.004%	0.004%
Use phase	99.696%	99.686%	99.922%	99.719%	99.981%	99.928%	99.715%	99.743%

Impact category	Climate change GWP 100 IPCC 2021	Particulate matter formation EF 3.1	Particulate matter formation ReCiPe 2016	Material resources: metals/ minerals EF 3.1	Material resources: metals/ minerals ReCiPe 2016	Human toxicity: carcinogenic EF 3.1	Energy resources: non-renewable EF 3.1	Cumulative energy demand: total
Unit	kg CO_2-eq	disease incidence	kg PM2.5-eq	kg Sb-eq	kg Cu-eq	CTUh	MJ	MJ-eq
Repair	0.004%	0.004%	0.009%	0.085%	0.002%	0.001%	0.004%	0.004%
End-of-Life	-0.080%	-0.311%	-1.147%	-9.351%	-0.130%	-0.178%	-0.099%	-0.114%
Total	**100%**	**100%**	**100%**	**100%**	**100%**	**100%**	**100%**	**100%**

The following Figure 5 illustrates the use-phase in more detail and indicates its four main elements: welding wire, shielding gas, overall energy usage and wear parts. The first three factors mentioned are primarily responsible for the carbon footprint of the use-phase. The steps preceding the use-phase (cradle to customer gate) shown in Figure 5, including the components, transport to Fronius, production and transport to customer, account for about 0.4% of the overall carbon footprint. With the selected waste scenario, a marginal credit (not listed in Figure 5) can be deducted from the resulting footprint of the preceding life cycle phases due to recycling instead of virgin production.

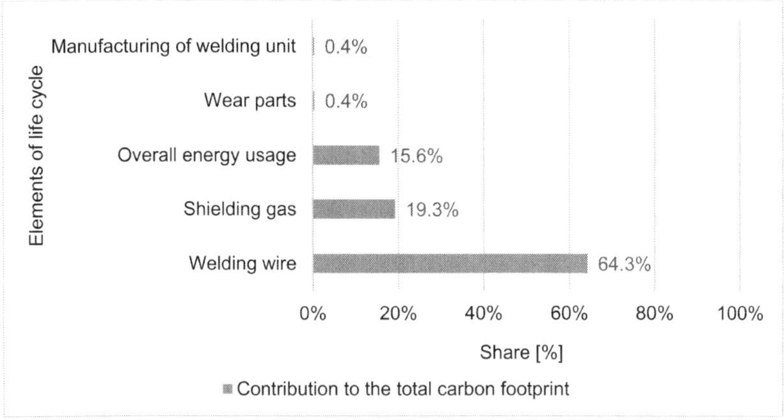

Figure 5: Percentage CO_2-eq results with split up use-phase. The bar "Manufacturing of welding unit" represents the footprint from cradle to customer gate (own illustration).

6. Implications

Summarizing the above presented LCA results for climate-hazardous emissions for the eight-year observation period show that only 0.8% of the total CO_2-eq are attributable to the manufacturing, repair (including wear parts), and disposal of the arc welding equipment itself. More than 99%, however, are caused by the welding process itself, with the electrical energy supplied to the welding arc, the shielding gas used, and the welding wire being the three emission drivers.

The LCA results therefore suggest the following approaches to decarbonize gas metal arc welding. The starting point for the proposed measures is the fact, that influencing the directly or indirectly required electrical energy can be expected to have a significant impact on reducing CO_2 emissions from the process of gas metal arc welding.

Regarding CO_2 emissions directly caused by the overall electrical energy required, the following options are obvious: On the one hand, manufacturers of welding power sources can further increase electrical efficiency, thus reducing the energy drawn from the power grid while maintaining the same deposition rate of the wire electrode. On the other hand, users can increasingly use electricity supply mixes with a high proportion of renewable energy to reduce emissions from grid electricity.

In addition, converting the internal power supplies of production buildings to industrial DC-microgrids offers promising potential for comprehensive overall power consumption reduction (Glasgo, Azevedo, & Hendrickson, 2016). Such DC-microgrids also enable the technically simplified integration of sustainable electrical energy sources such as photovoltaic systems, which can further increase the proportion of green electricity in the consumption systems of, for example, arc welding equipment (Elio, et al., 2021; Gebler, et al., 2020; Wei, et al., 2019; Worrell & Boyd, 2022).

With the shielding gases used, a reduction in the required gas quantity is primarily possible through using equipment for welding process-related gas consumption control. Furthermore, the usage of gases produced with an electrical power supply mix with a high proportion of renewable energy sources is a useful additional measure (He, Liu, Rehman, & Wang, 2021).

Regarding the welding wire used, it is already possible to reduce the required quantities of melted material through suitable design solutions during the design phase of metallic products (Sproesser, Chang, Pittner, Finkbeiner, & Rethmeier, 2015). During the ongoing production process, wire consumption can be reduced by measures to ensure welding process quality, for example, by avoiding defective welds (Mehta, 2019).

To reduce CO_2 emissions affected by the wire production process two possibilities can be mentioned. In addition to options related to the production of the base material (Souza Filho, Ma, Raabe, & Springer, 2023), the use of electrical energy during the wire drawing process itself could also offer a potential for reducing CO_2 emissions from gas metal arc welding. Further, specific LCA analyses for the welding wire itself are required to provide the necessary evidence.

7. Conclusion and Outlook

Overall, the previous sketched starting points are suitable for advancing the decarbonization of gas metal arc welding. Energy in form of electricity plays a pivotal role in the context of arc welding and this will offer new opportunities for technological innovations in the field of energy conversion and energy management solutions for welding applications. Taking also under consideration, that the mentioned courses of action are in the responsibility of different industrial players, it could be a "collective target" for all of them to gradually bring this basic industrial process closer to the technical vision of a "Green Electric Arc".

Abbreviations

BOM	Bill of materials
CFC-11	Trichlorofluoromethane
CO_2	Carbon dioxide
CTUe	Comparative toxic unit for aquatic ecotoxicity
CTUh	Comparative toxic unit for human
EF	Environmental Footprint Method
eq	Equivalents
EUR	Euro
GMAW	Gas Metal Arc Welding
GWP	Global warming potential
ILCD	International Reference Life Cycle Data System
IPCC	Intergovernmental Panel on Climate Change
LCA	Life cycle assessment

LCI	Life cycle inventory
NMVOC	Non-methane volatile organic carbon
PEF	Product Environmental Footprint Method
PM2.5	Particulate matter < 2.5 μm
ReCiPe	LCA-method for evaluating impact categories
UBP	Ecological scarcity unit (dt. Umweltbelastungspunkte)
UPT	Environmental consumption per person and day (dt. Umwelt-Personentage)

References

Bruyn, S. d. et al., 2018. *Environmental Prices Handbook.* EU 28 ed. Delft: CE Delft.

Crenna, E., Secchi, M., Benini, L. & Sala, S., 2019. Global environmental impacts: data sources and methodological choices for calculating normalization factors for LCA. *The International Journal of Life Cycle Assessment,* Volume 24, pp. 1851-1877.

Damiani, M., Ferrara, N. & Ardente, F., 2022. *Understanding Product Environmental Footprint and Organisation Environmental Footprint methods,* Luxembourg: Publications Office of the European Union.

Elio, J., Phelan, P., Villalobos, R. & Milcarek, R. J., 2021. A review of energy storage technologies for demand-side management in industrial facilities. *Journal of Cleaner Production,* Volume 307.

Europäisches Komitee für Normung, 2021. *(ÖNORM EN ISO 14040:2021-03): Umweltmanagement – Ökobilanz – Grundsätze und Rahmenbedingungen.* Wien: Austrian Standards International.

Europäisches Komitee für Normung, 2021. *(ÖNORM EN ISO 14044:2021-03): Umweltmanagement - Ökobilanz - Anforderungen und Ableitungen.* Wien: Austrian Standards International.

Frischknecht, R., 2020. *Lehrbuch der Ökobilanzierung.* Berlin: Springer-Verlag.

Frischknecht, R. & Büsser Knöpfel, S., 2013. *Ökofaktoren Schweiz 2013 gemäss der Methode der ökologischen Knappheit. Methodische Grundlagen und Anwendung auf die Schweiz,* Bern: Bundesamt für Umwelt.

Gebler, M., Cerdas, J. F., Thiede, S. & Herrmann, C., 2020. Life cycle assessment of an automotive factory: Identifying challenges for the decarbonization of automotive production – A case study. *Journal of Cleaner Production,* Volume 270.

Glasgo, B., Azevedo, I. L. & Hendrickson, C., 2016. How much electricity can we save by using direct current circuits in homes? Understanding the potential for electricity savings and assessing feasibility of a transition towards DC powered buildings. *Applied Energy,* Volume 180, pp. 66-75.

He, X., Liu, Y., Rehman, A. & Wang, L., 2021. A novel air separation unit with energy storage and generation and its energy efficiency and economy analysis. *Applied Energy*, Volume 281.

Huijbregts, M. et al., 2016. *A harmonized life cycle impact assessment method at midpoint and endpoint level*, Bilthoven: RIVM.

Mehta, K., 2019. Sustainability in Welding and Processing. In: K. Gupta, ed. *Innovations in Manufacturing for Sustainability*. Cham: Springer, pp. 125-145.

Mierzwa, M. et al., 2025. *Nachhaltigkeit in der schweißtechnischen Produktion*, Düsseldorf: DVS Media.

Pilz, H., 2023. *Fronius GEN24 & GEN24 Plus - A Benefit for the Environment*, s.l.: Fronius International GmbH.

Sala, S., Benini, L., Mancini, L. & Pant, R., 2015. Integrated assessment of environmental impact of Europe in 2010: data sources and extrapolation strategies for calculating normalisation factors. *The International Journal of Life Cycle Assessment*, Issue 20, pp. 1568-1585.

Sala, S., Cerutti, A. K. & Pant, R., 2018. *Development of a weighting approach for the Environmental Footprint*, Luxembourg: Publications Office of the European Union.

Souza Filho, I. R., Ma, Y., Raabe, D. & Springer, H., 2023. Fundamentals of Green Steel Production: On the Role of Gas Pressure During Hydrogen Reduction of Iron Ores. *JOM - The Journal of The Minerals, Metals & Materials Society*, 75(7), pp. 2274-2286.

Sproesser, G. et al., 2015. Life Cycle Assessment of welding technologies for thick metal plate welds. *Journal of Cleaner Production*, 108(A), pp. 46-53.

Wei, M., McMillan, C. A. & Rue du Can, S. d. l., 2019. Electrification of Industry: Potential, Challenges and Outlook. *Current Sustainable/Renewable Energy Reports*, Volume 6, pp. 140-148.

Wernet, G. et al., 2016. The ecoinvent database version 3 (part I): overview and methodology. *The International Journal of Life Cycle Assessment*, [online] 21(9), pp. 1218-1230.

Worrell, E. & Boyd, G., 2022. Bottom-up estimates of deep decarbonization of U.S. manufacturing in 2050. *Journal of Cleaner Production*, Volume 330.

Martin Schönberg

Chancen der EU-Nachhaltigkeitsberichterstattung

Vom Reporting zur Projektpraxis

Zusammenfassung: Die europäische Nachhaltigkeitsberichterstattung gemäß Corporate Sustainability Reporting Directive, den European Sustainability Standards und der EU-Taxonomie-Verordnung bietet neben Herausforderungen auch Chancen in der Projektpraxis. Der Konferenzbeitrag zeigt auf, dass Elemente des Nachhaltigkeitsreportings einen Beitrag für die Realisierung von tatsächlichen Projekten in Industrie und Energiewirtschaft leisten können. Dies erfolgt anhand einer demonstrativen Auflistung ausgewählter Best-Practice-Beispiele, wie der Klimarisiko- und Vulnerabilitätsbewertung, durch welche Anforderungen des Umweltverträglichkeitsprüfungsgesetzes 2000 in Bezug auf die Darstellung von Klimawandelfolgen erfüllt werden können; wie das Leistungsdichte-Kriterium (W/m^2) bei Wasserkraftreservoiren, durch welches die Einhaltung von Emissionsgrenzen nachgewiesen werden kann; und abgeleiteter Dimensionen aus den ESRS, wodurch sich Maßnahmen verorten lassen.

Keywords: Nachhaltigkeitsreporting, ESG, CSRD, EU-Taxonomie, Projektpraxis, Umweltverträglichkeitsprüfung.

1. Motivation

Die Einführung der europäischen Nachhaltigkeitsberichterstattung gemäß der Corporate Sustainability Reporting Directive (CSRD; Richtlinie (EU) 2022/2464) stellt Unternehmen vor tiefgreifende, strukturelle und organisatorische Herausforderungen. Die Richtlinie verpflichtet Unternehmen, die bestimmte Größen- und Schwellenwerte[1] überschreiten, zur Offenlegung

---

1 Von der Angabe bestimmter Größen- und Schwellenwerte wird auf Grund der sich schnell verändernden regulatorischen Rahmenbedingungen abgesehen. Die sog. Stop-the-Clock-Richtlinie (EU) 2025/794 (European Union, 2025) folgt dem Vorschlag des ersten Omnibus-Pakets. Sie streicht die (erwarteten) sektorspezifischen Standards und verschiebt die verpflichtende Nachhaltigkeitsberichterstattung für große Unternehmen, die noch nicht mit der Berichterstattung begonnen haben, sowie für börsennotierte kleinere und mittlere Unternehmen um zwei weitere Jahre.

umfassender Informationen über ökologische, soziale und Governance-Aspekte (European Union, 2022). Dies erfordert nicht nur neue Prozesse und Systeme, sondern auch erhebliche personelle und finanzielle Ressourcen.

Aktuell werden daher große Hoffnungen auf sog. Omnibus-Pakete der Europäischen Union gesetzt, die regulatorische Entlastungen bringen sollen, d.h. diese sollen Vereinfachungen oder zeitliche Streckung der Berichtspflichten ermöglichen. Diese Diskussionen über administrative Belastungen verdecken jedoch häufig das strategische Potenzial, das in der Nachhaltigkeitsberichterstattung selbst liegt.

Die im Rahmen der Berichterstattung generierten Inhalte sind nicht nur für externe Stakeholder:innen von Bedeutung, sondern können auch einen unmittelbaren operativen Nutzen entfalten – insbesondere in der Projektpraxis von Industrie und Energiewirtschaft.

Der vorliegende Beitrag greift diese Perspektive auf und zeigt anhand ausgewählter Best-Practice-Beispiele, wie Elemente der Nachhaltigkeitsberichterstattung nicht nur regulatorische Anforderungen adressieren, sondern auch zur erfolgreichen Planung und Umsetzung konkreter Projekte beitragen können.

Ziel des Beitrags ist es, Nachhaltigkeitsreporting nicht nur als Berichtspflicht, sondern als strategisches und operatives Werkzeug im unternehmerischen Kontext zu verstehen – und damit einen Beitrag zur Versachlichung der Debatte um regulatorische Anforderungen zu leisten.

2. Methodik

Der vorliegende Beitrag verfolgt einen anwendungsorientierten Ansatz, der auf einer Analyse und demonstrativen Darstellung von Best-Practice-Beispielen aus der Projektpraxis[2] basiert. Ziel ist es, konkrete Anknüpfungspunkte zwischen regulatorischen Anforderungen der europäischen Nachhaltigkeitsberichterstattung und deren operativer Umsetzung in österreichischen Industrie- und Energieversorgungsunternehmen (EVUs) aufzuzeigen. Die Methodik gliedert sich in drei zentrale Schritte:

1. **Identifikation relevanter regulatorischer Bezugspunkte**
   Im ersten Schritt werden die einschlägigen Rechtsgrundlagen definiert: Dazu zählen die EU-Taxonomie-Verordnung (VO (EU) 2020/852), mit Fokus auf technische Bewertungskriterien und sog. Do-No-Significant-

2 Die dargestellten Anwendungsfälle basieren auf realen Projekten aus der österreichischen Industrie und Energiewirtschaft. Aus Datenschutz- und Vertraulichkeitsgründen werden keine konkreten Projekt- oder Firmennamen angeführt.

Harm-(DNSH-)Kriterien, wie sie in den entsprechenden delegierten Rechtsakten festgelegt sind. Weitere Rechtsgrundlagen stellen die Corporate Sustainability Reporting Directive (CSRD; Richtlinie (EU) 2022/2464) mit den European Sustainability Reporting Standards (ESRS; Delegierte Verordnung (EU) 2023/2772) dar, wobei insbesondere die themenspezifischen Standards ESRS E1 (Klimawandel), ESRS E4 (Biodiversität und Ökosysteme) und ESRS S1 (Eigene Arbeitskräfte) für den gegenständlichen Beitrag herangezogen werden.

2. **Auswahl und Darstellung von Best-Practice-Beispielen**
   Ausgehend vom regulatorischen Rahmen werden konkrete Projekte aus der Energie- und Industriebranche ausgewählt, bei denen Elemente der Nachhaltigkeitsberichterstattung bereits in der Praxis Anwendung finden. Die Auswahlkriterien umfassen: Relevanz für die regulatorischen Anforderungen, Übertragbarkeit auf andere Projekte, Innovationsgrad und dokumentierter Nutzen.
3. **Resümee und Ableitung von Handlungsempfehlungen**
   Eine Zusammenfassung schließt die Ausführungen und leitet aus den analysierten Beispielen übertragbare Erkenntnisse und Handlungsempfehlungen ab.

Die Methodik folgt einem qualitativ-interpretativen Design, das bewusst auf die Verknüpfung von Projektpraxis und aktuellen, regulatorischen Entwicklungen abzielt. Durch die Verbindung von Theorie und Praxis kann auch ein Beitrag zur Operationalisierung der europäischen Nachhaltigkeitsziele im unternehmerischen Kontext geleistet werden.

2.1. Anwendungsbereich

Die im Beitrag dargestellten Best-Practice-Beispiele und Anwendungsfälle beziehen sich auf den europäischen Rechtsrahmen, insbesondere auf die Corporate Sustainability Reporting Directive (CSRD), die European Sustainability Reporting Standards (ESRS) sowie die EU-Taxonomie-Verordnung. Diese Regelwerke gelten unmittelbar oder mittelbar in allen Mitgliedstaaten der Europäischen Union und entfalten somit auch in Österreich rechtliche Wirkung.

In Österreich erfolgt die Umsetzung der CSRD durch Anpassungen im Unternehmensgesetzbuch (UGB) sowie durch die Novellierung des Nachhaltigkeits- und Diversitätsverbesserungsgesetz (NaDiVeG).[3] Die ESRS, die EU-

3 Anfang 2025 fand die Begutachtung eines neuen Nachhaltigkeitsberichtsgesetzes (NaBeG) statt, welches das NaDiVeG ablösen soll. Bisher ist dieses nicht verabschiedet worden.

Taxonomie-Verordnung und die entsprechenden delegierten Rechtsakte der EU-Taxonomie sind als Verordnungen unmittelbar anwendbar.

Die in diesem Beitrag dargestellten Beispiele gelten nicht nur exemplarisch für die österreichische Projektpraxis, sondern sind auch teilweise auf den gesamteuropäischen Raum übertragbar. Sie zeigen, wie europäische Nachhaltigkeitsvorgaben in nationale Verfahren und Entscheidungsprozesse integriert werden können – etwa in Umweltverträglichkeitsprüfungen, Genehmigungsverfahren oder im Bereich der strategischen Unternehmensführung. Damit wird ein praxisnaher Beitrag zur Operationalisierung europäischer Nachhaltigkeitsziele auf nationaler Ebene, mit besonderem Fokus auf die Industrie- und Energiewirtschaft in Österreich geleistet.

3. Regulatorischer Rahmen

Die zunehmende Bedeutung von Nachhaltigkeit in der Unternehmenspraxis, insbesondere des ESG-Tripels (Umwelt, Soziales und Governance), spiegelt sich in einer Vielzahl europäischer Rechtsakte wider, die Anforderungen an Identifikation, Bewertung, Steuerung und Transparenz tatsächlicher und möglicher Auswirkungen von bzw. auf Unternehmensaktivitäten vorgeben. Die folgenden Abschnitte bieten dazu einen einleitenden, kompakten Überblick über die EU-Taxonomie-Verordnung sowie die Corporate Sustainability Reporting Directive (CSRD).

3.1. EU-Taxonomie

Die EU-Taxonomie ist ein zentrales Instrument der europäischen Nachhaltigkeitsberichterstattung. Sie wurde mit der Verordnung (EU) 2020/852 eingeführt, um einheitlich zu definieren, welche Wirtschaftsaktivitäten als ökologisch nachhaltig gelten. Übergeordnetes Ziel ist es, im Sinne des Art. 2 (1) lit c. Pariser Abkommens (United Nations, 2015), Kapitalflüsse in nachhaltige Investitionen zu lenken. Die Verordnung legt sechs Umweltziele fest, darunter Klimaschutz, Anpassung an den Klimawandel und Schutz der Biodiversität (European Union, 2020).

Zur praktischen Anwendung der Taxonomie wurden ergänzende delegierte Rechtsakte erlassen. Die delegierte Verordnung (EU) 2021/2139 (European Commission, 2021) fokussiert auf die Umweltziele Klimaschutz und Anpassung an den Klimawandel und wird in Industrie und EVUs am häufigsten herangezogen, da in dieser die technischen Bewertungskriterien und DNSH-Kriterien für die entsprechenden Wirtschaftstätigkeiten definiert sind.

Unternehmen, die unter die entsprechenden Berichtspflichten fallen, müssen in ihrem Geschäftsbericht offenlegen, in welchem Umfang ihre wirtschaftlichen Aktivitäten mit den Taxonomiekriterien übereinstimmen, bzw. zu welchem Anteil ihr OPEX, CAPEX und Umsatz taxonomiekonform (bei Erfüllung aller Kriterien) oder fähig (bei der Erwähnung der Aktivität in einem der Rechtsakte, ohne Kriterienerfüllung) ist (European Commission, 2021). Damit wird die EU-Taxonomie zu einem verbindlichen Bewertungsrahmen für nachhaltige Unternehmens- und Investitionsentscheidungen – auch in der österreichischen Projektpraxis.

3.2. Corporate Sustainability Reporting Directive

Die Corporate Sustainability Reporting Directive (CSRD) – Richtlinie (EU) 2022/2464 (European Union, 2022) – ändert die bisherige Non-Financial Reporting Directive (NFRD) und erweitert den Anwendungsbereich, indem sie große Unternehmen sowie kapitalmarktorientierte KMUs zur umfassenden Offenlegung von Informationen zu Umwelt, Sozial- und Governance-Themen (ESG) verpflichtet. Ziel ist es, die Vergleichbarkeit, Qualität und Relevanz von Nachhaltigkeitsinformationen innerhalb der EU zu verbessern.

Die CSRD bildet den rechtlichen Rahmen für die Anwendung der European Sustainability Reporting Standards (ESRS) und ist eng mit der EU-Taxonomie-Verordnung verknüpft. Die European Sustainability Reporting Standards (ESRS), die durch die delegierte Verordnung (EU) 2023/2772 (European Union, 2025) erlassen wurden, definieren detaillierte Anforderungen an die Berichterstattung zu Themen wie Klimarisiken, Biodiversität oder Ressourceneffizienz (European Commission, 2023).

Die CSRD gilt ab dem Geschäftsjahr 2024 für große Unternehmen und wird schrittweise ausgeweitet. Durch die sogenannte *Stop-the-Clock-Richtlinie* (EU) 2025/794 (European Union, 2025) als Verrechtlichung des ersten *Omnibus-Pakets* wird aktuell (Juni 2025) die Ausweitung verzögert und einzelne Teile, wie die erwarteten, sektorspezifischen Standards werden gestrichen.

4. Best-Practice-Beispiele

Um die praktische Relevanz der europäischen Nachhaltigkeitsberichterstattung greifbar zu machen, werden im Folgenden ausgewählte Best-Practice-Beispiele aus der Industrie- und Energiewirtschaft vorgestellt. Diese Beispiele zeigen, wie sich Anforderungen aus der EU-Taxonomie, der CSRD und den ESRS konkret in Projekten umsetzen lassen – sei es im Rahmen von Genehmigungsverfahren oder strategischer Unternehmensführung. Die demonstrative Darstellung soll verdeutlichen, dass das aktuelle EU-Nachhaltigkeitsreporting nicht nur eine regulatorische Pflicht, sondern auch einen operativen Mehrwert darstellen kann.

4.1. Klimawandelfolgen und Resilienz

Die Berücksichtigung von Klimawandelfolgen und Resilienz gewinnt im Rahmen des europäischen Nachhaltigkeitsreportings zunehmend an Bedeutung. Sowohl die EU-Taxonomie-Verordnung (EU) 2020/852 als auch die Corporate Sustainability Reporting Directive (CSRD; Richtlinie (EU) 2022/2464) bzw. die ESRS E1 (Klimaschutz) fordern eine systematische Auseinandersetzung mit den physischen Risiken des Klimawandels.

Für sämtliche von der EU-Taxonomie erfassten Wirtschaftstätigkeiten ist eine sog. *Klimarisiko- und Vulnerabilitätsbewertung* (im Folgenden kurz als Klimarisikobewertung bezeichnet) entweder als DNSH-Kriterium oder als technisches Bewertungskriterium (bei Aktivitäten, die wesentlich zum Umweltziel *Anpassung an den Klimawandel* beitragen) durchzuführen. Im Wesentlichen basiert diese Bewertung auf den Vorgaben der delegierten Verordnung (EU) 2021/2139, Anhang I, Anlage A, wo chronische (bspw. Veränderung von Durchschnittstemperaturen oder von der Niederschlagsmustern) und akute (wie Starkregen, Hitzewellen oder Waldbrände) Klimagefahren aufgelistet sind (European Commission, 2021). Diese physischen Risiken müssen im Rahmen der Klimarisikobewertung unter verschiedenen Szenarien analysiert und Anpassungslösungen abgeleitet werden. Je nachdem, ob bestehende oder neu zu errichtende physische Anlagen zum Einsatz kommen, werden diese Lösungen innerhalb von fünf Jahren umgesetzt bzw. bereits in Planung und Bau integriert werden.

Auch im Rahmen der CSRD ist eine entsprechende Klimarisikoanalyse verpflichtend vorgesehen. Gemäß ESRS E1 sind Unternehmen angehalten, sowohl physische als auch transitorische Klimarisiken zu identifizieren und deren Auswirkungen auf die Geschäftstätigkeit zu bewerten. Die Methodik orientiert sich dabei an denselben Klimagefahren wie in der EU-Taxonomie und bildet somit eine konsistente Grundlage für unternehmensweite Klimaanpassungsstrategien. Es sei an dieser Stelle angemerkt, dass obwohl bei der Resilienzanalyse gemäß CSRD/ESRS auf die Klimagefahren gem. EU-Taxonomie verwiesen wird, sich bei dieser nicht um eine Klimarisiko- und Vulnerabilitätsbewertung gem. EU-Taxonomie handelt. Die Resilienzanalyse der CSRD/ESRS bezieht sich nicht auf die Bewertung physischer Risiken und deren Auswirkung auf die Wirtschaftsaktivität per se, sondern vor allem auf die Strategie und das Geschäftsmodell und wie diese durch Auswirkungen, Risiken, Chancen beeinflusst werden.

Unabhängig von den regulatorischen Anforderungen im Bereich der Nachhaltigkeitsberichterstattung fordert § 6 Abs. 1 Z 1 lit. f UVP-G 2000 (Bundeskanzleramt, 2023) in der Umweltverträglichkeitserklärung (UVE) u.a. die Anfälligkeit eines Vorhabens gegenüber Klimawandelfolgen darzustellen. Zusätzlich ist gemäß § 6 Abs. 1 Z 4 lit. e UVP-G eine Beschreibung der voraussichtlichen erheblichen Auswirkungen des Vorhabens auf die Umwelt infolge klimawandelbedingter Risiken zu verfassen.

Diese Anforderungen werden im UVE-Leitfaden des Bundesministeriums (BMNT, 2019) spezifiziert, da dort darauf verwiesen wird, dass zunehmend auch auf die Auswirkungen der Folgen des Klimawandels auf das Vorhaben und dessen Umgebung eingegangen werden soll. Dabei ist die Anfälligkeit eines Vorhabens gegenüber Klimawandelfolgen stark von dessen Lage und Umgebung abhängig.

Die Projektpraxis zeigt, dass Klimarisikobewertungen der Nachhaltigkeitsberichterstattung als Basis für UVE-Einreichungen, im Speziellen zur Erfüllung der österreichischen rechtlichen Anforderungen des UVP-G 2000 in Bezug auf die Anfälligkeit eines Vorhabens gegenüber Klimawandelfolgen, dienen können. Dabei folgt die Bewertungsmethodik den folgenden Schritten:

- Bewertung der Exposition (Identifikation relevanter physischer Klimagefahren, z. B. Hitze, Starkregen, Trockenheit und Abschätzung der Entwicklung bzw. Szenarien);
- Sensitivität (vorhabengebietsspezifische Relevanz, potenzielle Auswirkungen auf das Vorhaben durch mögliche Klimawandelfolgen, potenzielle Auswirkungen des Vorhabens auf Schutzgüter infolge des Klimawandels);
- Anpassungsfähigkeit des Vorhabens (Ableitung und Integration physischer und nicht-physischer Anpassungsmaßnahmen in Planung und Umsetzung).

Somit ist es ist möglich, Klimawandelfolgen und projekt- bzw. standortspezifische Klimaresilienzbewertungen im Rahmen von Umweltverträglichkeitserklärungen auf Basis durchgeführter Klimarisikobewertungen nach EU-Taxonomie bzw. nach CSRD darzustellen.

4.2. Emissionen aus Wasserkraftreservoiren

Im Rahmen der Nachhaltigkeitsbewertung von Wasserkraftprojekten stellt die Bewertung klimarelevanter Emissionen eine zentrale Herausforderung dar. Besonders im Zuge von Umweltverträglichkeitsprüfungen (UVP), der Einreichung von Umweltverträglichkeits-erklärungen (UVE) und im Speziellen bei der Erstellung von Klima- und Energiekonzepten[4] stellt sich auch national und regional öfters die Frage nach möglichen Emissionen aus Wasserkraftreservoiren.

Dies ist vor allem durch internationale Diskussionen bedingt, da Emissionen aus Wasserkraftreservoiren vor allem in tropischen Stauseen eine Rolle spielen. Mehrere Studien (Barros et al., 2011; Cole et al., 2007; Zhang et al., 2024) zeigen, dass höhere Methan- (CH_4) und Lachgas- (N_2O) Werte hauptsächlich in tropischen Gebieten gefunden werden und diese Gasbildungsprozesse in den gemäßigten Breiten, so auch im Alpenraum nicht deutlich ausgeprägt sind: Dies liegt an der geringen Menge überfluteter Biomasse, dem niedrigen Gehalt organischen Materials in Fließgewässern und den gemäßigten klimatischen Bedingungen, die die Methanbildung hemmen (Methan entsteht typischerweise durch die Zersetzung organischen Materials unter Sauerstoffmangel). Die höheren N_2O-Emissionen aus tropischen Stauseen im Vergleich zu temperaten (oder auch borealen) Gewässern sind auf eine höhere Stickstoffverfügbarkeit in dieser Region und eine höhere Temperatur zurückzuführen, die bestimmte chemische Prozesse (Nitrifikation und Denitrifikation) begünstigt. Folglich sind in Mitteleuropa CH_4- und N_2O-Emissionen aus Reservoiren in der Regel vernachlässigbar.

Im Zuge von Einreichprojekten gilt es teilweise dennoch nachzuweisen, dass bestimmte Schwellenwerte eingehalten und die Emissionen aus Wasserkraftreservoiren bewertet werden. Dazu kann das sogenannte *Leistungsdichte-Kriterium* (ausgedrückt in W/m^2) als Proxy-Indikator für die Emissionsintensität herangezogen werden. Dieses Kriterium beschreibt das Verhältnis zwischen installierter elektrischer Leistung und überfluteter Fläche und ist wissenschaftlich basiert, wobei Wasserkraftwerke mit hoher Leistungsdichte ($>10\ W/m^2$) in der Regel sehr geringe spezifische Emissionen aufweisen: Die United Nations Framework Convention on Climate Change (UNFCCC, 2020) hat zur Bewertung von Emissionen aus Wasserkraftreservoiren drei Kategorien unter Heranziehung des Leistungsdichtekriteriums definiert (Projekte $\leq 4\ W/m^2$ dürfen keine vereinfachten Methoden anwenden; Projekte > 4 bis $\leq 10\ W/m^2$ dürfen vereinfachte Methoden anwenden und bei Projekten $> 10\ W/m^2$ können Emissionen aus dem Reservoir vernachlässigt werden).

4 Die Erzeugung von Elektrizität aus Wasserkraftanlagen verursacht keine direkten CO_2-Emissionen. Indirekte CO_2-Emissionen werden in der Regel in der Bau- und Betriebsphase durch die Herstellung der Anlage und den damit verbunden Maschinen- und Geräteeinsatz, durch Fahrten im Zuge von Transport-, Betriebs- oder Wartungstätigkeiten und durch Landnutzungen bzw. -Änderungen verursacht. Diese werden bei UVP-pflichtigen Vorhaben in Klima- und Energiekonzepten als Teil der Umweltverträglichkeitserklärungen abgeschätzt.

Ebenfalls hat das Leistungsdichtekriterium den Weg in die EU-Taxonomie gefunden. Der *Schwellenwert von 5 W/m*^{2} ist nämlich ein technisches Bewertungskriterium für die Stromerzeugung aus Wasserkraft der EU-Taxonomie (European Commission, 2021) und dient als pragmatischer Bewertungsansatz im europäischen Kontext, wobei angenommen wird, dass solange der Wert über 5W/m^2 liegt, auch die Emissionen unter dem Schwellenwert von 100 gCO2eq/kWh sind.

Die Projektpraxis zeigt, dass das Leistungsdichte-Kriterium ein praktikables Instrument zur schnellen Emissionsabschätzung darstellt – insbesondere in Regionen mit geringer organischer Belastung und moderatem Klima wie in Österreich. Das Leistungsdichtekriterium aus der EU-Taxonomie kann einer einfachen, pragmatischen Bewertung möglicher Emissionen aus Wasserkraftreservoiren in Einreichprojekten (bspw. in Klima- und Energiekonzepten) dienen.

4.3. Verortung von Nachhaltigkeitsmaßnahmen

Die European Sustainability Reporting Standards (ESRS) definieren eine Vielzahl an Themenfeldern (Topics) und Unterthemen (Sub-Topics bzw. Sub-Sub-Topics) der Nachhaltigkeit, die Unternehmen im Rahmen ihrer Berichterstattung strukturiert adressieren müssen. Diese systematische Gliederung bietet nicht nur eine Grundlage für die externe Kommunikation, sondern kann auch unternehmensintern als strategisches Steuerungsinstrument genutzt werden.

Die Verortung von unternehmensspezifischen Maßnahmen entlang der ESRS-Themen (Topics, Sub-Topics, Sub-Sub-Topics) ermöglicht eine klare Zuordnung von Projekten, Zielen und Kennzahlen. So lassen sich etwa biodiversitätsbezogene Maßnahmen im Rahmen von *ESRS E4 Biodiversität und Ökosysteme* systematisch erfassen, bewerten und weiterentwickeln. Ebenso bietet *ESRS S1 Eigene Arbeitskräfte* eine umfassende Struktur zur Abbildung sozialer Aspekte wie Arbeitsbedingungen, Gleichstellung oder Weiterbildung. Aus den ESRS-Themen lassen sich entsprechend Dimensionen oder Cluster bspw. von Biodiversität oder zu Sicherheit und Gesundheit bei der Arbeit ableiten, wodurch sich unternehmensintern Projekte und Maßnahmen verorten lassen.

Diese durch die European Sustainability Reporting Standards vorgegebene, thematische Struktur kann in der Praxis vielfältig eingesetzt werden:

- Kommunikationspolitisch, etwa zur internen und externen Darstellung von Nachhaltigkeitsleistungen;

- Strategisch, etwa durch die Integration in ein Nachhaltigkeitsdashboard, das zentrale Kennzahlen (KPIs) und Zielerreichungsgrade abbildet;
- Operativ, etwa zur Priorisierung von Maßnahmen im Rahmen von Investitionsentscheidungen oder Projektbewertungen.

Die ESRS bieten damit nicht nur einen regulatorischen Rahmen, sondern auch eine strukturierte Grundlage für die systematische Verankerung von Nachhaltigkeit in der Unternehmensführung. Die Verortung von Maßnahmen entlang der ESRS-Themen kann somit als Brücke zwischen Berichtspflicht und strategischer Steuerung verstanden werden.

5. Resümee und Ableitung von Handlungsempfehlungen

Die europäische Nachhaltigkeitsberichterstattung – insbesondere im Rahmen der CSRD, der EU-Taxonomie und der ESRS – stellt Unternehmen vor neue Herausforderungen, eröffnet jedoch zugleich vielfältige Chancen für eine praxisnahe Umsetzung. Die Analyse zeigt, dass viele der regulatorisch geforderten Inhalte nicht nur für die Nachhaltigkeitsberichterstattung, sondern auch in der Projektpraxis anwendbar sind: Beispiele hierfür sind die Klimarisikobewertung, die in Umweltverträglichkeitserklärungen zur Erfüllung von Anforderungen des UVP-G 2000 herangezogen werden kann, die Beurteilung von Emissionen aus Wasserkraftreservoiren über das Leistungsdichtekriterium als Proxy für die Einhaltung von Emissionsgrenzwerten und die Nutzung der thematischen Struktur der European Sustainability Reporting Standards für die Verortung von Nachhaltigkeitsmaßnahmen.

Zusätzlich können folgende Handlungsempfehlungen aus der Analyse der Best-Practice-Beispiele abgeleitet werden:

- Stärkere unternehmensinterne Vernetzung fördern
  Ein zentrales Hemmnis in der Praxis stellt die mangelnde, interne Vernetzung in großen Unternehmungen dar: Nachhaltigkeitsberichterstattung wird häufig zentralisiert oder an externe Dienstleister ausgelagert, während relevante Informationen in Fachabteilungen oder Projektteams vorliegen. Dadurch bleiben Synergien ungenutzt, etwa bei der Wiederverwendung von Einreichunterlagen für Berichtszwecke oder bei der gemeinsamen Entwicklung von Bewertungsansätzen. Der Aufbau von Schnittstellen zwischen Nachhaltigkeitsverantwortlichen, Projektplanung, Projektkoordination, Genehmigungsmanagement und Controlling ist wesentlich, damit die Nachhaltigkeitsberichterstattung nicht als Parallelprozess gelebt werden.

- Projektunterlagen systematisch für das Reporting nutzen
  Einreichunterlagen können strukturierte Datenquellen für ESRS-konforme Berichterstattung darstellen. Ein bislang wenig genutzter, aber äußerst wirkungsvoller Ansatz besteht darin, Einreichunterlagen aus der Projektpraxis – etwa Umweltverträglichkeitserklärungen (UVE), darunter Klimarisikobewertungen oder Energie- und Klimakonzepte – systematisch als Datenquelle für die Nachhaltigkeitsberichterstattung gemäß ESRS heranzuziehen. Diese Unterlagen enthalten häufig bereits detaillierte Informationen zu Umweltauswirkungen, Klimarisiken, Emissionen oder Biodiversitätsaspekten, die sich direkt einzelnen ESRS-Themen zuordnen lassen. Durch eine strukturierte Erfassung und Integration dieser Inhalte in das unternehmensweite Reporting lassen sich Datenlücken schließen, Redundanzen vermeiden und Synergien zwischen Projektentwicklung und Berichtspflicht heben.
- ESRS-Themen als Steuerungsstruktur etablieren
  Die bestehende, regulatorische ESRS-Clusterung kann zur Verortung von Maßnahmen, Zieldefinitionen und KPI-Monitoring im Rahmen eines Nachhaltigkeitsmanagementsystems genutzt werden.
- Regulatorische Anforderungen als Innovationsimpuls verstehen
  Neue rechtliche Vorgaben können ein Anstoß für Innovationen sein, speziell wenn es um die Entwicklung unternehmensspezifischer Tools zur Unterstützung von Nachhaltigkeits-Monitoring und -Entscheidungen (z. B. in der Form von Dashboards) geht.
- Politik und Verwaltung einbinden
  Es gilt einen übergreifenden Dialog zur Harmonisierung von Gesetzen und zur Vermeidung von Doppelvorschreibungen zu schaffen. Dazu sind ein vernetztes Denken sowie eine intensivere, bereichsübergreifende Zusammenarbeit erforderlich – nicht nur bei der praktischen Umsetzung regulatorischer Vorgaben, sondern bereits auf legislativer Ebene. Es gilt vor allem redundante oder widersprüchliche Vorgaben zu identifizieren, harmonisieren und gegebenenfalls aufzuheben.

Abkürzungsverzeichnis

CH_4	Methan
CO_2eq	Kohlendioxidäquivalent
CSRD	Corporate Sustainability Reporting Directive
DNSH	Do No Significant Harm

ESG	Environmental, Social, Governance
ESRS	European Sustainability Reporting Standards
EU	Europäische Union
EVU	Energieversorgungsunternehmen
KPI	Key Performance Indicator
kWh	Kilowattstunde
LCA	Life Cycle Assessment
NaBeG	Nachhaltigkeitsberichtsgesetzes
NaDiVeG	Nachhaltigkeits- und Diversitätsverbesserungsgesetz
N_2O	Lachgas
UGB	Unternehmensgesetzbuch
UNFCCC	United Nations Framework Convention on Climate Change
UVP	Umweltverträglichkeitsprüfung
UVP-G	Umweltverträglichkeitsprüfungsgesetz
UVE	Umweltverträglichkeitserklärung

Literatur

Barros, N., Cole, J.J., Tranvik, L.J. et al. (2011): Carbon emission from hydroelectric reservoirs linked to reservoir age and latitude. Nature Geoscience, 4(9), 593–596.

BMNT (2019): UVE-LEITFADEN. Eine Information zur Umweltverträglichkeitserklärung. Über arbeitete Fassung 2019. [online] Verfügbar unter: https://www.bmk.gv.at/dam/jcr:ecaf18e1-a79c-4346-9f1e-5e2de2728ee3/UVE_Leitfaden_2019.pdf [Zugriff am 2. Juni 2025].

Bundeskanzleramt (2023): Umweltverträglichkeitsprüfungsgesetz 2000 (UVP-G 2000), BGBl. Nr. 697/1993 idgF. [online] Verfügbar unter: https://www.ris.bka.gv.at/Dokumente/Bundesnormen/NOR40209738/NOR40209738.pdf [Zugriff am 2. Juni 2025].

Cole, J.J., Prairie, Y.T., Caraco, N.F. et al. (2007): Plumbing the Global Carbon Cycle: Integrating Inland Waters into the Terrestrial Carbon Budget. Ecosystems, 10, 172–185.

European Union (2020): Regulation (EU) 2020/852 of the European Parliament and of the Council of 18 June 2020, Official Journal of the European Union, L 198/13. https://eur-lex.europa.eu/legal-content/DE/TXT/?uri=CELEX:32020R0852

European Commission (2021): Commission Delegated Regulation (EU) 2021/2139 of 4 June 2021 supplementing Regulation (EU) 2020/852 by establishing the technical screening criteria, Official Journal of the European Union. https://eur-lex.europa.eu/legal-content/DE/TXT/?uri=CELEX:32021R2139

European Union (2022): Directive (EU) 2022/2464 of the European Parliament and of the Council of 14 December 2022, Official Journal of the European Union, L 322/15. https://eur-lex.europa.eu/eli/dir/2022/2464/oj/eng

European Union (2023): Commission Delegated Regulation (EU) 2023/2772 of 31 July 2023 supplementing Directive 2013/34/EU as regards sustainability reporting standards. https://eur-lex.europa.eu/eli/reg_del/2023/2772/oj/eng

European Union (2025): Richtlinie (EU) 2025/794 des Europäischen Parlaments und des Rates vom 14. April 2025 zur Änderung der Richtlinie (EU) 2022/2464 und (EU) 2024/1760 bezüglich der Daten, ab denen die Mitgliedstaaten bestimmte Anforderungen an die Nachhaltigkeitsberichterstattung und die Sorgfaltspflichten von Unternehmen erfüllen müssen.

UNFCCC (2020): Methodological tool: Project emissions from reservoir. United Nations Framework Convention on Climate Change.

United Nations (2015). The Paris Agreement under the United Nations Framework Convention on Climate Change. [online] Verfügbar unter: https://unfccc.int/files/meetings/paris_nov_2015/application/pdf/paris_agreement_english_.pdf [Zugriff am 2. Juni 2025].

Zhang, Q., Li, L., Xu, H. et al. (2024): Estimation methods of wetland carbon sink and factors influencing wetland carbon cycle: a review. Carbon Research, 3, Article 50.

Kreislaufwirtschaft

Therese E. Bouvier-Schwarz, Martin Popowicz, Thomas Nigl

Klimapositive Kreislaufwirtschaft

Welchen Beitrag leistet die österreichische Abfallwirtschaft?

Zusammenfassung: Das Branchenprojekt „Klimapositive Abfallwirtschaft" konnte Spannungsbereiche zwischen Klimaschutz und Kreislaufwirtschaft identifizieren. Mittels eines Klimabilanztools wurde den abfallwirtschaftlichen Unternehmen eine einheitliche Berechnungsbasis für ausgewählte Stoffströme zur Verfügung gestellt. Abfallwirtschaftliche Aktivitäten sind Treiber für die Rückführung des Materials in den Kreislauf, jedoch ist die Berechnungsmethode für die damit erreichte Emissionseinsparung noch nicht vollständig mit den aktuellen Emissionsbilanzierungen akkordiert. Kreislaufwirtschafts- und Klimaziele werden in den strategischen Dokumenten meist getrennt betrachtet, da es sich um eine Ressourcen- oder Emissionsbasierte Bewertung handelt. Durch eine zukünftige Zusammenführung dieser Zielkriterien und Betrachtung der gesamten Lebenszyklen bis hin zur abfallwirtschaftlichen Tätigkeit inklusive Verwertung könnte ein gesamtheitliches Bild entstehen.

Keywords: Abfallwirtschaft, Klimaschutz, Stoffstromlenkung, Emissionsbilanzierung, Kreislaufführung.

1. Einleitung

Die Zielsetzungen des europäischen Green Deals forcieren einerseits einen Wandel von einer linearen zu einer zirkulären Wirtschaftsweise, andererseits wird bis 2030 eine Reduktion der Treibhausgasemissionen in allen Wirtschaftssektoren von 55 % (Vergleich 1990) sowie Klimaneutralität bis 2050 angestrebt (EU, 2021).

Kreislaufwirtschaft und Klimaschutz werden häufig als nicht eindeutig verschränkt gesehen, betrachtet das eine die Materialebene, das andere eine Emissionsebene. Die Zusammenhänge werden dann klar, wenn man die Emissionsbilanzen beider Bereiche vergleicht. Die Abfallwirtschaft als Teil der Kreislaufwirtschaft trägt durch die Sekundärrohstoffbereitstellung und den Einsatz von grünen Technologien bei die Ressourcenabhängigkeit zu reduzieren. Des Weiteren stellt sie lokale und regionale Wertschöpfung sicher und verkleinert den Emissionsrucksack der heimischen Wirtschaft.

Im von der österreichischen Forschungsförderungsgesellschaft unterstützten Branchenprojekt „Klimapositive Abfallwirtschaft – Klima+A" wurde den Partnerunternehmen des Verbandes österreichischer Entsorgungsbetriebe (VOEB) ein Berechnungstool zur Verfügung gestellt, um Emissionsbilanzen zu berechnen und den Einfluss der Abfallwirtschaft auf die österreichischen Klimaziele zu evaluieren.

2. Literatur und Datensammlung

In Österreich lag der Materialverbrauch (DMC) 2022 bei 17 Tonnen/Person/Jahr (Eisenmenger et al., 2024) und übersteigt somit wesentlich den durchschnittlichen nachhaltigen planetaren Rohstoffverbrauch. Kreislaufwirtschaftliche Aktivitäten können hier eingreifen, in dem sie den Primärmaterialverbrauch reduzieren und durch die Verlängerung von Produkt- und Materiallebenszyklen zur Ressourcenschonung beitragen.

In der österreichischen Kreislaufwirtschaftsstrategie (BMK, 2022) wurden neben vier strategischen Zielen (Ressourcenschonung, Vermeidung von Abfällen und Umweltverschmutzung durch Schadstoffe, Klimaschutz) auch sieben Transformationsschwerpunkte festgelegt. Diese Bereiche umfassen Bauwirtschaft, Mobilität, Kunststoffe und Verpackungen, Textilien, Elektronik, Biomasse sowie Abfallwirtschaft und Sekundärrohstoffe. Die Zusammenhänge dieser Sektoren mit der Abfallwirtschaft sind wesentlich, so zeigt sich das diese Sektoren entweder große Abfallmengen produzieren (Bauwirtschaft), komplexe Abfälle mit vielfältigen Inhaltsstoffen hinterlassen (Mobilität, Elektronik) oder auch noch keine vollständige Recyclierbarkeit gegeben ist (Textilien, Kunststoffe und teils Verpackungen).

Folgende quantitative Zielevorgaben der Kreislaufwirtschaftsstrategie (BMK, 2022) betreffen direkt bzw. indirekt auch die Abfallwirtschaft:

- Steigerung der inländischen Ressourcenproduktivität um 50 % bis 2030,
- Steigerung der Zirkularitätsrate auf 18 % bis 2030,
- Reduktion des Materialverbrauchs/Reduktion der Siedlungsabfallmengen um 10% bis 2030.

Die europäische Richtlinie (EU) 2018/851 legt Recyclingziele für Siedlungsabfälle fest, welche schrittweise in den nächsten Jahren ansteigen: bis 2025 müssen mindestens 55 %, bis 2030 mindestens 60 % und bis 2035 mindestens 65 % recycelt werden. Die österreichische Abfallwirtschaft mit ungefähr

3.000 Unternehmen ist somit ein wesentlicher Teil dieser Transformation zur Kreislaufwirtschaft (Schneider et al., 2025).

Eine Berechnung der abfallwirtschaftlichen Aktivitäten hinsichtlich deren Klimaschutzpotential ist bedeutend, jedoch geben die Emissionsbilanzen ein unvollständiges Bild. Die Treibhausgasemission (THG) aus der Abfallwirtschaft (Sektoreneinteilung laut Klimaschutzgesetz), welche 2022 3,4 % der Gesamtemissionen ausmachten, konnten von 1990 bis 2022 mehr als 50 % THG-Emissionen reduziert werden (BMK, 2024). Aktuell wird jedoch die Einsparung geringer. Dem Sektor Abfallwirtschaft wird nur ein Bruchteil der aktuellen eigentlichen Aktivitäten zugerechnet: Abfallverbrennung (Anteil der THG Emissionen am Sektor Abfallwirtschaft 47 %), Deponien (38 %) Biologische Abfallbehandlung (7 %) und Abwasserbehandlung und Entsorgung (THG Emissionen 8 %) zählen dazu (BMK, 2024). Recyclinganlagen und Transporte werden ausgenommen und zum Sektor Industrie bzw. Verkehr zugerechnet. Ebenso ist nur ein Teil der Industrieanlagen im Emissionshandel gemäß Klimaschutzgesetz (Bundesministerium, KSG BGBl. 1 Nr. 106/2011) verankert. Somit bilden sich die Emissionen eines Teils der Verwertungsanlagen im Emissionshandelssystem (ETS) ab, der restliche Teil sowie die gesamten Recyclingaktivitäten sind hier nicht inkludiert.

Die Studie „CO_2 reduction potential in European waste management" zeigt ein europäisches Bild. Drei Szenarien gehen von zukünftigen Einsparungen zwischen 150 Mio. Tonnen CO_2- Äquivalente bis zu 296 Mio. Tonnen CO_2-Äquivalente aus. Diese betrachten nicht nur die abfallwirtschaftlichen Aktivitäten selbst, sondern beziehen auch andere Industriezweige, welche Sekundärrohstoffe oder Ersatzbrennstoffe einsetzen und damit Emissionsreduziert arbeiten ein. Besonders der Einsatz von Sekundärmetallen, verbesserte Behandlung von Haushaltsabfällen sowie die Reduktion der Deponierung führt zu Emissionseinsparungen (CE Delft, Prognos, 2022).

Schebek et al. (2022) legen ebenso die Problematik der Zurechnung von Emissionen bzw. Einsparungen im Spannungsfeld zwischen Abfallwirtschaft und Industrie/Verwertern dar und resümiert, dass hier einerseits digitale andererseits auch politisch-wirtschaftliche Instrumente Lösungen sein könnten.

Wie beginnend gezeigt, wird der Anteil der gesamten Kreislaufwirtschaft derzeit in der nationalen Emissionsbilanzierung nicht eindeutig ausgewiesen. Betrachtet man Zahlen aus unterschiedlichen österreichischen Quellen, um ein Gesamtpotential abzuschätzen zu können, ergeben sich Emissionseinsparungen aufgrund der Substitution von Primärrohstoffen durch bereitgestellte Recyclingmaterialien im Jahr 2014 von 7,9 Mio. Tonnen CO_2-Äquivalente (Meyer et al., 2018). Durch verschiedene regulatorische und/oder technologische Änderungen (Deponieverbot, Einsatz von Ersatzbrennstoffen in der Zementindustrie etc.) in den letzten Jahren konnten 2022 3,4 %, das bedeutet ungefähr 70.000 Tonnen CO_2-Äquivalente im Sektor Abfallwirtschaft (exkl. Recycling- und Kreislaufwirtschaftstätigkeiten) eingespart werden (eigene Berechnung aufgrund der Daten des BMK, 2024). Im Bereich der Abfallvermeidung und des Re-Use konnten ungefähr weitere 178.000 Tonnen CO_2-Äquivalente reduziert werden (Neitsch, Wagner, 2024). Dieses Potential wird aktuell nicht konkret ausgewiesen noch die Zusammenhänge zwischen Sekundärrohstoffeinsatz und der Reduktion von Emissionszertifikaten für die betreffenden Industriezweige.

Auf dem großen Klimaschutzpotential der Kreislaufwirtschaft, aber auch der heterogenen und teils unklaren Berechnungsmethodik fußt das Branchen-Projekt des Verbands österreichischer Entsorgungsbetriebe „Klimapositive Abfallwirtschaft".

Ziel des Projektes ist es ein Berechnungstool für ausgewählte abfallwirtschaftliche Aktivitäten zu erstellen, um damit Emissionsszenarien rechnen zu können und Daten für die unternehmerischen Entscheidungen zu erhalten und darüber hinaus die Möglichkeiten einer Anrechnung/Abgeltung der von der Abfallwirtschaft ermöglichten Emissionseinsparungen zu eruieren.

3. Methodik

Das entwickelte Berechnungsinstrument basiert methodisch auf den Grundsätzen einer Klimabilanz mit Fokus auf Treibhausgasemissionen (CO_2-Äquivalente nach IPCC Methodik). Die Systemgrenzen umschließen alle innerbetrieblichen Maßnahmen (Gate-to-Gate) der zu betrachtenden Stoffströme: abfallwirtschaftliche Behandlung und Sortierung sowie Logistik. Aufgrund der Zielsetzung der Studie wurde dieser enge Rahmen gesetzt, es sollen die Einflüsse/Potentiale der abfallwirtschaftlichen Behandlung dargestellt werden. Die ausgewählten Abfallströme Ersatzbrennstoffe, Leichtverpackungen sowie biogene Abfälle, welche aufgrund des Vorkommens in den meisten österreichischen Abfallunternehmen von Bedeutung sind, weisen ein klares Kreislauf-, Emissionsreduktion- und/oder Mengenpotential auf. Als funktionale Einheit und Referenzfluss wurde eine Tonne behandelter Abfall angenommen.

Zu Beginn des Projektes wurde eine Realdatenerhebung bei den beteiligten Abfallunternehmen gestartet. Durch die verschiedene Größe, Ausrichtung bzw. auch vorhandene Datengrundlage war ein durchschnittlicher Unternehmensdatensatz für alle Stoffströme nicht erhebbar. Daher wurde auf Literatur, Branchendaten bzw. generische Datensätze zurückgegriffen. Um eine Vergleichbarkeit der gewählten Datensätze zu anderen bestehenden, frei zugänglichen Datenquellen zu ermöglichen, wurden Emissionsfaktoren für primär- und sekundär Rohstoffe sowie Emissionseinsparungen durch Einsatz von Sekundärrohstoffen recherchiert. In gemeinsamen Stakeholder-Workshops mit den beteiligten Unternehmen wurde zusätzlich eine strategische Ausrichtung zur Monetarisierung der Ergebnisse im Bereich der Abfallwirtschaft entwickelt. Diese zielen auf eine Rückführung der Abfallströme in den Kreislauf sowie höhere Qualitäten der Sekundärrohstoffe ab.

Im Berechnungstool, welches den VOEB Mitgliedsbetrieben zur Verfügung gestellt wird, können alle Datenquellen entnommen werden bzw. auch eigene Adaptierungen auf unternehmensspezifische Daten erfolgen. Dieses unterstützt die Unternehmen bei den ersten Abschätzungen zu Emissionen sowie Einsparungspotentialen.

4. Ergebnisse

Das Projekt „Klimapositive Abfallwirtschaft" zeigte, dass aktuell kreislaufwirtschaftliche Aktivitäten wie das Recycling nicht direkt der Abfallwirtschaft zugerechnet werden. Aktuell eingesetzte abfallwirtschaftliche Strategien und Instrumente müssen daher noch mit Kreislaufwirtschaftsaspekten ergänzt werden, wobei jedoch die Methoden zur Erfassung und Datengenerierung für Kreislaufwirtschaftsbemühungen noch nicht standardisiert vorliegend sind. Abbildung 1 zeigt die Abfallhierarchie, erweitert um die 10 R- Grundsätze der Kreislaufwirtschaft. Betrachtet man die Maßnahmen der einzelnen Hierarchie-Abschnitte sieht man das besonders die zwei ersten Bereiche erweitert bzw. genauer definiert gehören.

Zu überdenken ist, in wieweit eine Abfallhierarchie das gesamte Potential der Kreislaufwirtschaft abbilden kann, da die einzelnen Bereiche miteinander in Verbindung stehen. So kann zum Beispiel durch Recycling (Rückführung der Materialien in den Kreislauf) auch Abfallvermeidung indirekt passieren. Durch die Vorbereitung zur Wiederverwendung, im Speziellen Remanufacturing bzw. Refurbishing, werden einzelne Komponenten ausgebaut und einer qualitativeren Behandlung zuführbar, während der Großteil des Produktes im Lebenszyklus verbleibt. Dies ermöglicht ebenso Kreislaufwirtschaft. Betrachtet man die fünf Abschnitte der Abfallhierarchie sind auch nur drei dieser fünf Ebenen wirklich vollständig in der Abfallwirtschaft abgebildet.

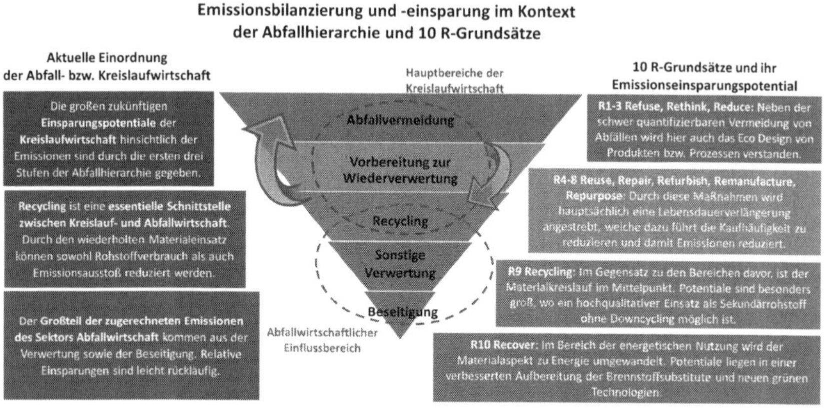

Abbildung 1: Darstellung der Zusammenhänge zwischen Emissionsbilanzierung und Einsparungen im Kontext der Abfallhierarchie und den R-Grundsätzen der Kreislaufwirtschaftsstrategie (eigene Darstellung).

Durch das erstellte Berechnungstool wurde den Partnerunternehmen die Möglichkeit gegeben, Emissionsszenarien darzustellen und hinsichtlich der zukünftig notwendigen ESG Reports Daten zu generieren. Wichtig ist dies auch in Bezug auf die hergestellten Qualitäten des Sekundärrohstoffes. Die Ergebnisse zeigten, dass durch die abfallwirtschaftliche Lenkung von Stoffströmen, Kreisläufe geschlossen und damit Emissionen über den gesamten Lebenszyklus eingespart werden können. Die Qualitätsentscheidung ist aber oftmals mit Mehremissionen bzw. aufwendiger Aufbereitungsschritte verbunden, welche in der Abfallwirtschaft entstehen, die Einsparung dadurch aber nicht dieser zugerechnet wird. Mit der CO_2-Steuer und anderen wirtschaftlichen Hemmnissen, wird somit die Kreislaufwirtschaft nicht gefördert.

Diese Erkenntnisse führten im Projekt zu Überlegungen wie die Emissions- bzw. Einsparungszuordnung funktionieren könnte bzw. auch von politischer Seite eine Förderung der auf Kreislauf-gerichteten Abfallwirtschaft entstehen kann. Die Modelle zur Monetarisierung stellen unternehmerische Einflussbereiche, aber auch politische Hebel dar. Zukünftig wird es von Bedeutung sein, die Bilanzgrenze mit dem kreislaufwirtschaftlichen Gedanken zu erweitern und gesamte Stoffstrompfade für die Bilanzierung bzw. auch die Zurechnung der Emissionen zu betrachten.

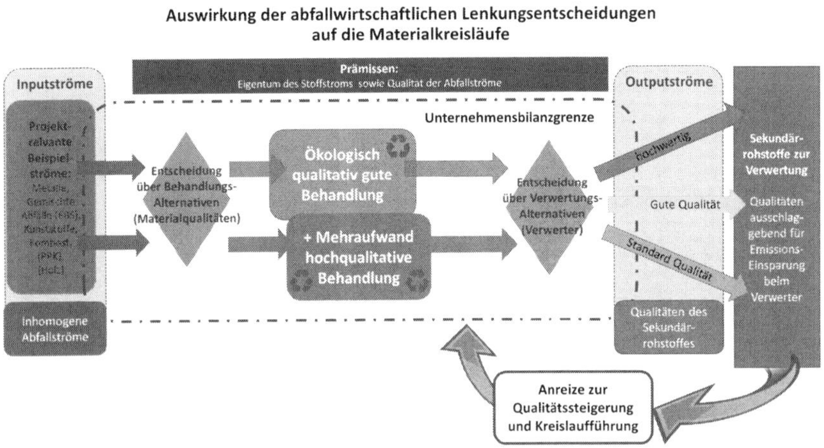

Abbildung 2: Darstellung des unternehmerischen Handlungsspielraumes in der Abfallwirtschaft für die Lenkung von Stoffströmen (eigene Darstellung).

5. Schlussfolgerung und Ausblick

Für eine weitere Schärfung des Tools wäre eine genaue Betrachtung der Verwertungsszenarien bzw. das Einpflegen von Realdaten nächste Schritte. Die Emissions-Kennzahlen sollten mittels des entwickelten Berechnungstools für die österreichischen Abfallunternehmen erleichtert zu errechnen sein und eine Vergleichbarkeit der Daten sicherstellen. Darüber hinaus hat das Projekt in den Diskussionen mit dem Mitgliedsbetrieben gezeigt, welche Informationen einfach zugänglich und erhebbar sind und welche nicht. Dieses Wissen kann auch für das ESG Reporting genutzt und weiter auf nationaler und europäischer Ebene eingebracht werden. Die finanzielle Zurechnung von Emissionsreduktionen ist darüber hinaus auf wirtschaftlicher und politischer Ebene zu klären. Die Abfallwirtschaft ist Schlüssel zu einer funktionierenden Kreislaufwirtschaft mit einer Schlüsselrolle des Recyclings und kann durch Einsatz von nachhaltigen Technologien bzw. den Lenkungsmaßnahmen einen wesentlichen Beitrag zur Klimaneutralität Österreichs liefern.

Abkürzungsverzeichnis

CO_2	Kohlenstoffdioxid
DMC	Domestic Material Consumption
ESG	Englisch für Environmental, Social, Governance
ETS	Emission trading system
FFG	Österreichische Forschungsförderungsgesellschaft
IPCC	Intergovernmental Panel on Climate Change
Mio.	Millionen
THG	Treibhausgasemissionen (Einheit CO_2-Äquivalente)
VOEB	Verband österreichischer Entsorgungsbetriebe
%	Prozent

Literatur

Bundesministerium für Klimaschutz, Umwelt, Energie, Mobilität, Innovation und Technologie (BMK) (2022), „Österreich auf dem Weg zu einer nachhaltigen und zirkulären Gesellschaft – die österreichische Kreislaufstrategie", verfügbar unter https://www.bmluk.gv.at/service/publikationen/klima-und-umwelt/oesterreich-auf-dem-weg--zu-einer-nachhaltigen-und--zirkulaeren-gesellschaft.html (Zugriff am 28.05.2025).

Bundesministerium für Klimaschutz, Umwelt, Energie, Mobilität, Innovation und Technologie (BMK) (2024) „Fortschrittsbericht 2024 – nach § 6 Klimaschutzgesetz", verfügbar unter: https://www.parlament.gv.at/gegenstand/XXVIII/III/62 (Zugriff am 26.05.2025).

CE Delft, Prognos (2022) „CO2 reduction potential in European waste management", verfügbar unter: https://cedelft.eu/publications/co2-reduction-potential-in-european-waste-management/ (Zugriff am 02.06.2025).

Eisenmenger Nina et. al. (2024), „Ressourcennutzung in Österreich 2024", im Auftrag des BMK und BMF, verfügbar unter https://www.bmf.gv.at/themen/bergbau/mineralrohstoffpolitik/oesterreich/ressourcennutzung-in-oesterreich.html (Zugriff am 27.05.2025).

Europäische Parlament, Rat der Europäischen Union (2018), „Richtline 2018/851 vom 30. Mai 2018 zur Änderung der Richtlinie 2008/98/EG über Abfälle", verfügbar unter: https://eur-lex.europa.eu/legal-content/DE/TXT/PDF/?uri=CELEX:32018L0851 (Zugriff am 28.05.2025).

Europäische Commision (2021), "European Green Deal – delivering on our targets", verfügbar unter https://ec.europa.eu/commission/presscorner/detail/en/fs_21_3688 (Zugriff am 14.05.2025).

Meyer Ina, Sommer Mark, Kratena Kurt (2018) „Volkswirtschaftliche Effekte durch Recycling ausgewählter Altstoffe und Abfälle", in Recycling und Rohstoffe, Band 11, verfügbar unter:

https://books.vivis.de/wp-content/uploads/2023/01/2018_RuR_049-064_Meyer.pdf (Zugriff am 02.06.2025).

Neitsch Matthias, Wagner Peter (2024) „Re-Use-Markterhebung 2023“, verfügbar unter: https://reuseaustria.at/markterhebungen/ (Zugriff am 27.05.2025).

Schebek Liselotte, Zeller Vanessa, Baehr Julian, Hagedorn Tabea, do Carmo Precci Lopes Alice (2022) „Vorstudie zur Klimaneutralität der Entsorgungswirtschaft“, TU Darmstadt, IWAR, verfügbar unter: https://tuprints.ulb.tu-darmstadt.de/21616/ (zugriff am 30.05.2025).

Schneider Herwig W. et al. (2025), „Branchenbild der österreichischen Abfallwirtschaft 2024“, Studie des Industrie wissenschaftlichen Instituts (IWI), verfügbar unter https://www.voeb.at/service/presse-news/presse-detail/show-article/studie-abfallbranche-erwirtschaftet-jaehrlich-neun-millarden-euro-umsatz/ (Zugriff am 02.06.2025).

Clara Kopeinig, Wolfgang Posch

Von der Emission zum Rohstoff – CO_2 in einer zirkulären Kohlenstoffwirtschaft

Zusammenfassung: In diesem Beitrag wird die Nutzung von Kohlendioxid (CO_2) als Rohstoff im Rahmen einer zirkulären Kohlenstoffwirtschaft untersucht. Im Gegensatz zur allgemeinen Kohlenstoffwirtschaft, die auch elementaren Kohlenstoff aus anderen Quellen umfasst, steht hierbei die Rückführung von CO_2 in industrielle Kreisläufe im Zentrum. Es werden stoffliche Nutzungsoptionen, wie die Herstellung von Treibstoffen, Chemikalien und Baustoffen, sowie prozessunterstützende Anwendungen, sogenannte Kohlenstoffdienstleistungen, betrachtet. Die zugrunde liegenden Technologien werden anhand ihres Technological Readiness Levels (TRLs) systematisch bewertet. Ergänzend analysiert der Beitrag die technischen, wirtschaftlichen und regulatorischen Voraussetzungen für den Aufbau einer funktionierenden CO_2 Value Chain. Ziel ist es, ein systemisches Verständnis für die Potenziale und Herausforderungen der CO_2-Nutzung in zirkulären Wertschöpfungssystemen zu schaffen.

Keywords: CO_2 Value Chain, Carbon Capture and Utilization (CCU), zirkuläre Kohlenstoffwirtschaft, Technological Readiness Level.

1. Einleitung

Trotz intensiver Bemühungen bleiben in vielen Industriezweigen, insbesondere in der Energie-, Chemie-, Zement- sowie Eisen- und Stahlindustrie, unvermeidbare CO_2-Emissionen bestehen (Kumar *et al.*, 2024). Das Konzept der zirkulären Kohlenstoffwirtschaft bietet hier einen vielversprechenden Ansatz: CO_2 wird dabei nicht länger als Abfallprodukt betrachtet, sondern als Rohstoff in industrielle Kreisläufe zurückgeführt. Dadurch eröffnen sich neben Emissionsminderungen auch neue Wertschöpfungspotenziale, beispielsweise in der Chemie-, Baustoff- und Energieindustrie.

Während die allgemeine Kohlenstoffwirtschaft sämtliche Formen industriell nutzbarer Kohlenstoffquellen, darunter fossile Rohstoffe, Biokohlenstoff oder elementarer Kohlenstoff (C) aus Verfahren wie der Methanpyrolyse, umfasst, fokussiert sich die zirkuläre Kohlenstoffwirtschaft (Circular Carbon Economy) in diesem Beitrag explizit auf die Rückführung und Nutzung von

Kohlendioxid (CO_2). Das Ziel besteht darin, CO_2 als bislang ungenutzten Stoffstrom in geschlossene industrielle Wertschöpfungsketten zu integrieren.

Zunächst werden die zentralen Voraussetzungen für die Entstehung eines funktionierenden Marktes für CO_2 als industriellen Rohstoff analysiert. Aufbauend darauf wird die CO_2 Value Chain als technisches Rückgrat einer zirkulären Kohlenstoffwirtschaft beschrieben. Im Zentrum steht die Bewertung relevanter CO_2-Nutzungstechnologien anhand ihres Technological Readiness Levels (TRL), um den jeweiligen Entwicklungsstand und das industrielle Umsetzungspotenzial systematisch und vergleichbar darzustellen.

Berücksichtigt werden neben der stofflichen Umwandlung von CO_2 in marktfähige Produkte wie synthetische Kraftstoffe, Baustoffe oder chemische Grundstoffe auch sogenannte Kohlenstoffdienstleistungen. Dabei handelt es sich um funktionale Anwendungen von CO_2, bei denen das Gas keine stoffliche Funktion im Endprodukt übernimmt, sondern prozessunterstützend wirkt, beispielsweise bei der Betonhärtung, als Lösungsmittel oder im Rahmen des Enhanced Oil Recovery. Abschließend werden technische, wirtschaftliche und regulatorische Hürden skizziert, die einer flächendeckenden Implementierung derzeit noch entgegenstehen.

2. Das Konzept der zirkulären Kohlenstoffwirtschaft

Um den Herausforderungen des 21. Jahrhunderts, insbesondere dem Klimawandel, wirksam zu begegnen, ist ein grundlegendes Umdenken auf gesellschaftlicher und wirtschaftlicher Ebene erforderlich. Daher ist ein Übergang von der bislang vorherrschenden linearen zur zirkulären Kohlenstoffwirtschaft unabdingbar. Die Kohlenstoffwirtschaft umfasst im Allgemeinen sämtliche stofflichen Kohlenstoffflüsse, unabhängig davon, ob der Kohlenstoff in Form von CO_2, als elementarer Kohlenstoff oder in organischen Verbindungen vorliegt und ob er fossilen, biogenen oder synthetischen Ursprungs ist. In diesem Beitrag wird CO_2 als Teilstrom der Kohlenstoffwirtschaft betrachtet. Im Fokus stehen dabei insbesondere dessen Rückführung und Nutzung im Sinne einer zirkulären Kohlenstoffwirtschaft.

In der linearen Kohlenstoffwirtschaft werden fossile Kohlenwasserstoffe gefördert und energetisch genutzt, wobei CO_2 durch Verbrennung freigesetzt wird. Zusätzlich entstehen in vielen Industriezweigen prozessbedingte Emissionen, die unabhängig vom Energieeinsatz auftreten, etwa durch chemische Reaktionen. Bislang gelangen beide Emissionstypen überwiegend ungefiltert in die Atmosphäre und werden nicht in einen geschlossenen Kohlenstoffkreislauf rückgeführt (KAPSARC, 2020). Um die externen Kosten, insbesondere die Klimafolgeschäden industrieller Emissionen, zu internalisieren, haben zahlreiche Staaten unterschiedliche Steuerungsinstrumente eingeführt, zu denen unter anderem CO_2-Steuern, Emissionshandelssysteme, Emissionsgrenzwerte sowie projektbasierte Kompensationsmechanismen gehören. In der Europäischen Union wurden mit dem Emissionshandelssystem (EU-ETS) und dem CO_2-Grenzausgleichsmechanismus (Carbon Border Adjustment Mechanism, CBAM) zwei zentrale Instrumente etabliert. Während das EU-ETS bereits seit 2005 Emissionen aus EU-internen Anlagen bepreist, soll der CBAM künftig auch Emissionen aus importierten, emissionsintensiven Produkten erfassen. Dadurch sollen Wettbewerbsverzerrungen zwischen europäischen und internationalen Produzenten verringert werden. Beide Mechanismen machen Treibhausgasemissionen zu einem wirtschaftlichen Risiko und Kostenfaktor für Unternehmen (European Commission, 2016, 2025).

Die zirkuläre Kohlenstoffwirtschaft stellt ein strategisches Gegenmodell zur linearen Kohlenstoffwirtschaft dar. Ihr Ziel ist es, Kohlenstoffflüsse möglichst vollständig im Kreislauf zu halten, um Emissionen zu vermeiden, CO_2 industriell zu nutzen oder langfristig zu binden. Insbesondere in der Nutzungsphase hat CO_2 das Potenzial, sich vom reinen Kostenfaktor zu einem wertvollen Rohstoff zu wandeln. Auf diese Weise soll ein Gleichgewicht zwischen emittiertem und rückgeführtem Kohlenstoff erreicht werden. Vier zentrale Strategien stehen dabei im Mittelpunkt: Reduzieren, Wiederverwenden, Recyceln und Entfernen (Reduce, Reuse, Recycle, Remove) (KAPSARC, 2020).

Die Strategie „Reduce" der zirkulären Kohlenstoffwirtschaft zielt darauf ab, Emissionen durch Energieeffizienz, den verstärkten Einsatz erneuerbarer Energien und die Optimierung industrieller Prozesse zu senken. Dadurch soll der Bedarf an Kohlenstoffmanagement von vornherein minimiert werden (IEA, 2020a; IRENA, 2020a).

Die Strategie der Entfernung, „Remove", beschreibt hingegen die dauerhafte Entfernung von CO_2 aus dem Kohlenstoffkreislauf im Rahmen von Carbon Capture and Storage (CCS). CCS bezeichnet eine Reihe von Technologien, mit denen CO_2 aus großen Punktquellen wie Industrieanlagen oder Kraftwerken abgeschieden und anschließend gespeichert wird. Weitere Maßnahmen innerhalb dieser Strategie umfassen die direkte Abscheidung aus der Atmosphäre (Direct Air Capture, DAC) sowie die Stärkung natürlicher Kohlenstoffsenken, beispielsweise in Wäldern und Böden. (Global CCS Institute, 2020). Im Zusammenhang mit zirkulären Kohlenstoffflüssen kommt jedoch den Strategien „Reuse" und „Recycle" in diesem Beitrag eine besondere Bedeutung zu. „Reuse" umfasst die industrielle Nutzung von CO_2 in direkter Form sowie die chemische Umwandlung zu neuen Produkten wie synthetischen Kraftstoffen, Chemikalien oder Baumaterialien (IEA, 2020b). Der Begriff „Recycling" bezieht sich auf den natürlichen Kohlenstoffkreislauf. In diesem wird Kohlenstoff aus der Atmosphäre durch Photosynthese in Biomasse umgewandelt, die wiederum zur Erzeugung von Bioenergie genutzt werden kann. Wird die Bioenergie mit der Carbon-Capture-and-Storage-Technologie (BECCS) kombiniert, gelangt das bei der energetischen Nutzung freigesetzte CO_2 nicht zurück in die Atmosphäre, sondern wird dauerhaft gespeichert. Dies führt zu einer Netto-Reduktion von CO_2, sogenannten negative Emissionen (IRENA, 2020b; KAPSARC, 2020).

Die zirkuläre Kohlenstoffwirtschaft ist ein ganzheitliches Konzept, das technologische, ökologische und ökonomische Ansätze vereint, um den Kohlenstoffkreislauf zu schließen. Durch die systematische Umsetzung der Strategien „Reduce, Reuse, Recycle und Remove" können Emissionen nicht nur vermieden oder dauerhaft entfernt, sondern auch in industrielle Nutzungspfade überführt werden. Insbesondere die Nutzung von CO_2 eröffnet dabei neue Potenziale für Wertschöpfung, da CO_2 als Ausgangsstoff für marktfähige Produkte genutzt wird.

3. Erforderliche Rahmenbedingungen für die Transformation zur CO_2-Nutzung im Kohlenstoffmarkt

Für die Etablierung einer wirtschaftlich tragfähigen CO_2-Nutzung im Sinne einer zirkulären Kohlenstoffwirtschaft ist mehr erforderlich als nur technologischer Fortschritt. Es handelt sich um einen komplexen, systemischen Transformationsprozess, der ökonomische, regulatorische und institutionelle Rahmenbedingungen miteinander verknüpft. Derzeit ist die wirtschaftliche Betrachtung von CO_2 durch einen fundamentalen Zielkonflikt geprägt. Einerseits spielt Kohlenstoff in vielfältigen industriellen Prozessen, beispielsweise in der Chemieindustrie, eine zentrale Rolle, andererseits wird seine Emission nach wie vor primär als externer Schaden behandelt, der mit Kosten verbunden ist. Das EU ETS und der CBAM sind zentrale Instrumente zur Internalisierung dieser externen Kosten. Sie setzen auf Preissignale, um Emissionen zu vermeiden, jedoch nicht, um CO_2 als potenzielle Ressource wirtschaftlich zu nutzen (European Commission, 2016, 2025).

In diesem Kontext bildet das Polluter-Pays-Prinzip die normative Grundlage. Es verpflichtet Emittenten dazu, für verursachte Umweltbelastungen zu zahlen (European Union, 2021). Um jedoch einen funktionsfähigen Markt für CO_2 als wirtschaftlich nutzbaren Rohstoff zu entwickeln, erscheint eine rein strafbasierte Bepreisung als unzureichend. Vielmehr wäre ein Paradigmenwechsel anzustreben, bei dem CO_2 als potenzieller Rohstoff mit ökonomischem Wert bewertet und handelbar gemacht wird (KAPSARC, 2020). Sobald die Nutzung und der Verkauf von CO_2 wirtschaftlich attraktiver sind als der reine Kauf von Emissionsrechten, kann eine Markttransformation einsetzen. Dies würde gezielte Investitionen in Technologien zur CO_2-Nutzung stimulieren und Emittenten zu aktiven Akteuren in einer zirkulären Kohlenstoffwirtschaft machen.

Dieser Anspruch wird in der regulatorischen Realität bislang nur unvollständig abgebildet. Zwar erkennt der aktuelle EU-Rechtsrahmen die stoffliche Nutzung von CO_2 punktuell an, beispielsweise im Rahmen der RED III, durch ReFuelEU Aviation oder FuelEU Maritime (European Union, 2023). Mit ReFuelEU Aviation werden Quoten für nachhaltige Flugkraftstoffe festgelegt, während FuelEU Maritime ähnliche Anforderungen für den Schiffsverkehr formuliert. In beiden Fällen ist eine Anrechnung CO_2-basierter E-Fuels möglich. Dennoch fehlt eine konsistente, skalierbare Systematik zur Etablierung eines eigenständigen Markts für Carbon Capture and Utilization (CCU). Anstelle klarer rechtlicher Rahmenbedingungen existiert eine fragmentierte Landschaft aus sektorspezifischen Quoten, projektbasierten Förderungen und unzureichenden Standards. Diese Inkonsistenz führt zu erhöhten Transaktionskosten, vermindert die Investitionssicherheit und behindert die wirtschaftliche Verwertung von CO_2.

Für einen funktionierenden Kohlenstoffmarkt sind differenzierte Preissignale notwendig: Neben der Bepreisung von Emissionen sollte auch die Nutzung von CO_2 honoriert werden. Instrumente wie Carbon Contracts for Difference (CCfDs) setzen genau hier an (Bundesministerium für Wirtschaft und Klimaschutz, 2024). Sie kompensieren die Differenz zwischen den tatsächlichen CO_2-Marktpreisen und den spezifischen Vermeidungskosten eines Projekts, beispielsweise bei der Herstellung synthetischer Kraftstoffe, und schaffen so Investitionssicherheit.

Gezielte Nachfrageimpulse könnten darüber hinaus eine zentrale Rolle bei der Entwicklung von Märkten für CO_2-basierte Produkte spielen. Erst wenn entsprechende Abnehmerstrukturen vorhanden sind, lässt sich ein funktionierender Markt etablieren. Sektorale Regelwerke wie ReFuelEU Aviation oder RED III bieten hier wichtige Anknüpfungspunkte. Es fehlen jedoch bislang übergreifende Zielquoten für CO_2-basierte Chemikalien, Kunststoffe oder Verpackungen.

Gleichzeitig braucht es gezielte Fördermaßnahmen, um das sogenannte „Tal der Enttäuschungen" zu überwinden (Gartner, 2025). Dabei handelt es sich um jene Phase im Technologiezyklus, in der vielversprechende Ansätze aufgrund fehlender Marktbedingungen wieder aufgegeben werden. Der EU Innovation Fund, das Programm „Horizon Europe" und grüne Anleihen können dabei helfen, private Investitionen zu mobilisieren und Risiken zu streuen. Darüber hinaus muss Carbon Capture Utilization and Storage als strategische Querschnittstechnologie anerkannt werden. Dies ist bereits im

Net Zero Industry Act und in der Industrial Carbon Management Strategy der EU (2024) angelegt (European Commission, 2024; European Union, 2024).

Ein weiteres zentrales Element ist die Reduktion der Transaktionskosten, die aktuell durch regulatorische Unsicherheiten, fehlende Standardisierung und mangelnde Markttransparenz entstehen. In einem funktionierenden Kohlenstoffmarkt erscheinen verlässliche, nachvollziehbare und digital verfügbare Informationen über die Herkunft, die Qualität, das Eigentum und die Wirkung von CO_2 als wichtig. Die Integration von digitalen Produktpässen, harmonisierten Zertifizierungsprozessen und einheitlichen CO_2-Bilanzen könnte hier Abhilfe schaffen und die Markteffizienz deutlich steigern. Geringere Transaktionskosten bedeuten dabei nicht nur niedrigere Hürden für Investitionen, sondern auch eine höhere Wettbewerbsfähigkeit zirkulärer CO_2-Lösungen im Vergleich zu fossilen Alternativen.

Neben den technologischen, regulatorischen und ökonomischen Voraussetzungen rückt zunehmend auch die strategische Kooperation zwischen Wettbewerbern in den Fokus. Insbesondere entlang der CO_2 Value Chain, wo einzelne Wertschöpfungsstufen wie Transportinfrastruktur, CO_2-Hubs oder standardisierte Zertifizierungssysteme erhebliche Anfangsinvestitionen und sektorübergreifende Abstimmungen erfordern, kann sich „Coopetition" – die Zusammenarbeit zwischen konkurrierenden Unternehmen – als entscheidender Faktor für die Marktentwicklung erweisen. Durch die gemeinsame Nutzung von CO_2-Pipelines, geteilte Logistiklösungen oder die kooperative Entwicklung industrieller Standards können Synergien genutzt und Transaktionskosten gesenkt werden, ohne dass der produktseitige Wettbewerb aufgehoben wird. Gerade in kapitalintensiven Bereichen, in denen sich Investitionen für einzelne Akteure kaum isoliert realisieren lassen, trägt „Coopetition" dazu bei, marktliche Fragmentierung zu überwinden und skalierbare Geschäftsmodelle auf Basis von CO_2 als Rohstoff zu etablieren (Walley, 2007).

Zusammenfassend zeigt sich, dass der Aufbau eines marktfähigen CO_2-Nutzungssystems weder durch technologische Reife noch durch isolierte Einzelmaßnahmen allein erreicht werden kann. Die Transformation zur zirkulären Kohlenstoffwirtschaft erfordert vielmehr ein systemisches Zusammenspiel aus politischem Gestaltungswillen, ökonomischen Anreizen und institutionellen Innovationsstrukturen. Erst wenn die Nutzung von CO_2 wirtschaftlich lohnender ist als dessen reine Emission, entstehen echte Marktimpulse mit positiven Effekten auf Innovation, Dekarbonisierung und industrielle Wertschöpfung. Ein funktionierender CO_2-Markt ist somit nicht nur ein ökologisches Instrument, sondern auch ein strategischer Hebel zur Sicherung der industriellen Wettbewerbsfähigkeit in einem zunehmend klimabezogenen Wirtschaftssystem. Die zirkuläre CO_2-Nutzung wird somit zur Schlüsselkomponente einer resilienten, klimaneutralen Industriepolitik.

4. Die CO_2 Value Chain – Von der Abscheidung zur Wertschöpfung

Die entlang der CO_2-Wertschöpfungskette eingesetzten Technologien, von der Abscheidung über den Transport bis zur stofflichen Nutzung, fungieren als technische Enabler für eine funktionierende zirkuläre Kohlenstoffwirtschaft. Nur wenn diese Prozesse nahtlos ineinandergreifen, können CO_2-Ströme wirtschaftlich nutzbar gemacht und dauerhaft in industrielle Materialflüsse rückgeführt werden. Die CO_2 Value Chain bildet somit das infrastrukturelle und technische Fundament für neue Geschäftsmodelle, regulatorische Innovationen und sektorübergreifende Kreislauflösungen in einem zukunftsfähigen Kohlenstoffmarkt.

Um die technische Realisierbarkeit einzelner Wertschöpfungsstufen zu bewerten, ist der Entwicklungsstand der zugrunde liegenden Technologien von entscheidender Bedeutung. Zur systematischen Einschätzung wird in diesem Beitrag das Konzept der Technology Readiness Levels (TRL) verwendet. Das ursprünglich von der NASA entwickelte Modell gliedert technologische Entwicklungen in neun Stufen – von der Grundlagenforschung (TRL 1) bis zur industriellen Einsatzreife (TRL 9) – und hat sich als anerkannter Standard im Innovationsmanagement etabliert (Mankins, 1995). Im Kontext der CO_2 Value Chain ermöglicht die TRL-Klassifikation eine vergleichbare Bewertung unterschiedlicher Technologien entlang der Wertschöpfungskette und unterstützt somit die Priorisierung von Investitionen und politischen Maßnahmen. Tabelle 1 zeigt die TRL-Stufen in der verwendeten Definition.

Tabelle 1: Einordnung der TRL gemäß NASA zur Beurteilung der technologischen Reife (Mankins, 1995).

TRL	Bezeichnung
1	Grundprinzipien wurden beobachtet
2	Technologiekonzept wurde formuliert
3	Technologiekonzept wurde experimentell nachgewiesen
4	Technologie wurde im Labor überprüft
5	Technologie wurde in relevanter Umgebung validiert
6	Technologie wurde in relevanter Umgebung getestet
7	System-Prototyp wurde im realen Einsatz getestet
8	System wurde vervollständigt und qualifiziert
9	System funktioniert in operationeller Umgebung

Die Wertschöpfungskette gliedert sich in mehrere aufeinander aufbauenden Stufen wie in Abbildung 1 illustriert. Ausgangspunkt dieser Wertschöpfungskette sind CO_2-Emissionen, die insbesondere in emissionsintensiven Industrien wie der Energie-, Stahl-, Zement- und Chemiebranche entstehen. Sie entstehen primär durch die Verbrennung fossiler Energieträger, sowohl in stationären industriellen Prozessen als auch in mobilen Anwendungen wie dem Straßen-, Luft- und Seeverkehr. Darüber hinaus fallen Emissionen auch prozessbedingt an, beispielsweise infolge chemischer Reaktionen bei der Zementherstellung. Während stationäre Punktquellen technisch gut mit Verfahren wie der Pre-Combustion-, der Post-Combustion- und der Oxy-Combustion-Methode sowie sorbent-, lösungsmittel- und membranbasierten Technologien adressiert werden können, ist die Abscheidung bei mobilen oder dezentralen Quellen deutlich komplexer. In solchen Fällen kann Direct Air Capture (DAC) eine relevante Lösung darstellen, um CO_2 direkt aus der Umgebungsluft abzuscheiden (European Commission. Joint Research Centre., 2024a).

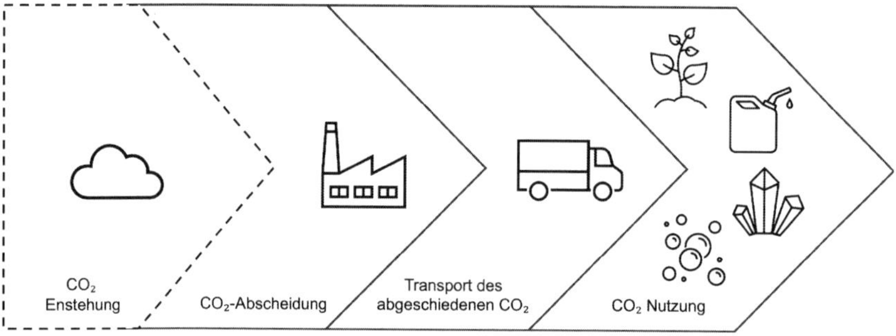

Abbildung 1: Schematische Darstellung der CO_2 Value Chain (Philbin, 2020a).

Der technologische Reifegrad der eingesetzten Abscheidungstechnologien variiert je nach Verfahren, Quelle und industrieller Anwendung erheblich. Erstgenerations-Technologien, zu denen aminbasierte Lösungsmittel, physikalische Absorptionsmittel und Membranen zur Aufbereitung von Erdgas zählen, gelten als weitgehend etabliert (TRL 9) und sind bereits kommerziell verfügbar. Diese Verfahren kommen insbesondere in der Ammoniak- oder Wasserstoffproduktion sowie bei der Erdgasaufbereitung erfolgreich zum Einsatz. Neuere Technologien wie hybride Membranen, Feststoff-Adsorber oder enzymbasierte Sorbentien befinden sich hingegen noch in der Forschungs- und Entwicklungs- oder Demonstrationsphase und erreichen im Durchschnitt lediglich TRL 5–7. Besonders deutlich wird dieser Unterschied im sektoralen Vergleich: Während in der Erdgasverarbeitung bereits TRL 9 erreicht wird, liegen die meisten Technologien in emissionsintensiven Industrien wie der Zement-, Stahl- oder Raffinerieindustrie lediglich im Bereich von TRL 6-7. Direct Air Capture (DAC) als Lösung für schwer abscheidbare Emissionsquellen erreicht aktuell im Durchschnitt TRL 6, ebenso wie Bioenergy with Carbon Capture and Storage (BECCS). Letzteres ist zwar konzeptionell gut verstanden, aber bislang kaum über Demonstrationsprojekte hinausgekommen (IEA, 2020c).

Im nächsten Schritt wird das abgeschiedene CO_2 über geeignete Infrastrukturen transportiert, darunter Pipelines sowie Transport auf Straße, Schiff oder Schiene. Hierbei müssen neben wirtschaftlichen Gesichtspunkten auch sicherheitsrelevante und ökologische Anforderungen berücksichtigt werden. Der technologische Reifegrad dieser Transportoptionen variiert leicht, insgesamt befindet er sich jedoch auf hohem Niveau. Während Pipelines und Kompressionsanlagen durchschnittlich den Reifegrad TRL 9 erreichen, liegen mobile Transportlösungen wie Bahn, Lkw und Schiff mit einem TRL 7-8 (European Commission. Joint Research Centre., 2024a).

Schließlich folgt die Nutzungsphase, in der das abgeschiedene CO_2 in verschiedenen industriellen Bereichen weiterverwertet wird. In dieser finalen Stufe der CO_2 Value Chain entsteht ein wesentlicher wirtschaftlicher Mehrwert, insbesondere durch die Herstellung sogenannter „Value-Added Products“ und Kohlenstoffdienstleistungen. Diese Stufe repräsentieren die Transformation von CO_2 als Emissions zu einem marktfähigen industriellen Rohstoff mit eigenständigem ökonomischem Nutzen (Naims, 2020; Philbin, 2020a).

Damit CO_2 dauerhaft in industriellen Kreisläufen zirkulieren kann, ist die CO_2 Value Chain auf ein tragfähiges Zusammenspiel technologischer und infrastruktureller Faktoren angewiesen. Technologische Enabler umfassen sämtliche Verfahren zur CO_2-Abscheidung, darunter klassische Ansätze wie Post-Combustion-, Pre-Combustion- oder Oxyfuel-Capture sowie neuere Lösungen wie Direct Air Capture (DAC). Für die stoffliche Nutzung stehen unterschiedliche Konversionspfade zur Verfügung, beispielsweise chemische Prozesse wie die Methanisierung, die Methanol- oder die Polymerproduktion und biologische Verfahren wie Algen- und Mikrobenreaktoren. Diese Technologien ermöglichen die Transformation von CO_2 in verwertbare Zwischen- oder Endprodukte und bilden das Rückgrat einer zirkulären Nutzung. Infrastrukturelle Enabler stellen sicher, dass diese Technologien miteinander vernetzt betrieben werden können. Dazu zählen CO_2-Transportnetze, insbesondere Pipelines, aber auch mobile Logistiklösungen per Straße, Schiene oder Schiff, zentrale CO_2-Hubs für Bündelung und Verteilung sowie geeignete Speicherstätten für die Zwischenlagerung oder die dauerhafte Speicherung.

In Europa gewinnt der Aufbau grenzüberschreitender Infrastrukturen an Bedeutung, etwa durch die EU-TEN-E-Verordnung und Projekte von gemeinsamem Interesse (PCI), die CO_2-Transport und -Speicherung erstmals als förderwürdige Infrastruktur anerkennen (European Union, 2022). Nur wenn diese technischen und logistischen Voraussetzungen flächendeckend verfügbar sind, kann die CO_2 Value Chain wirtschaftlich betrieben und sektorübergreifend implementiert werden.

Damit CO_2 jedoch dauerhaft als wirtschaftlich nutzbarer Rohstoff im industriellen Kreislauf zirkulieren kann, müssen nicht nur die technischen Voraussetzungen entlang der CO_2 Value Chain gegeben sein, sondern auch deren wirtschaftliche Tragfähigkeit gewährleistet werden. Die ökonomische Realisierbarkeit von CO_2-Nutzungstechnologien hängt maßgeblich von einer Vielzahl ineinandergreifender Rahmenbedingungen ab. Neben technologischen Fortschritten zur Effizienzsteigerung und Kostensenkung sind insbesondere verlässliche politische Anreize, funktionierende CO_2-Bepreisungssysteme und gezielte Forschungsförderung erforderlich. Ebenso essenziell ist der Aufbau geeigneter Infrastrukturen, etwa für den Transport, die Speicherung und Nutzung von CO_2, die Skaleneffekte ermöglichen und sektorübergreifende Kooperationen begünstigen. Regulatorische Klarheit, standardisierte Zertifizierungen und internationale Zusammenarbeit gelten als weitere zentrale Hebel, um Investitionssicherheit zu schaffen und die öffentliche Akzeptanz zu stärken. Erst im Zusammenspiel all dieser Faktoren kann die CO_2 Value Chain sowohl technologisch als auch wirtschaftlich geschlossen werden und eine tragfähige Grundlage für eine zirkuläre Kohlenstoffwirtschaft bilden (Taghizadeh-Hesary *et al.*, 2024).

5. Technologien der CO_2 Nutzung im Reifegradvergleich

Um eine zirkuläre Kohlenstoffwirtschaft umsetzen zu können, ist es entscheidend, den Entwicklungsstand der notwendigen Technologien zu kennen, da dieser maßgeblich darüber entscheidet, ob CO_2 tatsächlich im industriellen Maßstab abgeschieden, transportiert und wirtschaftlich verwertet werden kann. Ohne ausreichend entwickelte, skalierbare und integrierbare Technologien bleibt die Vision eines geschlossenen Kohlenstoffkreislaufs auf Demonstrationsprojekte beschränkt. Während sich Carbon Capture and Storage (CCS) auf die reine Reduktion von CO_2-Emissionen konzentriert, liegt der Fokus dieses Kapitels auf Carbon Capture and Utilization (CCU), also der stofflichen Nutzung von CO_2 als Ausgangsstoff. Mithilfe chemischer, biologischer, mineralischer oder physikalischer Verfahren kann CO_2 in Produkte wie Treibstoffe, Baustoffe oder Grundchemikalien umgewandelt und somit als industrieller Rohstoff in die Wertschöpfung integriert werden. Neben dieser stofflichen Nutzung gewinnen auch Kohlenstoffdienstleistungen an Bedeutung. Dabei wird CO_2 nicht als Rohstoff, sondern als prozessunterstützendes Medium eingesetzt, beispielsweise zur Betonhärtung, in der chemischen Verfahrenstechnik oder bei Enhanced Oil Recovery.

Die betrachteten Technologien wurden dabei in die vier Hauptbereiche chemische, biologische, mineralische und physikalische Nutzung gegliedert. Die Einteilung der CO_2-Nutzung in physikalische, chemische, biologische und mineralische Pfade orientiert sich an der Systematik aus der Arbeit von Shi et al. (2025), in der diese vier Hauptnutzungsformen als zentrale Kategorien der CO_2-Verwertung identifiziert wurden (Shi *et al.*, 2025).

Abbildung 2 zeigt eine systematische Darstellung der typischen Anwendungsfelder von CO_2 im Rahmen der Circular Carbon Economy. Innerhalb der vier identifizierten Kategorien sind jeweils beispielhafte Endprodukte oder Einsatzfelder aufgeführt, die in der aktuellen Literatur und in der Praxisdiskussion thematisiert werden.

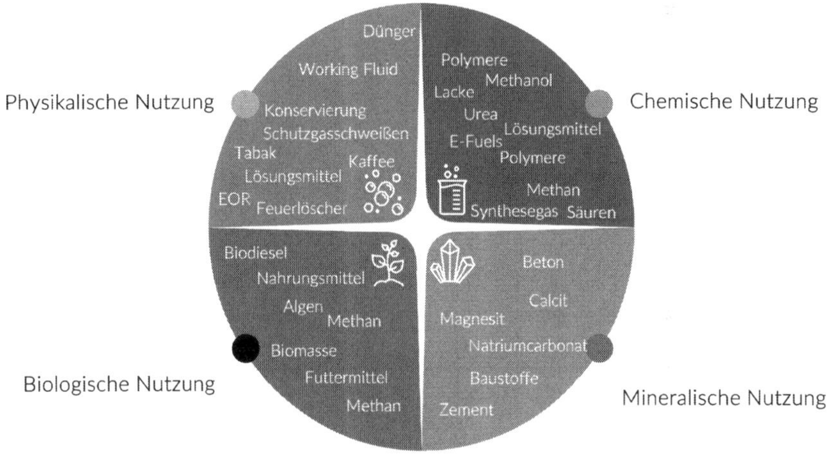

Abbildung 2: Endprodukte der CO_2-Verwertung nach Nutzungskategorien (eigene Darstellung).

5.1. Chemische Nutzung

Die chemische Nutzung ist derzeit das am breitesten untersuchte und industriell vielversprechendste Feld der CO_2-Verwertung. Dabei wird CO_2 als Kohlenstoffträger in chemische Syntheseprozesse eingebunden, beispielsweise zur Herstellung von Methanol, Polymeren oder synthetischen Kraftstoffen. Die Bandbreite reicht von voll etablierten Verfahren bis hin zu Ansätzen im experimentellen Stadium. In Tabelle 2 werden zentrale Technologien, ihr Reifegrad und die resultierenden Endprodukte zusammengefasst.

Tabelle 2: Chemische CO_2 Nutzung (eigene Darstellung).

	Technologie	TRL	Endprodukt
C1	Methanol Synthese	7-9	Methanol
C2	Sabatier-Reaktion	8-9	Methan, SNG
C3	Elektrochemische CO_2-Reduktion	2-5	Methan, Methanol, Ameisensäure, Ethanol, Formaldehyd
C4	Photokatalytische CO_2-Reduktion	3-4	Methan, Methanol, Ameisensäure, Ethanol
C5	Dimethylether-Synthese	4-9	DME Kraftstoff/Aerosol
C6	Dimethylcarbonat-Synthese	3-8	DMC
C7	CO_2-basierte Polymere	6-7	Polyurethane, Polyolefine, Polyoxymethylen, Elastomere
C8	Harnstoffsynthese	9	Urea/ Harnstoff
C9	Fischer-Tropsch-Synthese	5-9	E-Fuels
C10	Trockenreformierung	4-6	Synthesegas

Die chemische CO_2-Verwertung deckt ein breites TRL-Spektrum ab und reicht von voll industrialisierten Großprozessen bis zu Laboransätzen. Die Methanol-Synthese ist mit TRL 7–9 am weitesten fortgeschritten. Ihre Wirtschaftlichkeit hängt jedoch vom Preis für grünen Wasserstoff ab, der mittels Elektrolyse unter Einsatz erneuerbarer Energien klimaneutral hergestellt wird, sowie von einem ausreichenden CO_2-Preissignal (Dziejarski *et al.*, 2023; Garcia *et al.*, 2024; Jarvis und Samsatli, 2018). Die Sabatier-Reaktion (TRL 8–9) wandelt CO_2 und H_2 zu synthetischem Erdgas um. Hauptprobleme sind die Lebesdauer des Katalysators und die Kosten für H_2 (Garcia *et al.*, 2024; Jarvis und Samsatli, 2018).

Routen zur CO_2-Reduktion befinden sich deutlich früher in der Entwicklungsphase: Die elektrochemische CO_2-Reduktion (TRL 2–5) sowie die photokatalytische Variante (TRL 3–4) liefern zwar CO, Alkohole oder Säuren, leiden jedoch unter geringer Energieeffizienz und begrenzter Langzeitstabilität (Garcia *et al.*, 2024; Jarvis und Samsatli, 2018; Roh *et al.*, 2020; Rumayor *et al.*, 2018).

Für Dimethylether (DME) gilt: Die indirekte Route über Methanol ist vollständig kommerzialisiert (TRL 9), während die direkte Synthese aus Synthesegas erst bei TRL 4–5 steht Dimethylcarbonat (DMC) wird in Pilot- bis Demonstrationsanlagen (TRL 3–8) hergestellt. Die niedrige CO_2-Reaktivität und der Bedarf an robusten Katalysatoren bremsen jedoch die Entwicklung (Dziejarski *et al.*, 2023; Garcia *et al.*, 2024).

CO_2-basierte Polymere (Polycarbonate, Polyurethane, Polyolefine und POM) werden bereits im Demonstrationsmaßstab (TRL 6–7) eingesetzt, stoßen allerdings bei den Kosten für Katalysatoren, den Materialeigenschaften und der Marktdurchdringung auf Probleme (Philbin, 2020b; Raheem *et al.*, 2024). Die Urea-Synthese ist voll etabliert (TRL 9), bleibt jedoch indirekt an den CO_2-intensiven Haber-Bosch-Prozess zur Herstellung von Ammoniak gebunden (Dziejarski *et al.*, 2023; Jarvis und Samsatli, 2018; Philbin, 2020b).

Die Fischer-Tropsch-Synthese liefert E-Diesel, -Benzin und -Kerosin. Die Kerntechnik ist reif (TRL 9), doch CO_2-basierte Varianten mit erneuerbarem Syngas bewegen sich erst bei TRL 5–7 und kämpfen mit hohen Strom- und H_2-Kosten (Garcia *et al.*, 2024; Jarvis und Samsatli, 2018). Schließlich adressiert die Trocken-reformierung von CO_2 und Methan (TRL 4–6) die Herstellung Synthesegas das wiederum für die Methanol- oder Kraftstoffproduktion genutzt werden kann (Garcia *et al.*, 2024; vg. Jarvis und Samsatli, 2018).

5.2. Biologische Nutzung

Bei biologischen CO_2-Verwertungswegen wird die Fähigkeit von Mikroorganismen und Algen genutzt, CO_2 in organische Verbindungen umzuwandeln. Diese Ansätze sind insbesondere für die Produktion von biogenen Kraftstoffen, Nahrungsergänzungsmitteln oder Futtermitteln relevant. Allerdings stehen sie häufig vor Herausforderungen hinsichtlich Effizienz und Skalierbarkeit. Die nachfolgende Tabelle 3 zeigt ausgewählte Technologien und deren Entwicklungsstand.

Tabelle 3: Biologische CO_2 Nutzung (eigene Darstellung).

	Technologie	**TRL**	**Endprodukt**
B1	Biologische Sabatier-Reaktion	6	Methanol
B2	Mikroalgen	3-8	Biomasse, Biodiesel, Bioethanol, Futtermittel, Pharmazie

Die biologische CO_2-Verwertung beruht auf Mikroorganismen und Algen, die Kohlenstoff bei milden Bedingungen fixieren und in Energieträger oder Wertstoffe umwandeln. Am weitesten entwickelt ist die biologische Sabatier-Reaktion, eine hydrogenotrophe Methanisierung. In-situ oder ex-situ wird bei 30–60 °C CO_2 und H_2 zu Biomethan umgesetzt. Dabei werden Wirkungsgrade von bis zu 80 % erreicht. Diese Technologie befindet sich für Biogasanlagen auf Demonstrationsniveau (TRL 6). Engpässe sind die langsame Kinetik, pH-Stabilisierung, Gasreinigung und vor allem der kostspielige grüne Wasserstoff (Garcia *et al.*, 2024).

Ein weiterer relevanter Ansatz ist die Kultivierung von Mikroalgen, bei der CO_2 als Kohlenstoffquelle dient. Die Algen werden in Photobioreaktoren oder offenen Teichsystemen gezüchtet. Die gewonnene Biomasse kann auf verschiedene Weise genutzt werden. Einerseits besteht die Möglichkeit der energetischen Nutzung durch Trocknung, Pelletierung und anschließendes Co-Firing mit fossilen Brennstoffen in bestehenden Kraftwerken. Diese Technologie befindet sich auf TRL 4 und ermöglicht eine kurzfristige Emissionsminderung im konventionellen Energiesektor. Allerdings wird das zuvor fixierte CO_2 bei der Verbrennung wieder freigesetzt, sodass der Effekt der Emissionsminderung stark vom Gesamtsystem abhängt. Neben der energetischen Verwertung existieren zahlreiche stoffliche Nutzungsmöglichkeiten der getrockneten Algen. So kann die Biomasse zu Biokraftstoffen wie Biodiesel oder Bioethanol verarbeitet werden (TRL 3–5). Weitere stoffliche Anwendungen betreffen den Einsatz in der Tierfutter- und Kosmetikindustrie, in der Pharmazie sowie als Nahrungsergänzungsmittel. Zudem lassen sich Mikroalgen als Rohstoff zur Herstellung von Biokunststoffen und chemischen Zwischenprodukten nutzen. Je nach Produkt und Verwertungsweg erreichen diese stofflichen Anwendungen bereits Technologiereifegrade von bis zu TRL 8 (Dziejarski *et al.*, 2023; Jarvis und Samsatli, 2018; Roh *et al.*, 2020).

5.3. Mineralische Nutzung

Bei der mineralischen Nutzung von CO_2 reagiert das Gas mit mineralischen Substraten oder Industrieabfällen. Diese Prozesse bieten das Potenzial zur dauerhaften Bindung von CO_2 und zur gleichzeitigen Verwertung von Sekundärrohstoffen, was insbesondere im Bausektor von Bedeutung ist. Die Vielzahl der Mineralisierungswege und der eingesetzten Edukte führt zu einem breiten Spektrum an Reifegraden, wie Tabelle 4 verdeutlicht.

Tabelle 4: Mineralische CO_2 Nutzung (eigene Darstellung).

	Technologie	**TRL**	**Endprodukt**
M1	CCMC	2-8	Magnesiumkarbonat, Calciumkarbonat, Natriumkarbonat, CO_2 gehärteter Beton
M2	Karbonatisierung -Bauxit	9	Karbonatisierter Bauxitrückstand
M3	Karbonatisierung – Schlacken	6	Beton, Zusatzstoffe, Zementersatzstoffe, Natriumbicarbonat, Calcium- und Magnesiumcarbonat
M4	CO_2 Aushärtung – Beton	7-8	CO_2-gehärteter Beton

Bei den Carbon Capture and Mineral Carbonation (CCMC)-Technologien reagiert CO_2 mit natürlichen Mineralien oder Industrieabfällen, um stabile Carbonate zu bilden. Während reine Speicherprozesse sich auf TRL 2–6 befinden, ist die Produktion von Magnesiumcarbonaten (TRL 4), Calcium- und Natriumcarbonaten (TRL 7) und CO_2-gehärtetem Beton (TRL 8) bereits weiter entwickelt (Dziejarski *et al.*, 2023).

Anwendungen mit industriellen Abfallstoffen sind weiter fortgeschritten: Die Karbonatisierung von Bauxitrückständen zur Neutralisation ist kommerziell nutzbar (Philbin, 2020b). Auch die CO_2-Aushärtung von Beton befindet sich mit TRL 7–8 in einem fortgeschrittenen Entwicklungsstadium. Dabei reagiert CO_2 mit Zementbestandteilen oder Zuschlagstoffen, was die mechanischen Eigenschaften verbessert und die CO_2-Bilanz senkt (Dziejarski *et al.*, 2023; Philbin, 2020b).

Die direkte Karbonatisierung von Stahlwerkschlacken (TRL 6) wandelt CO_2 in karbonatisierte Zusatzstoffe für Beton, CO_2-negative Betonblöcke, Zementersatzstoffe, Natriumbicarbonat sowie Calcium- und Magnesiumcarbonate um (Watjanatepin *et al.*, 2024). Sie können unter anderem als Ersatz für Portlandzement oder zur Verbesserung der mechanischen Eigenschaften von Bauelementen verwendet werden. Herausforderungen sind die zum Teil geringe Reaktivität einzelner Schlacken, der hohe Energiebedarf für Aufbereitung und die begrenzte Marktverfügbarkeit mancher Endprodukte. Trotz dieser Hürden bietet die Technologie großen Nutzen für dauerhafte CO_2-Bindung und die Entwicklung zirkulärer Wertschöpfungssysteme in der Baustoffindustrie (Dziejarski *et al.*, 2023; Nimmas *et al.*, 2024).

5.4. Physikalische Nutzung

Bei physikalischen Nutzungen werden die chemisch inerten und thermodynamischen Eigenschaften von CO_2 genutzt, ohne dass eine stoffliche Umwandlung erfolgt. Die Anwendungen reichen von der Verwendung in der Lebensmittelindustrie bis hin zum Einsatz in Energiesystemen und industriellen Prozessen. Auch wenn das CO_2 dabei meist nur temporär gebunden wird, spielt diese Nutzungskategorie in zahlreichen etablierten Märkten eine bedeutende Rolle. Tabelle 5 bietet einen Überblick über relevante Anwendungen und deren technologische Reife.

Bei der physikalischen CO_2-Nutzung wird das Gas ohne chemische Umwandlung als Druckgas, Lösungsmittel oder Kühlmittel eingesetzt, vor allem in der Lebensmittel-, Energie- und Prozessindustrie. Da CO_2 dabei meist nur temporär gebunden wird, hängt der Klimanutzen von seiner Einbindung in zirkuläre Systeme ab.

Tabelle 5: Physikalische CO2 Nutzung (eigene Darstellung).

	Technologie	TRL	Endprodukt/Anwendung
P1	EOR	9	Erdöl
P2	Modified Atmosphere Packaging	9	Lebensmittel Konservierung
P3	Gewächshaus Dünger	9	Pflanzendüngung
P4	Schmelzkarbonat-Brennstoffzellen	5	Stromerzeugung
P5	Lignin Ausfällung Zellstoffindustrie	7-8	Lignin
P6	Kühlmedium	9	Kühlung,
P7	Schutzgasschweißen	9	Inertgas für Schweißprozesse
P8	Tabak Expansion	9	Tabak
P9	Superkritische CO2 Extraktion	6-7	Aromastoffe, entkoffeinierter Kaffee,
P10	CO2 als Arbeitsfluid in Kraftwerken	9	CO2 als Arbeitsfluid in Kraftwerken
P11	Karbonatisierung von Getränken	9	Karbonatisierte Getränke

Ein zentraler Anwendungsbereich ist das Enhanced Oil Recovery (EOR). Dabei wird CO_2 in erschöpfte Ölfelder injiziert, um zusätzliche Mengen Rohöl zu fördern. Ein Teil des injizierten CO_2 bleibt dabei dauerhaft im Gestein zurück, weshalb EOR als physikalische Nutzung mit potenzieller Langzeitspeicherung gilt (TRL 9)(Garcia *et al.*, 2024; Jarvis und Samsatli, 2018).

In der Lebensmittelindustrie wird CO_2 im Rahmen des Modified Atmosphere Packaging (MAP) eingesetzt, um die Haltbarkeit zu verlängern und Getränke wie Bier und Limonade zu karbonisieren (TRL 9)(Raheem *et al.*, 2024). In der Landwirtschaft kann CO_2 direkt zur Düngung in Gewächshäusern verwendet werden, um das Pflanzenwachstum zu fördern (TRL 9) (Philbin, 2020b).

Ein Sonderfall der physikalischen CO_2-Nutzung ist der Einsatz in Schmelzkarbonat-Brennstoffzellen (MCFC), bei denen CO_2 im Kreislauf mitverwertet wird. Diese Technologie verbindet Stromerzeugung mit CO_2-Abscheidung und befindet sich derzeit auf TRL 5. Herausforderungen bestehen in der Materialstabilität und der Komplexität des Betriebs (Garcia *et al.*, 2024).

Darüber hinaus wird CO_2 als Arbeits- oder Kühlmedium in Wärmepumpen, Laserkühlsystemen und beim Schweißen verwendet. In der Pharma- und Chemieindustrie dient es als Inertgas und in der Entkoffeinierung von Kaffee sowie der Extraktion von Aromastoffen kommt es als superkritisches Fluid zum Einsatz. Ein weiterer etablierter Anwendungsbereich ist der Einsatz als Druckgas, beispielsweise in Feuerlöschern, Aerosolen oder bei der Natriumkarbonat-Produktion in der Glasindustrie (Fu *et al.*, 2022; Garcia *et al.*, 2024).

In der Zellstoffindustrie wird CO_2 zur pH-Regulierung der Schwarzlauge eingesetzt, wodurch Lignin als Wertstoff rückgewonnen werden kann (TRL 7–8)(Philbin, 2020b).

5.5. Reifegradübersicht und Entwicklungsperspektiven: Die CO_2-Nutzung im S-Kurven-Modell

Die in Kapitel 5 dargestellten CO_2-Verwertungstechnologien lassen sich nicht nur anhand ihres technologischen Reifegrads differenzieren, sondern auch in Bezug auf ihre Funktion innerhalb der Wertschöpfung. Dabei treten zwei grundlegende Nutzungsformen hervor: einerseits die stoffliche Umwandlung von CO_2 in marktfähige Endprodukte und andererseits der Einsatz von CO_2 im Rahmen sogenannter Kohlenstoffdienstleistungen. Bei diesen nimmt das Gas eine unterstützende, aber keine stofflich wirksame Rolle im finalen Produkt ein.

Zur ersten Kategorie zählen Technologien, bei denen CO_2 in chemische Produkte eingebunden wird, die direkt als Rohstoffe oder Energieträger dienen. Beispiele hierfür sind die Methanol-Synthese, die Herstellung von E-Fuels über die Fischer-Tropsch-Synthese, CO_2-basierte Polymere oder die Harnstoff-Herstellung. Ebenso zählen hierzu die Nutzung von Mikroalgen zur Produktion von Biodiesel, Futtermitteln oder pharmazeutischen Inhaltsstoffen sowie die Karbonatisierung von Mineralien zu Baustoffen wie CO_2-gehärtetem Beton. Diese Technologien leisten einen direkten Beitrag zur Substitution fossiler Kohlenstoffquellen, indem sie CO_2 in zirkulären Produkten binden.

In der zweiten Kategorie, den Kohlenstoffdienstleistungen, wird CO_2 hingegen funktional in Produktionsprozesse integriert. Hier übernimmt CO_2 eine prozessuale Funktion, etwa als Reaktionsmedium, Katalyse Unterstützer oder physikalischer Trägerstoff. Zu den analysierten Anwendungen zählen das Enhanced Oil Recovery, bei dem CO_2 zur Druckerhöhung in Lagerstätten verwendet wird, sowie die CO_2-basierte Betonhärtung, die zur Festigkeitssteigerung und zu einer besseren CO_2-Bilanz beiträgt. Ebenso fällt der Einsatz von CO_2 als Schutzgas beim Schweißen, als Kühlmittel, als Arbeitsfluid in Kraftwerken oder als Lösungsmittel in der superkritischen Extraktion in diese Kategorie.

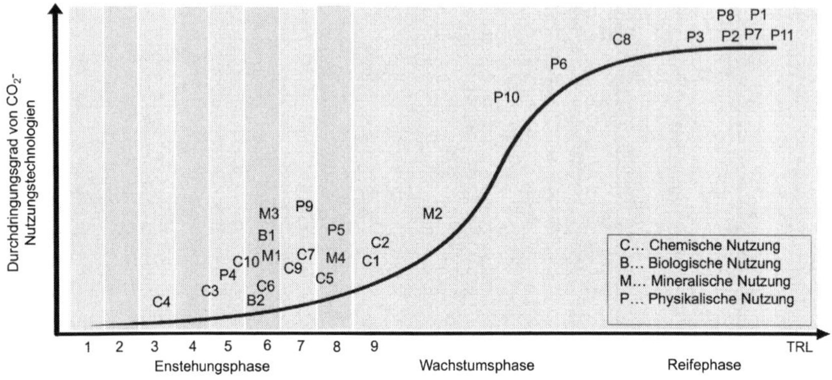

Abbildung 3: *CO_2-Nutzungstechnologien im Technologielebenszyklus des CCU; die Positionierung der Technologien erfolgt in Anlehnung an den jeweiligen Technologiereifegrad (eigene Ergänzungen).*

Abbildung 3 veranschaulicht den Entwicklungsstand verschiedener CO_2-Nutzungs-technologien entlang ihres technologischen Lebenszyklus. Die Abkürzungen der einzelnen Technologien entsprechen den Bezeichnungen in den vorangehenden Tabellen.

Die Einordnung der CO_2-Nutzungstechnologien erfolgt nach der Logik eines S-Kurven-Modells (Arthur D. Little International, 1986; Sommerlatte und Deschamps, 1985). Dieses Modell bildet die typischen Entwicklungs-, Wachstums- und Reifephasen im Technologielebenszyklus ab. Die Positionierung der Technologien basiert auf ihrem jeweiligen Technologiereifegrad. Technologien mit einem TRL zwischen 1 und 8 befinden sich noch in der Entwicklungsphase, da sie bislang nicht über den Pilot- oder Demonstrationsmaßstab hinausgehen und somit noch keine breite industrielle Anwendung erreicht haben. Erst ab TRL 9 gilt eine Technologie als vollständig einsatzbereit, wodurch der Übergang in die Wachstums- und Reifephase möglich wird. In der Grafik wurden alle Technologien mit TRL 9 entsprechend ihrer Marktdurchdringung diesen beiden Phasen zugeordnet. Die Abbildung gibt somit einen systematischen Überblick darüber, wie weit einzelne CO_2-Verwertungspfade im Hinblick auf ihren industriellen Einsatz und ihre potenzielle Skalierbarkeit fortgeschritten sind.

Die in diesem Kapitel dargestellten Reifegrade zeigen, dass zahlreiche technologische Ansätze zur CO_2-Nutzung bereits weit entwickelt sind und sich schrittweise für industrielle Anwendungen etablieren. Für die Realisierung dieser Vorhaben ist neben dem technischen Fortschritt auch die zukünftige Nachfrage nach CO_2 als Rohstoff von entscheidender Bedeutung. Prognosen zufolge wird der globale CO_2-Bedarf für CCU-Anwendungen bis 2050 deutlich ansteigen. Für die chemische Industrie wird ein jährlicher Bedarf von bis zu 3,1 Gigatonnen (Gt) CO_2 prognostiziert (Huo *et al.*, 2023), allein für die Methanol Produktion könnten global etwa 350 Megatonnen (Mt) CO_2 erforderlich sein (Deutsche Energie Agentur, 2024). Auch in Europa wird mit einem Anstieg des Bedarfs gerechnet, und zwar auf etwa 173 Mt CO_2 pro Jahr, wovon ein erheblicher Anteil auf die Herstellung von Chemikalien entfällt. Von 173 Mt CO_2 werden 50 % für die Herstellung von CCU-Kraftstoffen, 42 % für die chemische Produktion und 8 % für die Mineralisierung von Baumaterialien verwendet (Sapart *et al.*, 2024). Diese Zahlen verdeutlichen die zentrale Rolle von CO_2 in einer künftigen zirkulären Kohlenstoffwirtschaft und unterstreichen die Notwendigkeit, bereits heute gezielt skalierbare Infrastrukturen, nachhaltige CO_2-Quellen und wirtschaftlich tragfähige Nutzungspfade zu entwickeln.

6. Diskussion

Die Analyse des Technologiereifegrads zeigt, dass sich CO_2-Nutzungstechnologien in sehr unterschiedlichen Entwicklungsstadien befinden. Physikalische Anwendungen und etablierte chemische Prozesse, wie beispielsweise die Methanol- oder Harnstoffsynthese, sind bereits marktreif. Strom- und wasserstoffbasierte Verfahren sowie bestimmte biologische und mineralische Pfade befinden sich hingegen noch im Pilot- oder Demonstrationsstadium. Diese Unterschiede sind weniger auf technologische Limitierungen als auf systemische Faktoren wie Energiepreise, fehlende Infrastrukturen und unzureichende wirtschaftliche Anreize zurückzuführen.

Vor diesem Hintergrund wird deutlich, dass die Umsetzung einer zirkulären Kohlenstoffwirtschaft nicht allein von der technologischen Machbarkeit abhängen kann. Vielmehr erscheint ein koordinierter Ausbau der gesamten CO_2-Wertschöpfungskette – von der Abscheidung über die Aufbereitung und den Transport bis hin zur Nutzung und gegebenenfalls Speicherung – als entscheidend. Dabei sollten die Einzeltechnologien nicht nur technisch ausgereift, sondern auch ökonomisch tragfähig sein und sich in bestehende Infrastrukturen sowie Marktmechanismen integrieren lassen. Dies erfordert ein Zusammenspiel aus geeigneten politischen Rahmenbedingungen, gezielter Forschungsförderung und wirksamen ökonomischen Anreizen.

Ein wesentlicher Faktor für die wirtschaftliche Skalierung von CCU-Technologien ist die Etablierung verlässlicher Preissignale. Das bestehende EU-ETS fokussiert sich demgegenüber in erster Linie auf die Bepreisung von Emissionen, um deren Vermeidung zu fördern – nicht deren stoffliche Nutzung. Für CO_2, das als Rohstoff in Wertschöpfungspfade überführt wird, existiert bislang kein eigenständiger Marktpreis, der seinen wirtschaftlichen Beitrag zu Folgeprodukten widerspiegelt. Ein marktbasierter CO_2-Rohstoffpreis, der beispielsweise an Reinheit, Ursprung oder Transportentfernung gekoppelt ist, könnte die wirtschaftliche Verwertbarkeit von CCU-Pfaden verbessern.

Darüber hinaus erscheint eine abgestimmte Logistik entlang der gesamten CO_2 Value Chain als grundlegende Voraussetzung, um CO_2 von Emissionsquellen effizient zu den jeweiligen Nutzungs- oder Speicherstandorten zu transportieren. Der Aufbau grenzüberschreitender Pipelines, Hubs und Speicherinfrastrukturen könnte dazu beitragen, Transportkosten zu senken und industrielle Clusterbildungen zu fördern. Prognosen des Joint Research Centre der EU-Kommission zufolge könnte das CO_2-Pipelinenetz bis 2050 auf etwa 19.000 km anwachsen, was einen Investitionsbedarf von bis zu 23 Mrd. € mit sich bringt. Dabei spielen einheitliche Qualitätsstandards und gezielte öffentliche Förderung eine zentrale Rolle (European Commission. Joint Research Centre., 2024b). Gleichzeitig wird deutlich, dass der Ausbau der CO_2-Transport- und Speicherinfrastruktur eng mit der wirtschaftlichen Entwicklung CO_2-basierter Produkte verknüpft, ist: Unternehmen investieren nur dann in Infrastruktur, wenn ein stabiler Markt für die Nutzung von CO_2 besteht. Umgekehrt kann sich dieser Markt aber nur entwickeln, wenn bereits eine verlässliche und kosteneffiziente Infrastruktur vorhanden ist. Dieses wechselseitige Abhängigkeitsverhältnis stellt eine zentrale Herausforderung für die Etablierung des Systems dar. In Anlehnung an die Diskussion um natürliche Monopole, wie sie etwa bei Strom- oder Gasnetzen bestehen, wird deshalb häufig gefordert, den Aufbau grundlegender CO_2-Infrastrukturen durch staatliche Vorleistungen oder gezielte Regulierung anzustoßen. Nur so lassen sich die hohen Investitionskosten, technischen Abhängigkeiten und begrenzten Skaleneffekte überwinden, die mit großtechnischen Netzwerken verbunden sind.

Ein möglicher Ansatz zur Bewältigung dieser infrastrukturellen Herausforderungen ist die strategische Kooperation zwischen Wettbewerbern, auch „Coopetition" genannt. Durch gemeinsame Infrastrukturinvestitionen, beispielsweise in CO_2-Hubs, Pipelines oder Logistiklösungen, können Skaleneffekte genutzt, Investitionsrisiken geteilt und der Marktzugang für nachgelagerte Akteure erleichtert werden. Insbesondere in kapitalintensiven Bereichen, in denen sich der Infrastrukturausbau für einzelne Unternehmen kaum rechnet, kann „Coopetition" dazu beitragen, den Aufbau einer funktionsfähigen CO_2-Wertschöpfungskette systemisch voranzutreiben.

Ein weiterer kritischer Faktor, der aus der Analyse hervorgeht, ist der Zugang zu erneuerbaren Energiequellen und grünem Wasserstoff, insbesondere für strombasierte CCU-Verfahren wie die Methanol- oder E-Fuel-Synthese. Ohne eine kostengünstige und verlässliche Versorgung mit diesen Ressourcen lassen sich viele dieser Technologien kaum wirtschaftlich betreiben. Darüber hinaus ist aus klimapolitischer Sicht auch entscheidend, wie der für die Umwandlung benötigte Strom und Wasserstoff erzeugt wird. Wird etwa CO_2 mithilfe fossil erzeugter Energie verarbeitet, kann die resultierende CO_2-Bilanz negativ ausfallen, das heißt, es entsteht mehr CO_2, als vermieden wird. Damit die Nutzung tatsächlich als klimafreundlich gilt, muss sichergestellt sein, dass der gesamte Prozess überwiegend auf nachhaltigen Energiequellen basiert. Die Bewertung der CO_2-Nutzung sollte sich daher nicht nur auf das Endprodukt stützen, sondern den gesamten energetischen und stofflichen Aufwand entlang der Wertschöpfungskette einbeziehen. Dies unterstreicht die Notwendigkeit, Kohlenstoffnutzungstechnologien eng mit der Energiewende zu verzahnen, sowohl in technologischer als auch in regulatorischer Hinsicht.

Aus ökologischer Perspektive ist insbesondere der Umstand von signifikanter Relevanz, dass nicht jede Nutzungsweise automatisch zu einer anhaltenden Emissionsminderung beiträgt. In zahlreichen Anwendungsbereichen erfolgt die zeitverzögerte Freisetzung von CO_2, was die Effektivität hinsichtlich des Klimaschutzes in Frage stellt. Lebenszyklusanalysen (LCA) sind daher essenziell, um den tatsächlichen Beitrag einzelner Technologien zur Dekarbonisierung zu bewerten. Die Kriterien einer echten zirkulären Kohlenstoffwirtschaft werden nur erfüllt, wenn CO_2 dauerhaft gebunden bleibt und die zur Umsetzung verwendete Energie aus erneuerbaren Quellen stammt.

In diesem Kontext können digitale Instrumente wie Green Digital Twins (GDT) zusätzlich unterstützen, indem sie Umweltwirkungen, etwa den CO_2-Fußabdruck eines Produkts, entlang der gesamten Wertschöpfungskette dynamisch abbilden und bewerten. Dadurch lässt sich die Umsetzung zirkulärer Strategien datenbasiert steuern und transparenter gestalten (Feichtinger *et al.*, 2024).

Zusammenfassend lässt sich festhalten: Die ökonomische Realisierbarkeit von CCU-Technologien ist keine rein technologische, sondern eine systemische Herausforderung. Sie erfordert ein Zusammenspiel aus technologischer Reife, politischer Steuerung, Infrastrukturentwicklung, Marktintegration und Umweltbewertung. Nur unter diesen Voraussetzungen kann das Potenzial der CO_2 Value Chain wirtschaftlich erschlossen und als tragfähige Säule einer zukunftsfähigen, zirkulären Kohlenstoffwirtschaft etabliert werden.

7. Fazit und Ausblick

Die Ergebnisse der Forschung zeigen, dass die Nutzung von CO_2 nicht nur zur Reduktion von Emissionen beitragen kann, sondern auch das Potenzial besitzt, CO_2 von einem Abfallprodukt zu einem strategischen Rohstoff in zirkulären Wertschöpfungsketten zu transformieren. Einzelne Technologien sind zwar technologisch weit entwickelt, doch ihr Beitrag zur Dekarbonisierung hängt maßgeblich von der Systemintegration ab. Deutlich wird, dass nicht der technische Reifegrad allein über die Umsetzung entscheidet, sondern das Zusammenspiel von Technologie mit wirtschaftlicher Tragfähigkeit, politischer Steuerung und infrastrukturellen Voraussetzungen.

Für die weitere Forschung ergeben sich daraus zentrale Fragen. Wie lässt sich ein CO_2-Rohstoffmarkt mit verlässlichen Preissignalen gestalten, der Investitionen entlang der gesamten Wertschöpfungskette unterstützt? Welche regulatorischen und planerischen Instrumente sind notwendig, um eine koordinierte Infrastrukturentwicklung für CO_2-Transport und -Nutzung zu ermöglichen? Schließlich ist zu klären, wie sich Unternehmen strategisch in diesem entstehenden Markt positionieren können, sei es durch Technologieinvestitionen, Clusterbildung oder neue Geschäftsmodelle.

Um CO_2 Value Chains zusätzlich zu stärken, kann die Analyse industrieller Symbiosepotenziale einen wertvollen Beitrag leisten. Dabei stellt sich unter anderem die Frage, wie CO_2-Quellen und -Nutzer in regionalen Industriesystemen systematisch identifiziert, gekoppelt und wirtschaftlich bewertet werden können, um neue stoffliche Nutzungspfade strategisch nutzbar zu machen. Ebenso ist zu untersuchen, welche Synergiepotenziale durch industrielle Kooperationen im Rahmen einer Circular Carbon Economy entstehen können und wie sich diese systematisch erfassen und priorisieren lassen. In diesem Zusammenhang erscheint auch das Konzept der „Coopetition" als ein interessanter Untersuchungsansatz, insbesondere im Hinblick auf den gemeinsamen Aufbau und die Nutzung von CO_2-Infrastrukturen.

Die Transformation hin zu einer zirkulären Kohlenstoffwirtschaft erfordert nicht nur technologische Innovationen, sondern vor allem systemische Lösungsansätze, die Infrastruktur, Marktmechanismen und sektorale Zusammenarbeit integrieren. Nur so kann CO_2 nicht nur vermieden oder gespeichert, sondern auch aktiv in industrielle Wertschöpfungsprozesse integriert werden.

Abkürzungsverzeichnis

BECCS	Bioenergy with Carbon Capture and Storage
CBAM	Carbon Border Adjustment Mechanism
CCU	Carbon Capture and Utilization
CCUS	Carbon Capture, Utilization and Storage
CCS	Carbon Capture and Storage
CCMC	Carbon Capture and Mineral Carbonation
CO_2	Kohlendioxid (Carbon Dioxide)
DAC	Direct Air Capture
DMC	Dimethylcarbonat
DME	Dimethylether
E-Fuels	Elektrische synthetische Kraftstoffe
EOR	Enhanced Oil Recovery
EU-ETS	European Emissions Trading System
IEA	International Energy Agency
IRENA	International Renewable Energy Agency
JRC	Joint Research Centre
LCA	Life Cycle Assessment
MAP	Modified Atmosphere Packaging
MCFC	Molten Carbonate Fuel Cell (Schmelzkarbonat-Brennstoffzelle)
POM	Polyoxymethylen
SNG	Substitute Natural Gas
TRL	Technology Readiness Level

Literatur

Arthur D. Little International (Hrsg.). (1986), Management im Zeitalter der Strategischen Führung, Gabler Verlag, Wiesbaden, verfügbar unter:https://doi.org/10.1007/978-3-322-93117-7.

Bundesministerium für Wirtschaft und Klimaschutz. (2024), „Funding programme for carbon contracts for difference".

Deutsche Energie Agentur. (2024), „Erneuerbares Methanol".

Dziejarski, B., Krzyżyńska, R. und Andersson, K. (2023), „Current status of carbon capture, utilization, and storage technologies in the global economy: A survey of technical assessment“, Fuel, Vol. 342, S. 127776.

European Commission. (2016), „The EU Emission Trading System (EU ETS)“.

European Commission. (2024), „MITTEILUNG DER KOMMISSION AN DAS EUROPÄISCHE PARLAMENT, DEN RAT, DEN EUROPÄISCHEN WIRTSCHAFTS- UND SOZIALAUSSCHUSS UND DEN AUSSCHUSS DER REGIONEN Auf dem Weg zu einem ehrgeizigen industriellen CO2-Management in der EU“.

European Commission. (2025), „Carbon Border Adjustment Mechanism – European Commission“, verfügbar unter: https://taxation-customs.ec.europa.eu/carbon-border-adjustment-mechanism_en (zugegriffen 4 Juni 2025).

European Commission. Joint Research Centre. (2024a), Clean Energy Technology Observatory, Carbon Capture Utilisation and Storage in the European Union: Status Report on Technology Development, Trends, Value Chains and Markets : 2024., Publications Office, LU, verfügbar unter: https://data.europa.eu/doi/10.2760/0287566 (zugegriffen 20 Mai 2025).

European Commission. Joint Research Centre. (2024b), Shaping the Future CO2 Transport Network for Europe., Publications Office, LU, verfügbar unter: https://data.europa.eu/doi/10.2760/582433 (zugegriffen 15 Mai 2025).

European Union. (2021), „Special Report 12/2021: The Polluter Pays Principle: Inconsistent application across EU environmental policies and actions“.

European Union. (2022), „VERORDNUNG (EU) 2022/869 DES EUROPÄISCHEN PARLAMENTS UND DES RATES“.

European Union. (2023), „DIRECTIVE (EU) 2023/2413 OF THE EUROPEAN PARLIAMENT AND OF THE COUNCIL of 18 October 2023 amending Directive (EU) 2018/2001, Regulation (EU) 2018/1999 and Directive 98/70/EC as regards the promotion of energy from renewable sources, and repealing Council Directive (EU) 2015/652“, verfügbar unter: (zugegriffen 21 Juni 2025).

European Union. (2024), „Regulation (EU) 2024/1735 of the European Parliament and of the Council of 13 June 2024 on establishing a framework of measures for strengthening Europe's net-zero technology manufacturing ecosystem and amending Regulation (EU) 2018/1724Text with EEA relevance.“

Feichtinger, G., Posch, W., Mark, D. und Schlar, D. (2024), „Green Digital Twin for Organizations as Enabler for Carbon Management“, gehalten auf der 19th Conference on Sustainable Development of Energy, Water and Environment Systems (SDEWES 2024), Rome, Italy.

Fu, L., Ren, Z., Si, W., Ma, Q., Huang, W., Liao, K., Huang, Z., et al. (2022), „Research progress on CO2 capture and utilization technology“, Journal of CO2 Utilization, Vol. 66, S. 102260.

Garcia, J.A., Villen-Guzman, M., Rodriguez-Maroto, J.M. und Paz-Garcia, J.M. (2024), „Comparing CO2 Storage and Utilization: Enhancing Sustainability through Renewable Energy Integration“, Sustainability, Vol. 16 No. 15, S. 6639.

Gartner. (2025), „Gartner Hype Cycle Research Methodology“, Gartner, verfügbar unter: https://www.gartner.com/en/research/methodologies/gartner-hype-cycle (zugegriffen 21 Juni 2025).

Global CCS Institute. (2020), „GCCSI Remove“.

Huo, J., Wang, Z., Oberschelp, C., Guillén-Gosálbez, G. und Hellweg, S. (2023), „Net-zero transition of the global chemical industry with CO2 -feedstock by 2050: feasible yet challenging", Green Chemistry, Vol. 25 No. 1, S. 415–430.

IEA. (2020a), „IEA Reduce".

IEA. (2020b), „IEA Reuse".

IEA. (2020c), „CCUS in clean energy transitions", Energy Technology Perspectives.

IRENA. (2020a), „IRENA Reduce".

IRENA. (2020b), „IRENA Recycle".

Jarvis, S.M. und Samsatli, S. (2018), „Technologies and infrastructures underpinning future CO 2 value chains: A comprehensive review and comparative analysis", Renewable and Sustainable Energy Reviews, Vol. 85, S. 46–68.

KAPSARC. (2020), „CCE Guide Overview".

Kumar, A., Tiwari, A.K. und Milani, D. (2024), „Decarbonizing hard-to-abate heavy industries: Current status and pathways towards net-zero future", Process Safety and Environmental Protection, Vol. 187, S. 408–430.

Mankins, J.C. (1995), „TECHNOLOGY READINESS LEVELS".

Naims, H. (2020), „Economic aspirations connected to innovations in carbon capture and utilization value chains", Journal of Industrial Ecology, Vol. 24 No. 5, S. 1126–1139.

Nimmas, T., Wongsakulphasatch, S., Chanthanumataporn, M., Vacharanukrauh, T. und Assabumrungrat, S. (2024), „Thermochemical transformation of CO2 into high-value products", Current Opinion in Green and Sustainable Chemistry, Vol. 47, S. 100911.

Philbin, S.P. (2020a), „Critical Analysis and Evaluation of the Technology Pathways for Carbon Capture and Utilization", Clean Technologies, Vol. 2 No. 4, S. 492–512.

Philbin, S.P. (2020b), „Critical Analysis and Evaluation of the Technology Pathways for Carbon Capture and Utilization", Clean Technologies, Vol. 2 No. 4, S. 492–512.

Raheem, I., Tawai, A., Amornraksa, S., Sriariyanun, M., Joshi, A., Gupta, M., Pongprayoon, W., et al. (2024), „A Comprehensive Review of Approaches in Carbon Capture, and Utilization to Reduce Greenhouse Gases", Applied Science and Engineering Progress, verfügbar unter: https://doi.org/10.14416/j.asep.2024.11.004.

Roh, K., Bardow, A., Bongartz, D., Burre, J., Chung, W., Deutz, S., Han, D., et al. (2020), „Early-stage evaluation of emerging CO2 utilization technologies at low technology readiness levels", Green Chemistry, Vol. 22 No. 12, S. 3842–3859.

Rumayor, M., Dominguez-Ramos, A. und Irabien, A. (2018), „Formic Acid Manufacture: Carbon Dioxide Utilization Alternatives", Applied Sciences, Vol. 8 No. 6, S. 914.

Sapart, C., Perimenis, A. und Bernier, T. (2024), „The contribution of carbon capture & utilisation towards climate neutrality in Europe".

Shi, Y., Su, W., Xing, Y., Cui, Y., Liu, X., Guo, W. und Che, Z. (2025), „Research progress and future prospects of chemical utilization of CO2", Chemical Engineering Journal, Vol. 510, S. 161579.

Sommerlatte, T. und Deschamps, J.-P. (1985), „Der strategische Einsatz von Technologien".

Taghizadeh-Hesary, F., Vandercamme, L. und Phoumin, H. (2024), „Enhancing the Economic Feasibility of Carbon Capture, Utilisation, and Storage (CCUS) Projects", verfügbar unter: https://doi.org/10.1142/S1464333223500242.

Walley, K. (2007), „Coopetition: An Introduction to the Subject and an Agenda for Research“, International Studies of Management & Organization, Vol. 37 No. 2, S. 11–31.

Watjanatepin, P., Steinwidder, L., De Schutter, A., Miladinović, N., Granata, G., Vicca, S., Van Gerven, T., et al. (2024), „Preliminary Environmental and Economic Assessment of Mineral Carbonation of Steel Slags as a Carbon Capture, Utilization and Storage Technology“, Procedia CIRP, Vol. 122, S. 318–323.

Jacob Kopeinig, Mario Hoffelner,
Kevin Anton Kriechbaum, Helmut Zsifkovits

Von Linear zu Zirkulär: Die Rolle der End-of-Life-Collection in industriellen Kreisläufen

Zusammenfassung: Dieser Beitrag analysiert die zentrale Rolle der End-of-Life-Collection in industriellen Kreisläufen im Rahmen der Circular Economy. Trotz steigender globaler Rohstoffverbräuche verbleiben nur 7,2% der eingesetzten Materialien in funktionsfähigen Kreisläufen, was das vorherrschende lineare "take-make-waste"-Paradigma ökologisch und ökonomisch untragbar macht. Die Studie untersucht systematisch drei komplementäre Circular-Economy-Strategien: das Verengen, Verlangsamen und Schließen von Materialschleifen. Als zentrale strukturelle Schwachstelle wird der "Last-Mile-Gap" identifiziert – die unzureichende Rückführung von End-of-Life-Produkten trotz vorhandener Technologien. Durch eine Literaturanalyse werden fünf ineinandergreifende Barrierekategorien systematisch analysiert: mangelnde digitale Interoperabilität, ökonomische Unsicherheiten, organisatorische Fragmentierung, regulatorische Inkohärenz sowie unzureichende Verbraucheranreize. Die Forschung zeigt, dass End-of-Life-Collection nicht nur ein nachgelagerter Entsorgungsschritt ist, sondern eigentlich ein Katalysator für eine funktionierende Circular Economy. Ohne qualitativ hochwertige, flächendeckende Rückführung bleiben technische Recyclingpotenziale systematisch ungenutzt und Sekundärrohstoffmärkte strukturell unterfinanziert.

Keywords: Circular Economy, End-of-Life-Collection, Last-Mile-Gap.

1. Einleitung

Der weltweite Primärrohstoffverbrauch hat sich seit dem Jahr 2000 nahezu verdoppelt und wird Schätzungen zufolge bis 2060 auf mehr als 160 Mrd. t ansteigen (United Nations Environment Programme, 2020). Parallel dazu verbleiben lediglich 7,2 % der eingesetzten Materialien in Kreisläufen (Circle Economy, 2024). Diese Diskrepanz macht das lineare „take-make-waste"-Paradigma ökologisch, ökonomisch und sozial langfristig untragbar. Die Circular Economy (CE) gilt als systemischer Gegenentwurf. Kirchherr et al. definieren sie als Wirtschaftssystem, das konsequent auf Reduktion, Wiederverwendung, Recycling und Rückgewinnung abzielt (Kirchherr et al., 2017). Geissdoerfer et al. konkretisieren CE als System, das Ressourcenkreisläufe verengt, verlangsamt und schließt, womit sowohl die Verlängerung als auch die Effizienzsteigerung von Materialkreisläufen adressiert werden (Geissdoerfer et al., 2017).

In Europa erhält die CE politische Unterstützung durch den EU-Green Deal und den Circular Economy Action Plan. Beide Initiativen setzen verbindliche Leitplanken, darunter die geplante Ökodesign-Verordnung, das Right-to-Repair sowie den Digital Product Passport (DPP), um die Kreislauffähigkeit von Produkten entlang ihres gesamten Lebenszyklus zu erhöhen (European Commission. Directorate General for Environment., 2020). Die CE trägt wesentlich zur Schonung natürlicher Ressourcen bei und reduziert den Druck auf Ökosysteme („Circular economy – European Commission", 2025). Aber über die Umweltperspektive hinaus kann die CE auch wirtschaftlich attraktiv sein. Der Preis kritischer Rohstoffe wie Lithium stieg zwischen 2020 und 2024 um über 70 % („Global Critical Minerals Outlook 2024 – Analysis", 2024), während Importabhängigkeiten die Versorgungssicherheit europäischer Industrien beeinträchtigen (Establishing a Framework for Ensuring a Secure and Sustainable Supply of Critical Raw Materials, 2023). Zirkuläre Geschäftsmodelle werden heute vor allem als strategischer Hebel verstanden, um die Abhängigkeit von volatilen Rohstoffpreisen zu reduzieren, die Markenwahrnehmung bei Investoren und Kunden zu stärken und gleichzeitig die eigene Handlungsfähigkeit gegenüber zunehmend anspruchsvollen Nachhaltigkeitsvorgaben zu sichern (Ellen MacArthur Foundation, 2025; United Nations Environment Programme, 2020).

Dieser Beitrag analysiert, weshalb trotz klarer politischer Signale und vorhandener Technologieoptionen insbesondere die Rückführung als strukturelle Schwachstelle der Circular Economy gilt. Nach einem konzeptionellen Überblick über die komplementären Circular-Economy-Strategien des Verengens, Verlangsamens und Schließens beleuchtet Abschnitt 3 der „Last-Mile-Gap". Abschnitt 4 diskutiert die theoretischen und praktischen Implikationen dieses Beitrags für Industrie, Politik und Forschung und schließt mit konkreten Handlungsempfehlungen zur Schließung des Last-Mile-Gaps.

2. Kreisläufe schließen

In den vergangenen zehn Jahren ist die Forschung zur Circular Economy von einem vorwiegend visionären Leitbild zu einem empirisch validierten, handlungsorientierten Rahmen gereift. Eine der aktuell anerkanntesten Typologien bündelt die Handlungsoptionen in drei komplementäre Strategien –

Verengen, Verlangsamen und Schließen der Ressourcenschleifen (Bocken et al., 2016; Potting et al., 2017). Diese Logik erlaubt, technische Lösungen (z.B. Materialsubstitution oder Robot Disassembly), geschäftsmodellbezogene Innovationen wie Leasing und Product-as-a-Service, und politische Instrumente (z.B. Extended Producer Responsibility (EPR), Ökodesign) konsistent auf eine gemeinsame Zielsetzung auszurichten: die Reduktion primärer Ressourcenentnahmen (Kirchherr et al., 2017).

Gleichzeitig macht die Typologie klar, dass keine der drei Strategien allein ausreicht, um lineare Wertschöpfungssysteme zu transformieren. Effizienzgewinne durch Verengen können Rebound-Effekte erzeugen, während vermeintlich geschlossene Kreisläufe ohne verlässliche Rückführungs- und Aufbereitungsinfrastruktur technisch ins Leere laufen (Andrew und Pigosso, 2024; Geissdoerfer et al., 2017). Erst das gezielte Zusammenspiel der drei Strategien ermöglicht eine systemische Wirkung, die ökologische Zielgrößen wie Ressourcenschonung, Emissionsreduktion und Biodiversitätsschutz simultan adressiert. Daher gliedert der folgende Abschnitt die wesentlichen Erkenntnisse zu jeder der drei Strategien und beginnt mit dem Verengen der Materialflüsse.

Verengen (narrowing)

CE-Strategien zur Verengung zielen darauf ab, den absoluten Materialeinsatz pro erbrachter Funktionseinheit zu reduzieren. Laut Allwood et al. zielt diese Materialeffizienz darauf ab, materielle Dienstleistungen mit geringerer Materialherstellung und -verarbeitung zu erbringen. Praktisch bedeutet dies „weniger Material pro Einheit“ statt „mehr Output pro Input“ (Allwood et al., 2011). Realisiert wird dies durch Leichtbau, Materialsubstitution – etwa biobasierte Verbundwerkstoffe, oder additive Fertigung. Grenzen liegen jedoch im potenziellen Rebound-Effekt wo Effizienzgewinne Stückkosten senken und dadurch zusätzliche Nachfrage stimulieren können (Andrew und Pigosso, 2024). Daher muss „narrowing“ stets mit Strategien des Verlangsamens oder Schließens kombiniert werden, um absolute Verbrauchsreduktionen abzusichern.

Verlangsamen (slowing)

Die Verlangsamung von Ressourcenschleifen verfolgt das Ziel, die Nutzungsdauer und Auslastungsrate von Produkten zu steigern. Auf Design-Ebene geschieht dies durch Reparaturfreundlichkeit, Upgrade-Fähigkeit und modulare Architekturen (Haase und Lythje, 2022). Als praktische Umsetzung der Verlangsamungsstrategie ermöglicht beispielsweise Product-as-a-Service die

Realisierung längerer Nutzungsdauern und höherer Auslastungsraten durch die Verlagerung vom Produkteigentum hin zur Dienstleistungserbringung (Bertelli et al., 2024). Allerdings können kulturelle Eigentumsvorstellungen und wahrgenommene Interessenskonflikte zwischen Herstellern und Nutzern als Hindernisse für die Verbreitung dieser zirkulären Geschäftsmodelle wirken (Böcker und Meelen, 2017).

Schließen (closing)

Die Strategie des „Schließens" zielt darauf ab, Materialkreisläufe durch systematische Rückführung und Aufbereitung von End-of-Life-Produkten in neue Produktionszyklen zu vollenden. Technologisch entwickeln sich automatisierte Demontagesysteme, etwa Roboter-Disassembly und metallurgische Verfahren für kritische Metalle rasant. Governance-Instrumente wie die EPR verankern wirtschaftliche Verantwortung bei den Herstellern indem die Kosten für End-of-Life-Management von den Kommunen zu den Produzenten verschoben wird und schafft damit ökonomische Anreize für recyclingfreundliches Produktdesign (OECD, 2016). Die entscheidende Herausforderung besteht jedoch darin, End-of-Life-Produkte lückenlos zurückzuführen, sodass die technischen Potenziale nicht ungenutzt bleiben.

3. Der „Last-Mile-Gap"

Trotz technologischer Fortschritte bleibt die Rückführung der Engpass geschlossener Kreisläufe. Erstens fehlt eine breit anerkannte Dateninteroperabilität: Produktpässe entstehen bislang nur in einzelnen Pilotprojekten, und ohne einheitliche Datenmodelle lassen sich Materialinformationen nicht automatisiert in Sortier-/Aufbereitungsanlagen einbinden (Chaudhuri *et al.*, 2025). Zweitens sind die Anreize entlang der Wertschöpfungskette nicht aufeinander abgestimmt: Obwohl Product-as-a-Service-Modelle Eigentumsverantwortung bündeln, dringen sie nicht in alle Märkte gleichermaßen vor, etwa in den B2C-Kleingerätesektor, wo die Sammelquoten nahezu stagnieren (EUWID, 2022). Drittens erzeugen die aktuellen EPR-Regelungen verzerrte Preissignale. Die Gebühren bemessen sich meist nach dem Gewicht statt nach den tatsächlichen Umweltauswirkungen, sodass komplexe Verbundmaterialien möglicherweise zu niedrig bewertet werden (OECD, 2016). Viertens ist die Abhängigkeit von der Infrastruktur nicht zu übersehen, denn Sortier- und Recyclinganlagen entwickeln sich weiter, doch die letzte Meile der Sammlung bleibt problematisch.

Die fundamentale Schwachstelle der globalen Kreislaufwirtschaft manifestiert sich in dem sogenannten "Last-Mile-Gap" der Materialrückführung, der als strukturelles Versagen der Sammlung und Rückgewinnung von End-of-Life-Produkten verstanden werden kann. Diese Problematik zeigt sich besonders deutlich in der dramatischen Verschlechterung der globalen Zirkularitätsrate, die laut dem Circularity Gap Report 2024 von 9,1% (2018) auf nur noch 7,2% (2023) gesunken ist (Circle Economy, 2024), ein alarmierender Rückgang, der die zunehmende Linearität der Weltwirtschaft trotz wachsender Aufmerksamkeit für Kreislaufprinzipien verdeutlicht.

Der Last-Mile-Gap beschreibt konkret das Phänomen, dass trotz vorhandener technischer Recyclingkapazitäten die physische Sammlung und Rückführung von End-of-Life-Produkten nicht flächendeckend funktioniert. Diese Herausforderung wird besonders bei elektronischen Geräten sichtbar, wo trotz eines enormen Materialwertes von etwa 57 Milliarden USD nur 17,4% der jährlich anfallenden 53,6 Millionen Tonnen Elektroschrott fachgerecht zurückgeführt werden (Forti *et al.*, 2020). Ähnlich ernüchternd sind die Zahlen für Kunststoffe, deren historische Recyclingquote bei lediglich 9% liegt (Geyer *et al.*, 2017).

Die Überwindung des Last-Mile-Gaps erfordert daher nicht nur technologische Innovationen in adäquate Recyclingverfahren, sondern vor allem den systematischen Aufbau dezentraler Sammelstrukturen, die Implementierung digitaler Tracking-Systeme für Materialflüsse und die Schaffung wirtschaftlicher Anreize, die eine lückenlose Rückführung von Produkten ermöglichen. Ohne die Lösung dieser fundamentalen Sammelproblematik bleiben selbst die fortschrittlichsten Recyclingtechnologien weitgehend wirkungslos.

Die Rückführungs- oder End-of-Use-Phase entscheidet maßgeblich darüber, ob Produkte und Materialien in einen technisch und ökonomisch sinnvollen Kreislauf gelangen oder endgültig als Abfall enden. Obwohl politische Initiativen wie der Green Deal der EU ambitionierte Recycling- und Re-use-Quoten formulieren, liegt die tatsächliche Rücklaufleistung in vielen Branchen deutlich unter den Zielwerten. Eine Literaturrecherche zeigt, dass sich fünf miteinander verflochtene Barrierekategorien (Tabelle 1) zu einem systemischen Bottleneck verdichten: technologische Defizite, ökonomische Unsicherheiten, organisatorische Fragmentierung, regulatorische Inkohärenz sowie verhaltens- und nutzerbezogene Hindernisse.

Tabelle 1: Zentrale Barrieren der Rückführung und zugehörige Forschungslücken (eigene Darstellung).

Barrierekategorie	Kernproblem	Wirkung auf die Rückführung
Mangelnde digitale Interoperabilität	Proprietäre Produktpässe, fehlende Datenstandards	Medienbrüche, verzögerte Demontage, hohe Sortierkosten
Ökonomische Unsicherheiten	Hohe Anfangsinvestitionen, volatile Sekundärrohstoffpreise	Investitionsstau in Sammel- und Recyclinganlagen
Organisatorische Fragmentierung	Unklare Rollen von OEM, 3PL und Recyclern	Redundante Transporte, hohe Transaktionskosten
Regulatorische Inkohärenz	Uneinheitliche EPR-Gebühren, kaum Eco-Modulation	Fehlende Skaleneffekte, parallele Compliance-Systeme
Unzureichende verbraucherseitige Anreize	Datenschutzbedenken, „Hassle Costs", geringe monetäre Anreize	Niedrige Sammelquoten, Unterauslastung von Anlagen

Zunächst erschweren mangelnde Interoperabilität digitaler Produktpässe und proprietäre Schnittstellen den durchgängigen Informationsfluss entlang der Wertschöpfungskette (Chaudhuri *et al.*, 2025; García-Valderrama *et al.*, 2024). Während große Unternehmen eigene Datenökosysteme aufbauen, bleiben kleine und mittlere Unternehmen häufig außen vor und verlieren dadurch den Zugang zu rückführungsrelevanten Informationen wie Materialzusammensetzung oder Demontageanleitungen. Branchenweit validierte Readiness-Indizes, die den digitalen Reifegrad ganzer Sektoren abbilden, existieren bislang nicht (Pörtner *et al.*, 2025). Ebenso fehlt empirische Evidenz dazu, inwieweit standardisierte Datenformate die tatsächliche Rücklaufquote verbessern könnten – eine Lücke, die potenzielle Investoren in DPP-Infrastruktur verunsichert.

Hinzu kommt, dass hohe Anfangsinvestitionen und volatile Sekundärrohstoffpreise die Kapitalrendite zirkulärer Geschäftsmodelle verschlechtert (Ji-Hyland *et al.*, 2025; Sonar *et al.*, 2022). Anders als klassische Greenfield-Investitionen skalieren Rückführungsaktivitäten nicht linear, da sie stark von Stoffströmen abhängen, die ihrerseits durch Konsumtrends, Produktlebensdauern und Sammelsysteme bestimmt werden. Langfristige und standardisierte Bewertungsansätze liegen kaum vor, bzw. müssen für jeden Fall einzeln bestimmt werden, sodass Finanzierungsentscheidungen überwiegend auf kurzfristige Kalkulationen basieren (Schaubroeck, 2020). Diese Unsicherheit hemmt den Ausbau von Sammel-, Sortier- und Aufbereitungskapazitäten, welches wiederum den Rückführungsprozess zusätzlich verlangsamt.

Ein weiterer Engpass ergibt sich aus der organisatorischen Fragmentierung. Unklare Rollenverteilungen zwischen OEM, Third-Party-Logistics-

Dienstleistern und Recyclern resultieren in Medienbrüchen der Datenkette, redundanter Informationsbeschaffung und ineffizienten Transportwegen, die wiederum zu erheblichen Transaktionskosten führen (Mbago *et al.*, 2025). Zwar existieren punktuelle Kooperationsmodelle wie etwa Servitization-Ansätze, doch Multi-Actor-Netzwerkstudien, die systematisch Governance-Strukturen und Anreizmechanismen vermessen, sind bislang rar (Muzamwese *et al.*, 2024). Ohne ein solches Verständnis lassen sich jedoch weder faire Kosten- noch Erlösallokationen etablieren.

Darüber hinaus verschärft regulative Inkohärenz die bislang beschriebenen Herausforderungen. Die Ausgestaltung der erweiterten Herstellerverantwortung variiert in der EU ebenso wie in außereuropäischen Märkten erheblich. Eco-Modulation, also die Differenzierung von Gebühren nach ökologischer Produktperformance, wird bislang nur in einzelnen Pilotprojekten angewendet (Dey und Ashok S, 2025; Grandhi *et al.*, 2024). Das Ergebnis ist ein zersplittertes Regelwerk, der Skaleneffekte in Logistik und Recycling unterbindet und Unternehmen dazu zwingt, parallele Compliance-Systeme aufzubauen. Vergleichende Policy-Mix-Analysen, die Synergien etwa zwischen EPR, CO_2-Bepreisung und Beschaffungsstandards quantifizieren, fehlen nahezu vollständig (Di Santo *et al.*, 2024).

Schließlich bleiben Rückgabeentscheidungen auf der Verbraucherseite trotz potenziell vorhandener Infrastruktur häufig aus. Empirische Studien nennen Datenschutzbedenken, wahrgenommene Aufwände („hassle costs") und fehlende finanzielle oder Convenience-Anreize als zentrale Gründe für die geringe Partizipation (Keshavarz *et al.*, 2025; Marshall, 2015).

Die Wechselwirkungen dieser fünf Barrierekategorien verstärken sich gegenseitig. Technologische Inkompatibilitäten und organisatorische Rollenkonflikte generieren Datenlücken, die wiederum ökonomische Risiken vergrößern. Regulatorische Uneinheitlichkeit erschwert die Planungssicherheit, was wiederum Investitionen bremst. Unzureichende Anreize auf Nutzerebene reduzieren Rücklaufmengen, wodurch die Auslastung bestehender Anlagen sinkt und Skaleneffekte ausbleiben.

Aus dieser Diagnose ergeben sich drei wesentliche Forschungspunkte. Vorrangig sind gezielte technologische Fortschritte. Fehlende Dateninteroperabilität, vereinzelte Digital-Product-Passport-Pilotprojekte und noch nicht vernetzte Sortier- sowie Demontageverfahren müssen dringend überwunden werden, um die Rückführungsprozesse effizienter zu gestalten. Darüber hinaus wird ein konsistenter Governance-Rahmen benötigt; divergierende EPR-Vorgaben, kaum öko-modulierte Gebühren und uneinheitliche Beschaffungsstandards erschweren derzeit skalierbare Investitionen und Planungssicherheit. Schließlich sollten ökonomische und verhaltensbezogene Anreize entlang der gesamten Wertschöpfungskette miteinander harmonisiert werden, denn PaaS-Modelle erreichen längst nicht alle Marktsegmente, und die bestehenden Rückgabe- sowie Bonussysteme motivieren Verbraucher nur begrenzt zur aktiven Teilnahme.

4. Diskussion und Fazit

Die Analyse zeigt, dass die End-of-Life-Collection den zentralen Bottleneck industrieller Kreisläufe darstellt. Obwohl Strategien wie „narrowing" die Materialeffizienz steigern und „slowing" die Lebensdauer verlängert, entsteht tatsächliche Ressourcenschonung erst dort, wo Rücknahme, Sortierung und Aufbereitung nahtlos ineinandergreifen und geschlossene Kreisläufe ermöglichen. In den vergangenen Jahren hat sich allerdings gezeigt, dass gerade diese letzte Phase nicht zuverlässig funktioniert. Die globale Zirkularitätsrate ist gefallen, obwohl die technischen Recyclingkapazitäten gewachsen sind. Dieser sogenannte „Last-Mile-Gap" illustriert, dass selbst hochentwickelte Aufbereitungsverfahren wirkungslos bleiben, wenn ausgediente Produkte nicht oder nicht rechtzeitig bei den Anlagenbetreibern ankommen.

Die Schlüsselrolle der Sammlung lässt sich an mehreren Wirkungszusammenhängen verdeutlichen. Erstens bestimmt die Höhe der Rücklaufquoten direkt die Menge an Sekundärmaterial, die in neuen Produktgenerationen zirkulieren kann, wodurch jeder zusätzliche Prozentpunkt an End-of-Life-Collection eine Steigerung des Substitutionspotenzials bewirkt. Zweitens führen kontinuierliche und planbare Rückführungen zu Skaleneffekten bei Sortier- und Recyclinganlagen; sie senken potenziell die spezifischen Verarbeitungskosten, erhöhen die Wirtschaftlichkeit und erleichtern Investitionen in modernere Technologien (OECD, 2016). Drittens fungiert die Sammlung als wichtigstes Feedback-System für Design-for-Circularity, weil nur unter Rückführung die notwendigen Material-, Demontage- und Schadstoffdaten vollständig erfasst und an OEMs zurückgespielt werden können (Chaudhuri *et al.*, 2025). Nicht zuletzt verringert eine stabile End-of-Life-Collection die Abhängigkeit von volatilen Rohstoffmärkten; angesichts einer Preissteigerung kritischer Metalle von über 70% zwischen 2020 und 2024 lässt sich End-of-Life-Collection daher auch als strategische Versicherung gegen Lieferengpässe interpretieren („Global Critical Minerals Outlook 2024 – Analysis", 2024)

Warum diese potenzielle Hebelwirkung bislang weitgehend ungenutzt bleibt, erklären fünf ineinandergreifende Barrierekategorien. Mangelnde digitale Interoperabilität verhindert einen durchgängigen Informationsfluss über Materialzusammensetzung und Demontageanleitungen; Investitions- und Preisunsicherheiten auf den Sekundärrohstoffmärkten schwächen die

Rentabilität von Sammel- und Sortieranlagen; unklare Rollenzuweisungen zwischen Herstellern, Logistikdienstleistern und Recyclern erzeugen Medienbrüche sowie redundante Transporte; heterogene EPR-Regelungen und kaum eco-modulierte Gebühren verzerren Preissignale und erschweren die Skalierbarkeit; schließlich bremsen Datenschutzbedenken, wahrgenommene „Hassle-Costs" und fehlende materielle Anreize das Rückgabeverhalten der Nutzerinnen und Nutzer.

Die End-of-Life-Collection erweist sich damit nicht als nachgelagerter Entsorgungsschritt, sondern als eigentlicher Katalysator der Circular Economy. Ohne eine qualitativ hochwertige, flächendeckende und datenbasierte Rückführung verpuffen technische Recyclingpotenziale, digitale Produktpässe verlieren ihren Nutzen und der Ausbau von Sekundärrohstoffmärkten bleibt unterfinanziert. Für die betriebliche Praxis bedeutet dies, dass Herstellerkonsortien gemeinsam mit kommunalen Akteuren prioritär in dezentrale Sammel- und Erfassungssysteme investieren und gleichzeitig offene Schnittstellen für den Digital Product Passport etablieren sollten, damit Sortieranlagen ohne Medienbruch Material- und Demontagedaten übernehmen können. Eine Anreizarchitektur, die reale Umweltexternalitäten über öko-modulierte EPR-Gebühren, Pfand- und Bonusmodelle sowie CO_2-Preisaufschläge internalisiert, kann diese Infrastruktur zusätzlich stützen.

Die Forschung sollte parallel dazu zuverlässige Indikatoren entwickeln, welche die Effektivität der Rückführung messbar machen, interdisziplinäre Untersuchungen zu sozialen und verhaltensbezogenen Determinanten des Sammelverhaltens durchführen und Policy-Mix-Analysen etablieren, mit denen sich Synergien zwischen EPR, Right-to-Repair, Beschaffungsstandards und CO_2-Bepreisung evaluieren lassen. Gelingt es, diese Hebel gleichzeitig anzusteuern, wird die Sammlung zur Schließstelle statt zur Bruchstelle industrieller Kreisläufe und ermöglicht erst dann die ökologischen, ökonomischen und sozialen Versprechen der Circular Economy in vollem Umfang einzulösen.

Literatur

Allwood, J.M., Ashby, M.F., Gutowski, T.G. und Worrell, E. (2011), „Material efficiency: A white paper", Resources, Conservation and Recycling, Vol. 55 No. 3, S. 362–381.

Andrew, E. und Pigosso, D.C.A. (2024), „Multidisciplinary perspectives on rebound effects in sustainability: A systematic review", Journal of Cleaner Production, Vol. 470, S. 143366.

Bertelli, A., West, S. und Rapaccini, M. (2024), „Navigating the Shift: From Traditional Sales to Product-as-a-Service (PaaS)", in Thürer, M., Riedel, R., Von Cieminski, G. und Romero, D. (Hrsg.), Advances in Production Management Systems. Production Management Systems for Volatile, Uncertain, Complex, and Ambiguous Environments, Bd. 732, Springer Nature Switzerland, Cham, S. 215–228.

Bocken, N.M.P., De Pauw, I., Bakker, C. und Van Der Grinten, B. (2016), „Product design and business model strategies for a circular economy", Journal of Industrial and Production Engineering, Vol. 33 No. 5, S. 308–320.

Böcker, L. und Meelen, T. (2017), „Sharing for people, planet or profit? Analysing motivations for intended sharing economy participation", Environmental Innovation and Societal Transitions, Vol. 23, S. 28–39.

Chaudhuri, A., Wæhrens, B.V., Treiblmaier, H. und Jensen, S.F. (2025), „Impact pathways: digital product passport for embedding circularity in electronics supply chains", International Journal of Operations & Production Management, Vol. 45 No. 6, S. 1213–1226.

Circle Economy. (2024), „CGR 2024", verfügbar unter: https://www.circularity-gap.world/2024 (zugegriffen 11 Juni 2025).

„Circular economy – European Commission". (2025), 5 Juni, verfügbar unter: https://environment.ec.europa.eu/topics/circular-economy_en (zugegriffen 12 Juni 2025).

Dey, A. und Ashok S, D. (2025), „Policy pathways utilizing extended producer responsibility and eco-modulation frameworks for sustainable food packaging waste management in India: A review", Results in Engineering, Vol. 26, S. 104885.

Di Santo, N., Del Giudice, T. und Sisto, R. (2024), „Policy mixes in rural areas: a scoping literature review", RIVISTA DI ECONOMIA AGRARIA, Vol. 79 No. 3, S. 83–99.

Ellen MacArthur Foundation. (2025), „Circular economy introduction", verfügbar unter: https://www.ellenmacarthurfoundation.org/topics/circular-economy-introduction/overview (zugegriffen 16 März 2025).

Establishing a Framework for Ensuring a Secure and Sustainable Supply of Critical Raw Materials. (2023), verfügbar unter: https://eur-lex.europa.eu/legal-content/EN/TXT/?uri=CELEX:52023PC0160 (zugegriffen 11 Juni 2025).

European Commission. Directorate General for Environment. (2020), 2020 Circular Economy Action Plan: International Aspects., Publications Office, LU, verfügbar unter: https://data.europa.eu/doi/10.2779/085517 (zugegriffen 11 Juni 2025).

EUWID, T.W. (2022), „Sammelmengen von Altgeräten und Gerätebatterien stagnieren in Österreich", 19 Oktober, verfügbar unter: https://www.euwid-recycling.de/news/international/sammelmengen-von-altgeraeten-und-geraetebatterien-stagnieren-in-oesterreich-251022/ (zugegriffen 11 Juni 2025).

Forti, V., Baldé, C.P., Kuehr, R. und Bel, G. (2020), „The Global E-waste Monitor 2020".

García-Valderrama, T., Pérez-González, M.C., Puentes-Graña, C. und Sánchez-Ortiz, J. (2024), „Developing an efficiency evaluation model for the circular economy in Europe", European Planning Studies, Vol. 32 No. 10, S. 2160–2181.

Geissdoerfer, M., Savaget, P., Bocken, N.M.P. und Hultink, E.J. (2017), „The Circular Economy – A new sustainability paradigm?", Journal of Cleaner Production, Vol. 143, S. 757–768.

Geyer, R., Jambeck, J.R. und Law, K.L. (2017), „Production, use, and fate of all plastics ever made", Science Advances, Vol. 3 No. 7, S. e1700782.

„Global Critical Minerals Outlook 2024 – Analysis". (2024), IEA, 17 Mai, verfügbar unter: https://www.iea.org/reports/global-critical-minerals-outlook-2024 (zugegriffen 11 Juni 2025).

Grandhi, S.P., Dagwar, P.P. und Dutta, D. (2024), „Policy pathways to sustainable E-waste management: A global review", Journal of Hazardous Materials Advances, Vol. 16, S. 100473.

Haase, L.M. und Lythje, L.S. (2022), „User Strategies for Prolonging Product Lifetimes: A New Starting Point for Circular Conceptual Design", Sustainability, Vol. 14 No. 22, S. 15133.

Ji-Hyland, C., White, D. und Khaydarov, R. (2025), „The impact of circular economy practices on sustainable logistics performance", International Journal of Logistics Research and Applications, S. 1–27.

Keshavarz, K., Alvarez, M.J. und Garcia, C.J. (2025), „The Role of Consumers in Transitioning to a Circular Economy", Circular Economy and Sustainability, verfügbar unter:https://doi.org/10.1007/s43615-025-00617-0.

Kirchherr, J., Reike, D. und Hekkert, M. (2017), „Conceptualizing the circular economy: An analysis of 114 definitions", Resources, Conservation and Recycling, Vol. 127, S. 221–232.

Marshall, G. (2015), „Hassle Costs and Price Discrimination: An Empirical Welfare Analysis", American Economic Journal: Applied Economics, Vol. 7 No. 3, S. 123–146.

Mbago, M., Ntayi, J.M., Mkansi, M., Namagembe, S., Tukamuhabwa, B.R. und Mwelu, N. (2025), „Implementing reverse logistics practices in the supply chain: a case study analysis of recycling firms", Modern Supply Chain Research and Applications, verfügbar unter:https://doi.org/10.1108/MSCRA-01-2025-0003.

Muzamwese, T.C., Franco-Garcia, L. und Heldeweg, M.A. (2024), „The role of sustainable business networks in promoting a Circular Economy in Africa—A systematic literature review", WIREs Energy and Environment, Vol. 13 No. 1, S. e506.

OECD. (2016), Extended Producer Responsibility: Updated Guidance for Efficient Waste Management, OECD, verfügbar unter:https://doi.org/10.1787/9789264256385-en.

Pörtner, L., Riel, A., Schmidt, B., Leclaire, M. und Möske, R. (2025), „Data Management Maturity Model—Process Dimensions and Capabilities to Leverage Data-Driven Organizations Towards Industry 5.0", Applied System Innovation, Vol. 8 No. 2, S. 41.

Potting, J., Hekkert, M.P., Worrell, E. und Hanemaaijer, A. (2017), Circular Economy: Measuring innovation in the product chain.

Schaubroeck, T. (2020), „Circular economy practices may not always lead to lower criticality or more sustainability; analysis and guidance is needed per case", Resources, Conservation and Recycling, Vol. 162, S. 104977.

Sonar, H., Mukherjee, A., Gunasekaran, A. und Singh, R.K. (2022), „Sustainable supply chain management of automotive sector in context to the circular economy: A strategic framework", Business Strategy and the Environment, John Wiley and Sons Ltd, Vol. 31 No. 7, S. 3635–3648.

United Nations Environment Programme. (2020), Global Resources Outlook 2019: Natural Resources for the Future We Want, UN, verfügbar unter:https://doi.org/10.18356/689a1a17-en.

Industrielle Transformation

Patrick Kuballa, Gerald Katterbauer, Andreas Zehetner

Sustainable Hall Conditioning: Ein ganzheitlicher Ansatz zur energieeffizienten Hallenklimatisierung

Innovative Luftkonditionierungstechnologien zur Reduktion von CO_2-Emissionen und Betriebskosten in der Industrie

Zusammenfassung: Der Gebäudesektor steht vor einer zentralen Herausforderung: Der Energiebedarf für Kälteerzeugung wächst rasant und trägt erheblich zum CO_2-Ausstoß bei. In Österreich wird der urbane Kältebedarf bis 2050 voraussichtlich 1–2 % des nationalen Energieverbrauchs ausmachen. Vor diesem Hintergrund zeigt dieser Beitrag, wie innovative Ansätze wie Sustainable Hall Conditioning helfen können, industrielle Klimatisierung neu zu denken. Die vorgestellten Maßnahmen ermöglichen bis zu 95 % CO_2-Einsparung und leisten einen Beitrag zur nachhaltigen Transformation der Industrie.

Keywords: Nachhaltigkeit, CO_2 Reduktion, Energieeffizienz, Green Transition, Industrielle Konditionierung.

1. Industrie unter Druck: Energieverbauch, CO_2 – Ausstoß und die Suche nach Lösungen

Die wirtschaftlichen Herausforderungen in Zeiten einer Rezession treffen Unternehmen oft mit voller Wucht. Sinkende Auftragsvolumen, steigender Kostendruck und eine unsichere Marktdynamik erfordern schnelles Handeln und durchdachte Investitionen. Gleichzeitig stehen Unternehmen vor der Verpflichtung, ihre Nachhaltigkeitsziele einzuhalten – nicht nur aus regulatorischen Gründen, sondern auch, um gesellschaftliche Verantwortung zu übernehmen und wettbewerbsfähig zu bleiben.

Ein besonders drängendes Thema in diesem Zusammenhang ist die Kälteerzeugung: Sie zählt zu den am stärksten wachsenden Energieverbrauchern im Gebäudesektor – mit erheblichen Auswirkungen auf Umwelt und Energieversorgung. Laut aktuellen Prognosen wird der urbane Kältebedarf in Österreich bis 2050 auf 3,5 bis 6,3 TWh pro Jahr ansteigen, was etwa 1 bis 2 %

des gesamten nationalen Energieverbrauchs (derzeit rund 335 TWh) entspricht. Diese Entwicklung macht deutlich, wie wichtig es ist, bereits heute auf effiziente, ressourcenschonende Kühlsysteme zu setzen – insbesondere in Industrie- und Gewerbegebieten mit hohem Energiebedarf. (Abart-Heriszt et al., 2024, S. 7)

Genau hier setzt das Sustainable Hall Conditioning (SHC)-System von INFRANORM® an. SHC kombiniert innovative Technologien aus den Bereichen Kühlung, Heizung, Luftreinigung und Energieeffizienz in einem einzigen modularen Gesamtsystem. Es ermöglicht Unternehmen, Kosten erheblich zu reduzieren und gleichzeitig einen signifikanten Beitrag zum Klimaschutz zu leisten. Mit SHC können Produktionshallen 365 Tage im Jahr optimal temperiert und mit frischer, sauberer Luft versorgt werden – ein entscheidender Faktor für stabile Produktionsbedingungen, die Motivation der Mitarbeitenden und die Produktqualität.

Dieser Beitrag zeigt, wie SHC nicht nur eine technologische Innovation darstellt, sondern auch eine strategische Lösung für Unternehmen, die ihre Betriebskosten senken und gleichzeitig umweltfreundliche Praktiken umsetzen möchten. Es wird detailliert beschrieben, wie SHC in wirtschaftlich schwierigen Zeiten als effektives Instrument eingesetzt werden kann, um finanzielle Stabilität und ökologische Verantwortung miteinander zu verbinden. Die folgenden Kapitel beleuchten die wirtschaftlichen Vorteile, die ökologischen Effekte und die strategische Bedeutung von SHC.

Mit SHC eröffnen sich völlig neue Möglichkeiten, die wirtschaftlichen und ökologischen Herausforderungen einer Rezession zu meistern. Es ist eine Einladung an Unternehmen, ihre Infrastrukturen neu zu denken – für eine zukunftssichere, nachhaltige und wirtschaftlich erfolgreiche Produktion.

1.1. Die doppelte Herausforderung: Kosten und Nachhaltigkeit

In wirtschaftlich turbulenten Zeiten stehen Unternehmen vor einer schwierigen Doppelaufgabe: Einerseits müssen sie Kosten senken, um ihre finanzielle Stabilität zu sichern und wettbewerbsfähig zu bleiben. Andererseits wächst der Druck, ökologische Verantwortung zu übernehmen und strenge Umweltauflagen zu erfüllen. Diese beiden Anforderungen scheinen auf den ersten Blick widersprüchlich zu sein, denn nachhaltige Maßnahmen werden oft mit höheren Investitionen und laufenden Kosten assoziiert. Doch die Realität zeigt, dass der richtige technologische Ansatz beide Ziele gleichzeitig erreichen kann.

Die wirtschaftlichen Herausforderungen einer Rezession zwingen Unternehmen dazu, innovative Lösungen zu finden, um Betriebskosten zu senken, ohne dabei Qualität oder Effizienz zu opfern. Gleichzeitig verlangen Marktteilnehmer – von Regierungen bis zu Konsumenten – immer stärker nach umweltfreundlichen Produktionsprozessen. Unternehmen, die in der Lage sind, diese Anforderungen zu erfüllen, sichern sich nicht nur finanzielle Vorteile, sondern positionieren sich auch als Vorreiter einer nachhaltigen Industrie.

Sustainable Hall Conditioning (SHC) bietet eine Lösung für diese Herausforderung, indem es beide Ziele – Kostenreduktion und Umweltverantwortung – miteinander verbindet. Das System kombiniert modernste Technologien aus den Bereichen Kühlung, Heizung und Luftreinigung, um eine energieeffiziente und umweltfreundliche Hallenklimatisierung zu ermöglichen. Durch die Integration von Funktionen wie zweistufiger adiabater Kühlung, Heizung und effizienter Frischluftzufuhr schafft SHC ein optimales Arbeitsumfeld, das sowohl die Betriebskosten senkt als auch die CO2-Bilanz erheblich verbessert.

Die Fähigkeit, Kosten zu sparen und gleichzeitig Umweltziele zu erreichen, ist nicht nur ein technologischer Vorteil, sondern auch ein strategischer Wettbewerbsvorteil. Unternehmen, die ihre Produktionsstätten mit SHC ausrüsten, zeigen, dass wirtschaftlicher Erfolg und ökologische Verantwortung Hand in Hand gehen können. Dieses Whitepaper untersucht detailliert, wie SHC diese doppelte Herausforderung meistert und welche Vorteile es Unternehmen in einer zunehmend komplexen und umweltbewussten Geschäftswelt bietet.

1.2. Wirtschaftliche Vorteile von SHC

In wirtschaftlich herausfordernden Zeiten liegt der Fokus vieler Unternehmen auf der Reduzierung von Kosten, um die Wettbewerbsfähigkeit zu sichern und finanzielle Stabilität zu gewährleisten. Hier setzt Sustainable Hall Conditioning (SHC) mit einer Vielzahl von wirtschaftlichen Vorteilen an, die nicht nur kurzfristige Einsparungen ermöglichen, sondern auch langfristige betriebliche Effizienz fördern. SHC bietet eine umfassende Lösung, die die Betriebskosten signifikant senkt, Ausfallzeiten reduziert und gleichzeitig die Produktivität steigert.

Reduzierung der Energiekosten

Ein entscheidender Vorteil von SHC ist die drastische Senkung der Energiekosten. Durch den Einsatz der zweistufigen adiabaten Kühlung wird die Energieeffizienz erheblich gesteigert, was zu Einsparungen von bis zu 80 % im Vergleich zu herkömmlichen Kühlsystemen führt. Statt auf Umluftverfahren oder energieintensive konventionelle Klimaanlagen zu setzen, nutzt SHC gefilterte Frischluft und innovative Kühltechnologien, die den Stromverbrauch auf ein Minimum reduzieren. Diese Einsparungen sind besonders in einer Rezession von großer Bedeutung, da sie die finanzielle Belastung durch steigende Energiekosten mindern.

Geringere Betriebs- und Wartungskosten

SHC-Systeme sind so konzipiert, dass sie wartungsarm und langlebig sind. Selbstreinigende Komponenten sowie langlebige Filtertechnologien und patentierte Verdunstungsmedien minimieren den Wartungsaufwand und verlängern die Lebensdauer der Systeme. Dadurch werden teure Ausfallzeiten reduziert, und die Gesamtbetriebskosten können um bis zu 80 % gesenkt werden. Insbesondere in Branchen mit kontinuierlichem Produktionsbetrieb sorgt SHC für eine zuverlässige und störungsfreie Klimatisierung.

Steigerung der Produktivität

Neben den direkten Kosteneinsparungen trägt SHC auch zur Verbesserung der Arbeitsbedingungen und Produktionsprozesse bei. Stabile Hallentemperaturen und eine saubere, angenehme Luftqualität erhöhen die Leistungsfähigkeit von Maschinen und Mitarbeitenden gleichermaßen. Durch die Vermeidung von Überhitzung oder unzureichender Kühlung wird die Zahl der Produktionsfehler reduziert, und es entstehen weniger Ausschussprodukte. Gleichzeitig steigt die Mitarbeiterzufriedenheit, was langfristig zu einer höheren Produktivität und geringeren Krankenständen führt.

Die wirtschaftlichen Vorteile von SHC machen es zu einer unverzichtbaren Lösung für Unternehmen, die ihre Betriebskosten senken und ihre Effizienz steigern möchten. Es ist eine Investition, die sich nicht nur durch direkte Einsparungen, sondern auch durch nachhaltige betriebliche Verbesserungen auszahlt. Die Kombination aus reduzierten Energiekosten, minimalem Wartungsaufwand und einer gesteigerten Produktivität unterstreicht den Wert von SHC als strategische Ressource für Unternehmen, die ihre wirtschaftlichen Ziele auch in schwierigen Zeiten erreichen wollen.

Abbildung 1: Verbaute SHC-Anlage für nachhaltige und wirtschaftlich temperierte saubere Hallenluft (eigene Darstellung).

1.3. Ökologische Vorteile: Nachhaltigkeit erreichen

In Zeiten, in denen ökologische Verantwortung ein zentraler Bestandteil unternehmerischen Handelns ist, stehen Unternehmen vor der Herausforderung, ihre Umweltbilanz zu verbessern, ohne die Wirtschaftlichkeit zu gefährden. Sustainable Hall Conditioning (SHC) bietet eine innovative Lösung, die ökologische und wirtschaftliche Ziele miteinander verbindet. Mit modernster Technologie reduziert SHC nicht nur den Energieverbrauch und die CO2-Emissionen, sondern trägt auch zur Ressourcenschonung und Verbesserung der Luftqualität bei.

Signifikante CO2-Einsparungen

Ein herausragendes Merkmal von SHC ist die Reduzierung der CO2-Emissionen um bis zu 95 %. Dies wird durch den Einsatz der zweistufigen adiabaten Kühlung erreicht, die nicht nur hocheffizient arbeitet, sondern auch auf klimaschädliche Kältemittel verzichtet. Stattdessen nutzt das System die natürliche Kühlwirkung von Wasser, wodurch es einen minimalen ökologischen Fußabdruck hinterlässt. Diese CO2-Einsparungen sind nicht nur ein Gewinn für die Umwelt, sondern auch ein Beitrag zur Einhaltung globaler Klimaziele und zur Erfüllung strenger Umweltauflagen.

Effiziente Ressourcennutzung

SHC setzt auf maximale Effizienz bei der Nutzung von Ressourcen wie Wasser und Energie. Im Vergleich zu traditionellen adiabaten Kühlsystemen verbraucht SHC bis zu 30 % weniger Wasser, da die Kühleffizienz erheblich gesteigert wurde. Darüber hinaus wird die Abwärme effizient genutzt, um den Heizbedarf im Winter zu reduzieren. Dies spart bis zu 40 % der Heizkosten und minimiert gleichzeitig die Umweltbelastung durch fossile Brennstoffe.

Einhaltung höchster Hygienestandards

Neben der Energieeffizienz überzeugt SHC durch seine hohe Luftqualität. Das System erfüllt die strengen Anforderungen der VDI 6022 und ist damit für Anwendungen geeignet, die höchste Hygienestandards erfordern, wie beispielsweise in der Lebensmittel- oder Pharmaindustrie. Der patentierte Kühlwabenaufbau, eine antibakterielle Beschichtung und ein umfassendes Hygienekonzept in Design und Regelung sorgt dafür, dass die Luft frei von jeglichen Schadstoffen bleibt. Dies schützt nicht nur die Mitarbeitenden, sondern auch die Produktionsanlagen vor Verunreinigungen und verlängert deren Lebensdauer.

Die ökologischen Vorteile von SHC gehen weit über die bloße Reduzierung von Emissionen hinaus. Sie zeigen, wie Technologie und Innovation Unternehmen dabei unterstützen können, eine führende Rolle im Umweltschutz einzunehmen und gleichzeitig betriebliche Effizienz zu maximieren. SHC ist ein Beweis dafür, dass Nachhaltigkeit und Wirtschaftlichkeit kein Widerspruch sind, sondern gemeinsam zu einer besseren Zukunft beitragen können.

1.4. SHC als strategische Investition in Krisenzeiten

In wirtschaftlich schwierigen Zeiten, wie während einer Rezession, suchen Unternehmen nach Investitionen, die nicht nur kurzfristige Entlastung bieten, sondern auch langfristig strategischen Nutzen bringen. Sustainable Hall Conditioning (SHC) erfüllt genau diese Anforderungen, indem es Kosteneinsparungen ermöglicht, ökologische Verantwortung fördert und die Wettbewerbsfähigkeit sichert. Mit SHC wird die Hallenkonditionierung zu einem zentralen Baustein für wirtschaftlichen Erfolg und nachhaltige Entwicklung.

Schnelle Amortisation

Ein entscheidender Vorteil von SHC sind bei Neuanlagen die niedrigeren Investitionskosten als bei herkömmlichen Systemen. Beim Umstieg von bisherigen Lösungen auf die nachhaltige SHC Lösung (Retrofit) ist die kurze Amortisationszeit entscheidend. Durch signifikante Einsparungen bei Energie-, Wartungs- und Betriebskosten amortisiert sich die Investition in der Regel innerhalb von 6 Monaten bis 3 Jahren. Diese schnelle Rentabilität macht SHC zu einer idealen Lösung, selbst für Unternehmen, die in einer Rezession ihre finanziellen Mittel gezielt einsetzen müssen. Unternehmen profitieren direkt von niedrigeren Betriebskosten, ohne langfristige finanzielle Belastungen einzugehen.

Flexible und skalierbare Lösungen

SHC wurde entwickelt, um sich an die individuellen Bedürfnisse von Unternehmen anzupassen. Die modulare Bauweise des Systems ermöglicht maßgeschneiderte Lösungen, die sowohl für kleine Produktionshallen als auch für großflächige Industrieanlagen geeignet sind. Zudem können bestehende Anlagen problemlos nachgerüstet werden, ohne dass umfassende strukturelle Änderungen erforderlich sind. Diese Flexibilität und Skalierbarkeit machen SHC zu einer zukunftssicheren Investition, die mit den Anforderungen eines Unternehmens wachsen kann.

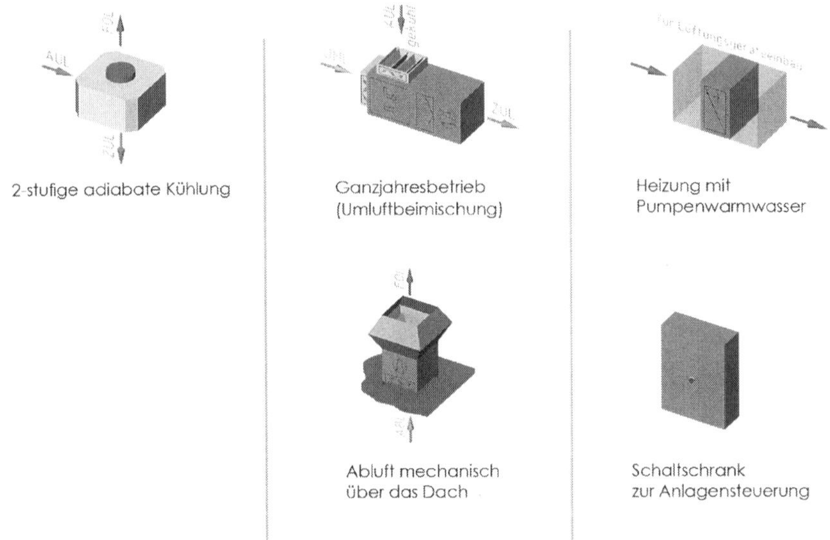

Abbildung 2: Flexibilität durch Modularität – SHC Module Beispielhaft (eigene Darstellung).

Zukunftssicherheit

Mit der zunehmenden Verschärfung von Umweltauflagen und dem wachsenden Druck, nachhaltige Praktiken umzusetzen, bietet SHC eine klare Antwort auf die Herausforderungen der Zukunft. Das System erfüllt nicht nur aktuelle Umweltstandards, sondern ist auch darauf ausgelegt, zukünftige Anforderungen zu erfüllen. Unternehmen, die in SHC investieren, positionieren sich als Vorreiter im Umweltschutz und stärken gleichzeitig ihr Image als verantwortungsbewusste Marktakteure. Dies schafft Vertrauen bei Kunden, Partnern und Mitarbeitenden gleichermaßen.

Sustainable Hall Conditioning ist mehr als nur eine technische Lösung – es ist eine strategische Ressource für Unternehmen, die in Krisenzeiten sowohl wirtschaftlich als auch ökologisch nachhaltig agieren möchten. Indem es schnelle finanzielle Entlastung, betriebliche Flexibilität und langfristige Zukunftssicherheit bietet, wird SHC zu einem unverzichtbaren Werkzeug, um Herausforderungen in einer dynamischen Geschäftswelt erfolgreich zu meistern.

Ob in der Automobil-, Lebensmittel- oder Schwerindustrie – die Erfolgsgeschichten von SHC zeigen, dass diese Technologie Unternehmen dabei unterstützt, wettbewerbsfähig zu bleiben und gleichzeitig einen aktiven Beitrag zum Umweltschutz zu leisten. Mit jedem erfolgreichen Projekt beweist SHC, dass wirtschaftliche Effizienz und ökologische Verantwortung Hand in Hand gehen können.

2. Vorgehensweise zur Systembewertung

Die Entwicklung und Implementierung von Sustainable Hall Conditioning (SHC) basieren auf einem methodisch fundierten Validierungsprozess, der sowohl theoretische als auch praxisbezogene Elemente vereint. Ziel war es, die tatsächliche Energieeffizienz und ökologische Wirkung des Systems unter realen Produktionsbedingungen wissenschaftlich zu überprüfen.

Grundlage der Methodik bildete ein mehrstufiger Validierungsansatz: Zunächst wurden detaillierte Berechnungsmodelle zur Ermittlung der Kühl- und Heizleistung sowie zur Analyse von Energieverbrauch, Betriebskosten und CO_2-Emissionen entwickelt. Diese Modelle wurden auf Basis konkreter Hallengeometrien, Standortklimadaten sowie typischer interner Wärmelasten parametrisiert und in realitätsnahen Szenarien simuliert.

Zur Überprüfung der Modellvalidität erfolgte anschließend eine praxisnahe Feldanalyse. In mehreren Industrieunternehmen – unter anderem bei der Firma Senoplast – wurden SHC-Systeme installiert und messtechnisch überwacht. Dabei kamen Sensoren zur Raumklimaerfassung, Volumenstrommessung sowie zur Verbrauchs- und CO_2-Bilanzierung zum Einsatz. Die ermittelten Realdaten dienten sowohl der Bestätigung der vorhergesagten Energieeinsparungen als auch der kontinuierlichen Systemoptimierung.

Zur Bewertung der relativen Effizienz wurde das SHC-System zudem mit klassischen Kältemaschinenlösungen verglichen – sowohl in Bezug auf energetische Kennzahlen als auch auf Betriebskosten. Dieser Vergleich diente als objektiver Referenzrahmen zur Einordnung der Systemleistung im industriellen Umfeld.

Ergänzt wurde die Methodik durch eine kontinuierliche Begleitforschung, bei der Nutzerfeedback, Wartungsaufwand und Systemverfügbarkeit systematisch erfasst und ausgewertet wurden. Dies ermöglichte eine ganzheitliche Beurteilung der Praxistauglichkeit von SHC – sowohl aus technischer als auch aus wirtschaftlicher und organisatorischer Sicht.

In Summe zeigt sich: Die Kombination aus modellbasierter Vorausberechnung, realer Systemmessung und praxisorientierter Vergleichsanalyse stellt sicher, dass SHC nicht nur theoretisch, sondern auch unter realen Bedingungen als hocheffiziente und nachhaltige Klimatisierungslösung überzeugt.

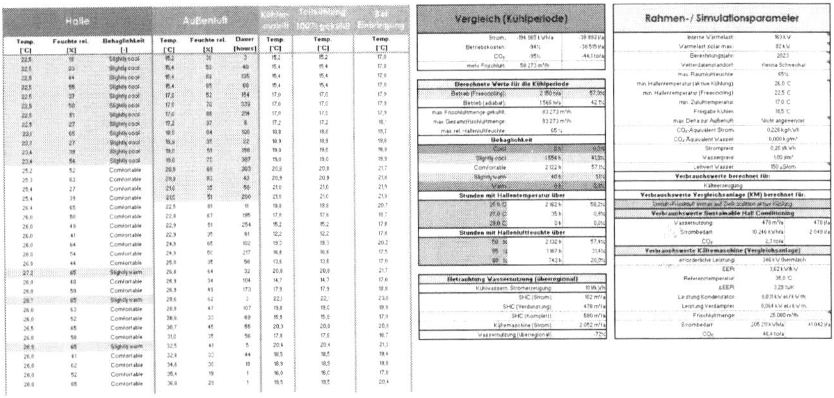

Abbildung 3: Simulationsmodell Hallenbedingungen (eigene Darstellung).

3. Fazit

Sustainable Hall Conditioning (SHC) bietet Unternehmen eine einzigartige Möglichkeit, die Herausforderungen von Kostenreduktion und Nachhaltigkeit erfolgreich zu bewältigen. In einer Zeit, in der wirtschaftlicher Druck und ökologische Verantwortung gleichermaßen im Fokus stehen, zeigt SHC, dass beides nicht nur vereinbar, sondern auch gemeinsam erreichbar ist.

Mit seinen zahlreichen Vorteilen – von der drastischen Senkung der Energiekosten bis hin zur Verbesserung der Produktionsbedingungen – ist SHC weit mehr als ein technologisches System. Es ist ein strategischer Ansatz, der Unternehmen dabei unterstützt, sowohl kurzfristige Einsparungen als auch langfristige Effizienzgewinne zu erzielen. Durch den modularen Aufbau und die Flexibilität des Systems können individuelle Anforderungen erfüllt werden, was SHC zu einer universellen Lösung für verschiedenste Branchen macht.

Darüber hinaus trägt SHC aktiv zum Umweltschutz bei. Mit einer CO2-Reduktion von bis zu 95 %, effizienter Ressourcennutzung und der Einhaltung höchster Hygienestandards positioniert sich SHC als Vorreiter in Sachen nachhaltiger Technologien. Unternehmen, die SHC implementieren, profitieren nicht nur von niedrigeren Betriebskosten und einem positiven ROI, sondern stärken auch ihre Wettbewerbsfähigkeit und ihr Image als verantwortungsbewusste Akteure am Markt.

Diese Innovationskraft wurde auch extern mehrfach bestätigt: SHC wurde mit dem Umweltmanagementpreis 2023 als „Beste Umweltschutzmaßnahme“ in Deutschland und Österreich ausgezeichnet und darüber hinaus als IÖB-Klimaschutz-Innovation gelistet – eine besondere Anerkennung durch die Innovationsplattform der österreichischen Bundesregierung für zukunftsweisende Umwelttechnologien im öffentlichen Beschaffungswesen. Beide Auszeichnungen unterstreichen die hohe Relevanz von SHC für die Green Transition und bestätigen seine Rolle als Benchmark im Bereich energieeffizienter Hallenklimatisierung.

Abschließend lässt sich festhalten: Sustainable Hall Conditioning ist ein wegweisendes System, das Unternehmen in wirtschaftlich schwierigen Zeiten dabei unterstützt, Kosten zu senken, ökologische Verantwortung zu übernehmen und ihre Wettbewerbsfähigkeit zu sichern. Es ist die perfekte Wahl für Unternehmen, die nicht nur heute, sondern auch morgen erfolgreich sein wollen.

Abkürzungsverzeichnis

BMK	Bundesministerium für Klimaschutz
CO_2	Kohlenstoffdioxid
IÖB	Innovationsplattform Öffentliche Beschaffung (Österreich)
ROI	Return on Investment
SHC	Sustainable Hall Conditioning
VDI	Verein Deutscher Ingenieure

Literatur

Abart-Heriszt, L., Beigelböck, B., Eder, K., Holzer, P., Keller, T., Kling, B., Pummer, A., Rzihacek, C., Wimmer, F. & Wolf, M. (2024) Urbaner Kältebedarf in Österreich 2030/2050. Wien: Bundesministerium für Klimaschutz (BMK), S. 7.

Andreas Meltzer, Daniel Dantine, Heinz Nusser

Decarbonization in Times of Crisis?

Investment Decisions under Uncertainty

Summary: Uncertainty significantly hinders industrial investments in decarbonization. Current decarbonization-roadmaps often lack the ability to systematically address uncertainty in assessing decarbonization measures. An enhanced Decision Quality framework can help to account for uncertainty in decision-making processes. This supports the decision-making process itself, as well as the communication of findings to key stakeholders and management executives. The complex task of prioritising decarbonization measures amongst several production sites can be facilitated by a software tool. The proposed scenario planning approach allows to assess and future-proof current roadmaps against future developments.

Keywords: Decarbonization, Industry, Uncertainty, Decision Quality, Finance, Investments.

1. Introduction

Uncertain economic and energy policy conditions are among the most significant barriers to corporate investment in climate neutrality. These uncertainties include, on the one hand, highly volatile forecasts regarding the future prices of renewable energy sources – such as hydrogen - and, on the other hand, geopolitical disruptions that are putting increasing pressure on Europe's industrial competitiveness. (*Draghi-Report*, 2024)

Achieving the European climate targets requires timely investments in decarbonization infrastructure. Due to the long lead times required for technological development and the ramp-up of infrastructure, it is imperative that measures and pilot projects are initiated without delay. However, we are currently observing significant delays in decarbonization projects across many sectors. These delays are partly attributable to the prevailing economic situation in Europe, and partly to volatile political framework conditions. Discussions are underway regarding the reduction or withdrawal of subsidies for decarbonization. Yet, without such financial support, many decarbonization projects are not economically viable. Political delays are being driven, for instance, by national budget deficits as well as unexpectedly high prices for renewable energy carriers, such as green hydrogen.

At the same time, the deadlines for achieving decarbonization targets are rapidly approaching. This is especially relevant for companies that have committed to emissions reductions under the Science Based Targets initiative (SBTi). The ongoing and accelerating pace of global climate change underscores the urgent need for timely implementation of mitigation measures.

Most high-emission companies already have a CO_2 roadmap – i.e. a strategic plan outlining how they aim to reduce greenhouse gas emissions over time to meet climate targets or specific reduction commitments. In structured dialogues with representatives from the industrial sector, we found that the insufficient integration of uncertainty and the necessity to update economic and regulatory assumptions are perceived as key barrier towards climate action.

To address this challenge, we further developed the decision-theoretical concept of "Decision Quality" (DQ) and implemented it in a practical modelling framework (see:(Daniel Kahneman, 2012; Lum, 2016; Nutt, 2002; Paul Papayoanou, 2010; Spetzler *et al.*, 2016; Tetlock *et al.*, 2016)). This enhanced framework enables comprehensive consideration of uncertainties in investment decisions, allowing for an objective and systematic risk assessment and reprioritization of decarbonisation investment projects. On the following pages we outline the theoretical pillars of our concept and suggest the use of software tools to handle complex decision processes.

2. Method

Our methodological approach is grounded in the decision-theoretical concept of DQ, which we applied to assess corporate investments in decarbonization.

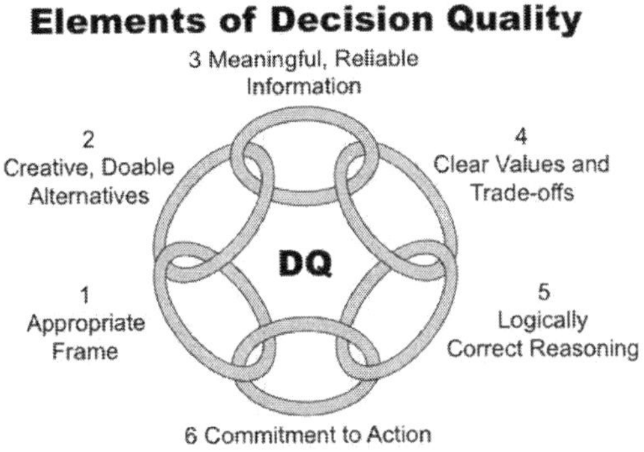

Figure 1: The six key-elements of decision-making. Based on (Spetzler et al., 2016) and retrieved from: https://accendoreliability.com/why-environmental-decision-making-is-difficult-and-what-to-do-about-it/

Figure 1 shows the six key-elements of decision-making, as defined by Carl Spetzler. They provide a structured framework for making sound, strategic decisions under uncertainty. A high-quality decision requires: an appropriate frame to define the context and purpose; creative, feasible alternatives to ensure choice; meaningful, reliable information to ground analysis; clear values and trade-offs to guide prioritization; logically correct reasoning to ensure analytical soundness; and a commitment to action to translate decisions into results. It is important to note that each element is necessary but not sufficient on its own - all six must be present for a decision to be considered high quality. This fact is illustrated by the six links of a chain in the figure. The decision is only as strong, as each individual link.

We recommend implementing this concept in a structured process, supported by in-house build or commercial software tools. The main advantage lies in the transparency and simplification of the decision-making process for decision-makers such as sustainability managers.

A structured process using a software tool yields several benefits:

- The creation of varying sets of alternatives – e.g. different decarbonization roadmaps with a focus on H_2, electrification, or other strategies, respectively.
- The collection and structuring of relevant information, such as financial and technical KPIs of the decarbonization measures, as well as the prioritization of measures (e.g. using CO_2-abatement costs as key indicator).

- The definition of clear values (e.g. acceptable costs vs. reduced CO_2-emissions).
- The logically correct reasoning. The human brain is prone to biases in decision-making, especially when uncertainty is to be involved.(Spetzler *et al.*, 2016) As decision-makers in the field of decarbonization are often confronted with a considerable amount of different alternatives for the individual production sites of international companies, and a broad range of uncertainty regarding e.g. CAPEX and OPEX of decarbonization technologies, a software tool can be extremely beneficial to avoid biased decisions and to identify the financially most beneficial measures.
- Ensuring a sustained commitment to action requires the active integration of all relevant stakeholders. This integration can be facilitated through participatory decision-making enabled by a centralized software platform. For example, site-level managers can contribute directly to corporate sustainability efforts by submitting relevant data and proposed measures through a shared tool. Furthermore, the platform should enable transparent progress monitoring by documenting key milestones and decision points – such as budget approvals, project planning stages, and due diligence status – thereby enhancing accountability and coordination across organizational levels.

3. Handling Uncertainty in Decarbonization Projects

We developed a framework that allows to manage the steps 2-6 of the DQ approach, as these steps usually lie in the influence of sustainability managers and related positions. A detailed description of a possible application of our concept for planning and implementation of decarbonization roadmaps is provided on the following pages.

3.1. Appropriate Frame

We assume that the framing step is performed and prescribed by executive management. This step ensures, that the right problem is addressed and decision-makers have aligned on purpose, perspective, and scope of the decision problem. In the field of decarbonization, we regularly see that executive management sets the frame for sustainability managers and others, e.g. by a general commitment to climate neutrality in a certain time frame and certain constraints that must be met, such as financial viability.

3.2. Creative Alternatives

In practice, it is a demanding task for sustainability managers to create alternatives for the variety of international locations that use different processes and energy carriers. We found that on-site workshops with plant managers can be helpful to identify a first set of realistic decarbonization alternatives. However, the alternatives are often updated regularly, as new information, technologies, or alternatives become available. We recommend an online collaboration platform to integrate local stakeholders in the transformation process and keep the backlog of different alternatives up to date.

3.3. Reliable Information and Uncertainty

Handling uncertainty in complex investment decisions is one of the key barriers in developing optimised decarbonisation pathways. To account for uncertainty regarding certain parameters, such as future raw material costs, energy prices, or market demand, we recommend the use of ranges instead of single values. By simulating the full range of these parameters from the assumed minimum to maximum values, the influence of individual factors on the investment's economic viability can be assessed, enabling the identification of the most relevant uncertainties.

Figure 2 illustrates this, using the example of a biomethane plant intended to substitute natural gas in an industrial decarbonization context. The width of each bar represents the extent to which each parameter (such as e.g. the market price for biomethane) influences the investment's net present value (NPV). We see that the uncertainty regarding the future market price of biomethane, as well as future feedstock cost have the highest influence on the overall profitability of the project. On the other hand, uncertainty regarding the total output of the plant or lifetime of the plant have a comparably low influence. This indicates that it is beneficial to focus on the most influential factors, such as future market prices. In the concrete example, it could be beneficial to collect further and more reliable information on future biomethane market prices (e.g. by performing a market study) or by developing a hedge to reduce the risk of high feedstock costs (e.g. by long-term contracts with suppliers).

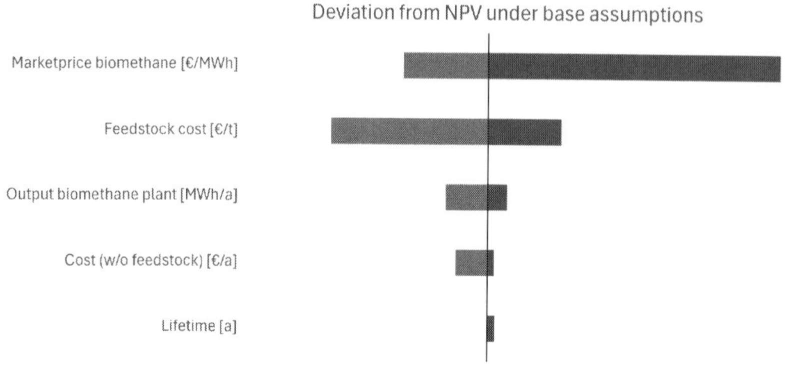

Figure 2: Major influencing factors on NPV, using a biomethane plant as an example. The bar width indicates the impact of each parameter on investment viability. Source: Own illustration based on: (energy-messenger, 2024; Hermeling et al., 2022; MOŽINA, 2023; Možina et al., 2024; Stangl et al., 2024; Wlcek et al., 2023)

Another important concept to deal with uncertainty is the use of "scenarios planning". To clarify: In practice, we regularly see the usage of the word "scenario" in the meaning of "bundle of decarbonisation measures". In our theoretical concept, we define scenarios as "possible future states of the world that we cannot influence directly". Hence, as a company it is possible to define a decarbonization strategy/roadmap and to create different "bundles of decarbonization measures". However, it lies outside the influence sphere of the company, how the market/energy prices/legislation will develop in the future (we define this as possible scenario). As these aspects have a major impact on the companies, it is advised to explore multiple future scenarios and their effects on the company performance, given a specific decarbonization strategy.

The scenario planning approach is illustrated in Figure 3. In this example, four possible future states of the company environment are illustrated. The two main drivers "cost of renewable energy carriers" and "global cooperation" are highly relevant for e.g. export oriented industries with a high energy demand. The actual developments cannot be foreseen; however, it is possible to assess different decarbonization strategies against the four scenarios. This enables companies to optimize their decarbonization strategies so that they are successful in all four scenarios or at least to mitigate risks.

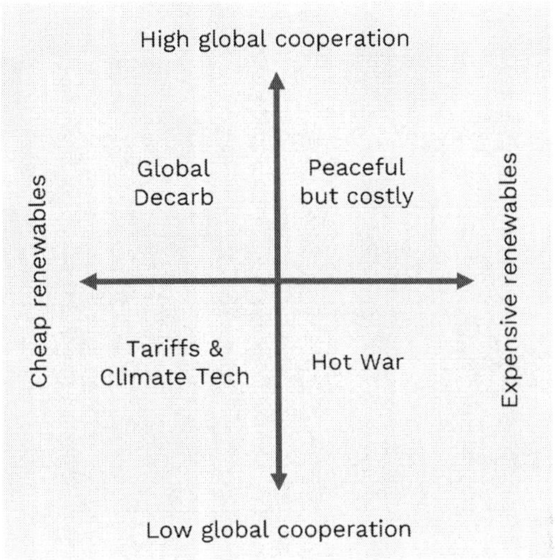

Figure 3: Four exemplary scenarios that might impact the performance of a company decarbonization strategy. In this fictional example, the price of renewable energy carriers and the level of global (economic) collaboration could have a major influence on company performance.

3.4. Clear values

In decarbonization projects, decision-makers are regularly confronted with conflicting goals/values – e.g. financial optimization vs. high CO_2-emission reduction. Some measures are beneficial in terms of both goals. Others might save significant emissions, but might be costly. In cases where a significant amount of decarbonization measures have to be managed, it can be highly beneficial to graphically depict the measures amongst those values. Figure 4 shows a set of decarbonization measures of a fictional industry company with several production sites. It allows the prioritization of measures given the company values.

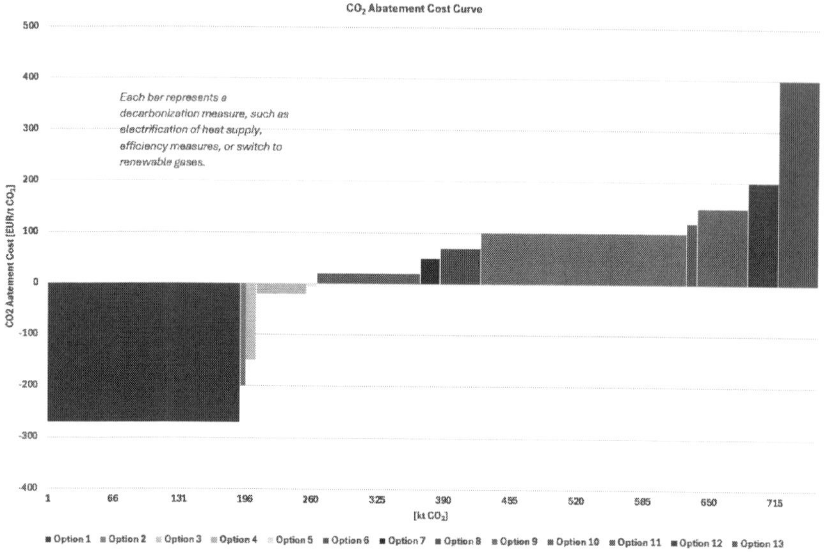

Figure 4: Fictional abatement cost curve of a set of decarbonization measures for a fictional international industry company. Measures on the lower left side are beneficial in terms of cost, but have a low emission reduction potential. Measures depicted in the upper right part have a high emission reduction potential, but are also related to high economic costs per saved ton CO_2.

3.5. Logically correct reasoning

A major challenge in decarbonization projects is the handling of large datasets and uncertainty. The optimization of a decarbonization roadmap for several sites and the consideration of the relevant uncertainties and the consideration of the relevant framework conditions at the individual sites (e.g. availability of H2-infrastructure, costs for energy carriers, environmental legislation, etc.) can be challenging. The use of software to support this complex decision-making process is highly beneficial. We recommend the use of at least three assumptions (low, base, high) for each relevant and uncertain parameter, as depicted in Figure 5.

Country	Market Assumption	Scenario	Forecast Date	2023	2025	2030	2050
Austria	CO2 ETS (EUR/t)	All	All	All	All	All	
Austria	CO2 ETS (EUR/t)	Base	2024-Dec-13	72	85	150	250
Austria	CO2 ETS (EUR/t)	High	2024-Dec-13	72	85	250	400
Austria	CO2 ETS (EUR/t)	Low	2024-Dec-13	72	85	100	200

Figure 5: Exemplary input mask of a software tool to consider uncertainty of key-parameters in decarbonization roadmaps.

Table 1 shows scenario planning as possible feature in a decarbonization software tool. The ability to assign the custom scenarios with the corresponding low/base/high assumptions of the uncertain key-parameters allows to check on the robustness of the decarbonization strategy under possible future framework conditions.

Table 1: Scenario planning allows to describe possible future states of the company environment. The definition of key assumptions serves as input for assessing impacts of the company environment on the performance of the company and potential success of its decarbonization strategy.

	Global Decarb	Peaceful but costly	Tariffs and climate tech	Hot war
Bio methane (EUR/MWh)	Low	High	High	Base
CO2 ETS (EUR/t)	High	High	Base	Low
Green hydrogen (EUR/MWh)	Low	High	Low	High
Natural gas (EUR/MWh)	Base	Base	High	High
Power (EUR/MWh)	Base	Base	Base	Low
Renewable power (EUR/MWh)	Low	High	Low	High
Critical raw materials [EUR/t]	Low	High	High	Low

Based on assumptions as illustrated in Table 1, the results for individual decarbonization measures, or bundle of measures (decarbonization strategies) can be calculated. For the calculation minimum, base case, and maximum values are used as input for the financial estimations. Table 2 presents the results of the economic analysis under base assumptions and under the four before defined scenarios. It can be seen, that the financial viability of some measures is highly dependent upon external framework conditions. With relatively high costs for renewable energy and low global cooperation, several measures would have a negative NPV. Depending on the individual demand of the companies for decarbonization planning, further results can be retrieved from the underlying datasets.

3.6. Commitment to action

The effectiveness of a decision is influenced not only by the choice itself but also by the willingness to follow through with it. We clearly see a delay in the implementation of decarbonization projects in the recent years. It is vital to transport the findings of reporting and roadmap-creation into concrete investments and measures. In our work with companies, we see the need to close the gap between reporting and definition of roadmaps on the one hand, and the decision-making, allocation of budget and resources, as well as the implementation itself, on the other hand. In the sound communication of uncertainty and elaborated estimations of key financial indicators such as net-present-value or abatement cost-curves, we see the potential to create a common understanding amongst different stakeholders (e.g. finance, sustainability and management teams) and to move from mere roadmaps into concrete investment projects.

Table 2: Key Performance Indicators (KPIs) for different decarbonization measures under base assumptions (upper part of the table) and economic performance indicated by net present value (NVP) in lower part. Green cells signify that the measure reaches a positive NPV, red signifies a negative NPV.

		Efficiency Measures	Fuel Switch to Biomethane	Large Heat Storage (90°C)	Heat Pump
KPIs in Base Scenario	CapEx [EUR]	540 000	33 000	4 602 299	1 093 750
	NPV [EUR]	3 246 192	-123 000	13 938 972	-129 653
	Payback [Years]	1,20	0,00	2,30	3,60
	IRR [%]	16	0	3	-2
	CO_2 Abatement Cost [EUR/tCO_2]	-1	4	-305	282
	Scope 1,2,3 CO_2 [t]	-4 790	-80	-644	-537
NPV in Scenarios	Global Decarb	+	+	+	+
	Peaceful but costly	+	+	+	-
	Tariffs and climate tech	+	-	+	+
	Hot war	+	-	-	-

4. Conclusion

Company representatives and literature identify uncertainty as one key barrier for investments in decarbonization of industry sites. To integrate uncertainty in the current often rather static models for roadmap planning, we propose a refined version of the DQ framework. The framework supports the structuring and assessment of decarbonization-related investment decisions in industrial settings. Particularly in times of heightened uncertainty, it is crucial to understand the impact of those uncertainties on the business case of decarbonization measures and to proactively implement risk-mitigation strategies. Our framework allows to identify most influential, but uncertain parameters into roadmap planning. Using a scenario-planning approach, it is possible to identify possible future states of the company environment ant their impacts on the decarbonization strategy. The principles of DQ allow to enhance current decision-making processes in decarbonization management and to move from mere theoretical planning and reporting towards informed decision making under uncertainty. For exemplary purposes, we provided fictional examples of challenges that companies are currently confronted with and proposed the representation and management of uncertainty in a software tool.

By integrating the theoretical foundations of DQ into a software solution, uncertainties within the corporate decision-making context can be made transparent and clearly communicated. Specific biases, that threaten sound decision-making can be reduced by structuring the decision-making process according to scientific findings of DQ. This facilitates more informed and robust investment decisions in support of industrial decarbonization.

Further efforts are necessary in finalizing software tools for practial implementation of the enhanced DQ process and the refinement of the framework with industry stakeholders. Although the framework has been successfully tested with industry partners, it has not yet been empirically validated using a scientific approach. Future research could benefit from an in-depth validation of the framework as well as from a comparison with alternative decision-making approaches.

List of abbreviations

DQ	Decision Quality
NPV	Net Present Value
SBTi	Science Based Targets initiative

References

Daniel Kahneman. (2012), *Schnelles Denken, Langsames Denken*, Siedler Verlag.

energy-messenger. (2024), "agriportance - Preisentwicklung Biomethan", 15 October, available at: https://agriportance.com/de/preisentwicklung/biomethan-entwicklung-preise/ (accessed 22 October 2024).

Hermeling, W., Nachtmamm, K. and Scholwin, F. (2022), *Biogas - Ein Taschenbuch Für Die Erzeugerpraxis*, Springer Verlag.

Lum, R. (2016), *4 Steps to the Future: A Quick and Clean Guide to Creating Foresight*, Vision Foresight Strategy LLC.

MOŽINA, F.M. (2023), B*iomethananlagen Zur Bereitstellung Erneuerbarer Energie in Niederösterreich – Potenziale, Handlungsempfehlungen Und Identifikation von Potenziellen Anlagenstandorten.*

Možina, F.M., Windsperger, B., Papadokonstantakis, S. and Windsperger, A. (2024), *Strategic Analysis of Regional Biomethane Injection Potential from Agricultural Residues: Leveraging LP Optimization for Economic Assessment.*

Nutt, P. (2002), *Why Decisions Fail: Avoiding the Blunders and Traps That Lead to Debacles*, Berrett-Koehler.

Paul Papayoanou. (2010), *Game Theory for Business: A Primer in Strategic Gaming*, Probabilistic Publishing.

Spetzler, C., Winter, H. and Meyer, J. (2016), *Decision Quality: Value Creation from Better Business Decisions, Wiley.*

Stangl, F., Fliedl, M.M. and Seidl, M.S. (2024), *Handelbarkeit Und Anrechenbarkeit von Erneuerbaren Gasen*, available at: https://www.erneuerbaresgas.at/jart/prj3/erneuerbare_gase/data/uploads/SEG%20Leitfaden%20Handelbarkeit%20und%20Anrechenbarkeit.pdf.

Tetlock, P., Gardner, D. and Neubauer, J. (2016), *Superforecasting – Die Kunst Der Richtigen Prognose*, Fischer.

The Future of European Competitiveness. (2024), European Comission, available at: https://commission.europa.eu/document/download/97e481fd-2dc3-412d-be4c-f152a8232961_en?filename=The%20future%20of%20European%20competitiveness%20_%20A%20competitiveness%20strategy%20for%20Europe.pdf.

Wlcek, B., Furtwängler, C. and Knaus, K. (2023), *Marktbericht 2023*, Servicestelle Erneuerbare Gase, available at: (accessed 22 November 2024).

Viorel Nita, Paulina Fernández, Michael Tost

Ways to improve the limited data and transparency of lithium-ion batteries supply chains

Summary: Due to i) incomplete coverage of mineral-containing commodities along their supply chains, ii) insufficient information provided by country-of-origin reporting, and iii) discrepancies in bilateral trade data reporting, the limitations in trade statistics necessitate identifying complementary ways for obtaining more data and information on the supply chains. In the case of lithium-ion batteries placed on the EU market, consolidation of data from i) existing public statistics, ii) application of more unified standards and end-to-end voluntary certification schemes incorporating traceability systems, and iii) the due diligence reports to be submitted by large companies within the framework of the EU Battery Regulation can increase their supply chain transparency.

Keywords: Raw materials, Lithium-ion batteries, Supply chain transparency, Trade statistics, Traceability, EU Battery Regulation.

1. Context

The transport sector accounts for around 14 per cent of global GHG emissions (Climate Watch data). The expanding interest in batteries is driven by the high environmental impact of road transport, which is responsible for 89% of the transport sector's global GHG emissions (Climate Watch data). Electric vehicles can significantly reduce road transport emissions through zero direct emissions or lowering the whole-life-cycle emissions, and batteries play an important role here.

However, battery manufacturing requires large quantities of raw material inputs and poses significant supply risks throughout the supply chain, especially for countries highly reliant on imports of minerals and metals, as is the case of the EU (see Figure 1).

Production of lithium-ion batteries, the most commonly used battery type nowadays, requires extraction and further processing of high amounts of cobalt, graphite, lithium, manganese, and nickel, depending on the battery type.[1] As for lithium, battery manufacturing consumes 87 per cent of lithium

1 E.g., LFP, LMO, NCA, or NMC battery; for details, Capliez et al., (2025).

mined worldwide (USGS, 2025), and its rising demand will lead to significant growth of lithium production capacity in the coming years (Alonso et al., 2025).

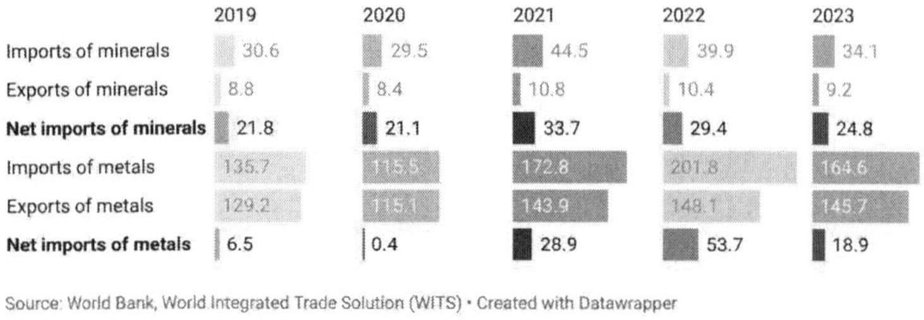

Figure 1 EU27′s net imports of minerals and metals over the period 2019-2023 (own representation; bn USD; (World Integrated Trade Solution)).[2]

As far as cobalt is concerned, the DRC is by far the world's leading producer, with 72 percent of the world's estimated potential production capacity in 2024 (Alonso et al., 2025); its main use is in lithium-ion battery cathode materials.

Production of lithium-ion batteries induces significant environmental impact along the entire battery life cycle; mining and refining stages are major contributors, accounting together for around 40% of average battery emissions (McKinsey & Company, 2024b).

The most social, governance-related, and human rights violations take place in the same two upstream supply chain segments. Mancini et al. (2020) discuss risks associated with cobalt, graphite and lithium. González and de Haan (2020) provide a detailed review of the worldwide environmental impacts and human rights violations caused by the extraction of lithium, cobalt, nickel, graphite, and manganese. Amnesty International (2024) reports additional human rights violations induced by mining expansion and illegal mining, such as forced evictions in DRC; malnutrition, contamination, and use of violence in Brazil; violation of indigenous people's rights in Venezuela. More recent examples of human rights and international law violations related to minerals can be found in the individual CAHRA reports published by DG Trade (European Commission, 2025).

According to the estimations of McKinsey & Company (2023), driven mainly by the expansion of batteries for electric mobility, the global demand

2 "Minerals" product covers HS chapters 25 and 26; "Metals" product group cover HS chapters 72-83.

for lithium-ion batteries is expected to have an annual growth of around 33 percent up to 2030. That will entail soaring raw material extraction and increasing production throughout the battery supply chain and induce additional ESG risks worldwide.

2. Overview of the lithium-ion battery supply chain

The lithium-ion battery supply chain covers six broad segments: i) extraction, ii) processing, iii) cathode active materials (CAM), iv) cell components, v) cells, and vi) battery assembling (González and de Haan, 2020). A simplified overview of the lithium-ion battery supply chain is provided in Table 1. A detailed overview would be manifold, by battery type; in fact, the lithium-ion battery supply chain is more complex, involving numerous commodities, transactions and players involved in extraction, processing, refining, manufacture, trading, distribution, end use, etc.[3]

Table 1: Overview of lithium-ion battery supply chain (own compilation; Severiano et al., 2024; González and de Haan, 2020; Carrara et al., 2023).

<table>
<tr><th colspan="3">Upstream segments</th><th colspan="4">Downstream segments</th></tr>
<tr><th>Raw material</th><th>Extraction</th><th>Processing</th><th>Cathode active materials</th><th>Cell components</th><th>Cells</th><th>Battery pack</th></tr>
<tr><td>Lithium</td><td>Brine ores
Spodumene</td><td>Conversion and purification:
battery-grade lithium compounds (lithium carbonate; lithium hydroxide)</td><td rowspan="4">NCA (nickel-cobalt-aluminum)
NMC (nickel-manganese-cobalt; currently preeminent)
LMO (lithium-manganese-oxide)
L(M)FP (lithium-(manganese)-iron-phosphate, emerging as preeminent)
LCO (lithium-cobalt-oxide; traditional)</td><td rowspan="4">Cathodes
Anodes
Electrolytes
Separators</td><td rowspan="4"></td><td rowspan="4">NCA
NMC
LMO
LFP
LCO</td></tr>
<tr><td>Cobalt</td><td>Cobalt mining</td><td>Refining</td></tr>
<tr><td>Nickel</td><td>Nickel sulphide
Nickel laterite</td><td>Leaching/ Smelting
Refining</td></tr>
<tr><td>Manganese</td><td>Manganese</td><td>Roasting/ Leaching
Refining</td></tr>
</table>

3 Donelly et al. (2023), Section 3.1, for further details.

Upstream segments			Downstream segments			
Raw material	**Extraction**	**Processing**	**Cathode active materials**	**Cell components**	**Cells**	**Battery pack**
Others	Copper, graphite, rare earths, aluminum and others	Refining/ Processing	Natural graphite anode Synthetic graphite anode Lithium hexafluorophosphate			

Two features of the current global lithium-ion battery market stand out: i) oversupply[4] and ii) clear domination of China, Japan and South Korea, in terms of both domestic production and presence of companies on markets outside Asia, including on the EU market.[5] The Asian producers account for between 90 and 96% of the world´s production of cathode, anode, electrolyte and separator materials (McKinsey & Company, 2024). CATL (China), LG Chem (South Korea), BYD (China), Panasonic (Japan) and Samsung (South Korea) are among the biggest battery cell manufacturers.

China dominates all supply chain segments, accounting for around 80% of global natural graphite production; producing 18% and controlling around 60% of worldwide lithium production; controlling more than half of the official cobalt production in the DRC; refining 80% of the raw materials used in electric vehicles; and accounting for more than half of global production and around 86% of global exports of lithium-ion batteries in 2023.[6]

Excepting the lithium carbonate – for which Chile is the major EU supplier, China remains by far the EU's leading supplier to the EU of lithium hydroxide, lithium primary cells and batteries, and lithium-ion electric accumulators (Figure 2).

Thus, due to the EU's high reliance on imports, responsible supply for many segments of lithium-ion battery supply chain becomes an issue of high relevance.

4 As of 2023, China´s production of lithium-ion batteries was around twice as high as the global demand (Alonso et al., 2025).

5 E.g., CATL in Germany; Guotai-Huarong and LG Chem in Poland; Samsung SDI in Hungary.

6 Sources of data: Capliez et al. (2025) and S&P Global (2024).

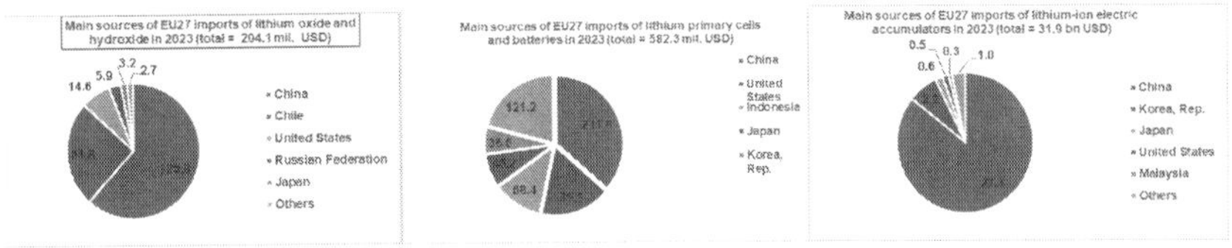

Figure 2: The five main suppliers of lithium hydroxide, lithium primary cells and batteries, and lithium-ion accumulators to the EU in 2023 (own representation; mil. USD; bn USD for electric accumulators; source of data: World Bank, World Trade Integrated Solution).[7]

3. Supply chain transparency

A supply chain is a network of nodes and links, characterized by a bounded visibility for each participating actor (Carter et al., 2015), usually limited to its immediate suppliers and customers.

In the context of the mineral supply chains, it refers to "*moving the mineral from the extraction site downstream to its incorporation in the final product for end consumers*" (OECD, 2016). Transparency in mineral supply chains has gained increasing relevance, driven by concerns related to environmental degradation, severe human rights abuses, support for armed groups, bribery and fraud associated with mining (OECD, 2019; Rüttinger and Corder, 2020).

A prerequisite of more responsible supply chains is increasing their transparency. Supply chain mapping is first needed for i) obtaining more data and information on commodity's origin, successive transformations, and the sequence of transactions between the involved actors, and then for ii) identifying and addressing potential ESG risks associated with its supply chain.[8] As Gardner et al. (2019) put it, "*transparency can demystify complex supply chains, and help different actors identify and minimize risks and improve conditions on the ground*". Especially in the politically unstable, conflict-affected or under-regulated areas, limited or unreliable data on production and trade flows could hide the occurrence of illicit production and trade, alongside environmental and social risks (as in the case of coltan in Central Africa – Bleischwitz et al., 2012). Against this backdrop, OECD (2016) recommends that compa-

7 No HS and CN codes were identified – and thus no data were available – for CAM and cell components, i. e., cathode, anode, electrolytes and separators. See section 3.1 for the limited statistical commodity coverage.

8 IEA (2025) for more details about the role of supply chain mapping, including that of traceability, in increasing supply chain transparency.

nies implement a "*system of controls and transparency*" over their upstream mineral supply chain as a building block of their risk-based due diligence management.

4. Several statistical limitations on mirroring the real-world lithium-ion battery supply chains

The accuracy of trade data is essential for further trade analyses and trade policies based on them. In this section we discuss several existing limitations related to incomplete statistical coverage of mineral-containing commodities and country-of-origin reporting, which call for the use of additional data.

4.1. Capturing of real-world supply chains in trade statistics

There are several limitations concerning the coverage of battery-related commodities in trade classifications in both the World Customs Organization's Harmonized System (HS) and the Eurostat's Combined Nomenclature (CN), which hinder a collection and sound analysis of cross-country trade data for all supply chain segments. In the area of raw materials, some clarification was brought by Georgitzikis (2023) on issues such as i) identification of trade codes of commodities incorporating raw materials, ii) determination of their material content, and iii) assignment of the supply chain segment certain products belong to. Below we discuss two major shortcomings in both the HS and CN relevant to our topic.

S1) Heterogeneous products classified under a unique HS subheading or CN code make it difficult to collect trade data for certain products. An example is the six-digit HS heading 2615, Niobium, tantalum, vanadium or zirconium ores and concentrates, further divided into two subheadings – 2615.10, Zirconium ores and concentrates, and 2615.90, Other; in CN, the eight-digit CN codes 2615.10.00 and 2615.90.00 do not add further product specification. The second example is particularly relevant to the lithium-ion battery supply chains: a single collective code for lithium-containing ores is allocated in CN 2025, i.e., CN 2530.90.40, Spodumene, petalite, lepidolite, amblygonite, hectorite, jadarite and similar minerals, suitable for the extraction of lithium. This is not the case in the HS, where they are mixed with other types of ores (such as those related to rare-earth metals, scandium or yttrium) in the HS subheading 2530.90, Mineral substances not elsewhere specified or included – Other. This lack of trade codes in HS hinders the collection of cross-country trade flows of extracted lithium; the limited specificity in CN requires the use of additional public or private data sources for the EU-related trade flows.

S2) *Incomplete statistical coverage of midstream lithium-containing commodities*. In the case of the lithium-ion battery supply chain, not all commodities are covered by trade statistics. While the cathode precursor materials are partly covered, their specificity remains unsatisfactory; however, no trade codes for cathode active materials were identified. There are HS codes for compounds such as lithium oxide and hydroxide (HS 282540), lithium carbonates (HS 283691) and nickel oxides and hydroxide (HS 282540), but no separate codes are assigned to compounds such as iron phosphate, manganese sulphates and dioxides, or lithium cobalt oxide in either HS 2022 or CN 2025.

4.2. Country-of-origin reporting and bilateral asymmetries

The limited information provided by country-of-origin reporting and the use of different methods for attribution of country of origin pose additional difficulties in tracking the ultimate origin and sequence of transactions of cross-country traded commodities.

For imported commodities, the attribution of country of origin is based on two main criteria: i) the supplying country criterion, when the commodity is entirely produced in a single country; and ii) the last substantial transformation criterion, applicable when more than one country contributed to the manufacturing of a commodity. In spite of the technical work carried out so far, there are still discrepancies in the application of country-of-origin reporting since i) some countries do not apply it at all; ii) when applied, it is for limited purposes such as preferential customs duties and other trade measures that require documented proof of origin; iii) its application is not harmonized worldwide (UN DESA, 1998). Most importantly, the last substantial transformation criterion only accounts for the last supply chain segment.

Further complications arise in the case of the EU as a trade bloc, which records the extra-EU27 imports on country-of-origin basis, and the imports between member states on country-of-consignment principle (Eurostat, 2023).[9] In the case of intra-EU27 imports, even if UN DESA (1998) strongly recommends reporting using the former reporting method, the partner country attribution only accounts for the member state of consignment, while collection of country-of-origin information remains optional (Eurostat, 2023).

Thus, even in the ideal case of a harmonized use of the last substantial transformation criterion, tracking bilateral transactions along the supply chain ends at the country in which the last substantial transformation took place. A good illustration of this limitation is the case of an imported assem-

9 Cotterlaz and Vicard (2023) for a detailed discussion on the consequences of this reporting standard.

bled battery: while raw materials are extracted and its components are produced in various countries, its import origin is attributed to the country where the battery is assembled.

The existing asymmetries in reporting bilateral trade transactions in the UNSD Comtrade database have been extensively discussed, e.g., Markhonko (2014) and Mitikj and Kaushik (2024). First, one of the main reasons for their occurrences lies in the use of different rules for trade partner attribution. Second, even the use of the same UNSD-recommended reporting method, i.e., reporting the commodity import partner based on the country-of-origin rule, and the export partner based on the last-known-destination rule, intrinsically leads to "structural" discrepancies. Moreover, there are also "non-structural" causes of the bilateral discrepancies, such as deliberate misreporting or misclassification errors, as discussed by Mitikj and Kaushik (2024).

Fortunately, some of these shortcomings can be used to spotlight areas of insufficient supply chain transparency, where more examination would be needed. In this respect, Saka et al. (2024) propose a methodology for measuring the extent of supply chain transparency using bilateral asymmetries in the UN Comtrade database as a proxy. By applying it to 14 commodities related to the lithium battery supply chain, they spotlighted opaque country- and commodity-related areas that need further investigation and policy actions. Since bilateral discrepancies in the reported trade flows are caused by both structural and non-structural factors (Mitikj and Kaushik, 2024), further research on how to separate them would bring more accuracy in determining the transparency degree of a certain supply chain. Also, further research into how the magnitude of missing data can be an indication of supply chain opacity, as in the case of the DRC's lack of reported data on the exports of cobalt ores and concentrates, would also bring useful clarification.

5. Voluntary initiatives and regulations

Since 2010, following the California Transparency in Supply Chains Act, numerous private initiatives, standards and certification schemes have been developed, thereby contributing to increasing the transparency of global mineral supply chains. Deberdt and Le Billonfor (2021) and Fernández et al. (2024a) provide reviews of them. An important driver of their proliferation is the rising pressure from civil society, downstream producers and consumers to address the environmental, social and political risks occurring in the mineral supply chains. Attempting to prevent any "*reputational damages*" (Vermeulen, 2013) and "*maintain market access*" (Severiano et al., 2024), the companies operating in extraction and processing segments, which are more exposed to underregulated or conflict areas, have increasingly adhered to certification schemes.

Despite their importance, many certification standards face significant limitations. First, they often lack a comprehensive approach, failing to cover all stages of the supply chain or to integrate small-scale actors and less-traded minerals (Dietrich and Melcher, 2022). Nevertheless, in a context of evolving regulation, certification standards continue to advance, expanding to include a broader set of minerals and socio-environmental issues. Notably, efforts have been made to integrate artisanal mining by providing technical assistance and reducing barriers to entry.

There is still significant opacity related to the origins and flows of mineral commodities sourced from conflict areas (e.g., Bleischwitz et al., 2012), caused by two major factors: i) underregulation or governance vacuum in some mining areas and ii) difficulty of tracking minerals in the mid- and downstream segments (Hofmann et al., 2015). As Severiano et al. (2024) show, in spite of the proliferation of corporate-focused self-regulatory frameworks, their heterogeneity makes them less effective (Hiete et al., 2019). This is the reason why regulations come into play.

6. Traceability of the mineral supply chains

Traceability is the capacity to determining where a particular product originates, where it has travelled, who has handled it, and what modifications it has undergone (OECD and IEA, 2025). It is an essential instrument for increasing supply chains transparency, helping companies obtain better data and information on their supply chains and associated environmental and human rights impacts (Gustafsson et al., 2023).

Some certification schemes, such as IRMA and RMI, incorporate traceability systems. A key component of these systems is the chain of custody, which provides information on the sequence of entities that have handled a product, including miners, transporters, exporters, processors and manufacturers (OECD and IEA, 2025). As the chain of custody alone does not guarantee complete traceability, its effectiveness depends on proper integration with other tracing mechanisms (Erdmann and Franken, 2022).

Digital technologies have also gained traction in enhancing the efficiency and reliability of traceability mechanisms. These include i) blockchain, which enables decentralized and secure transaction records, improving data integrity along the supply chain (Mugurusi and Ahishakiye, 2022; Onifade et al., 2024); ii) RFID, widely used for physical material tracking (Tian, 2016); iii) mineralogical fingerprinting, based on geochemical and isotopic signatures that can confirm the origin of a mineral (Desaulty et al., 2022); and iv) artificial fingerprinting, which involves embedding unique tracer particles into materials to verify their identity and origin throughout the chain (Laurence et al., 2024). While these technologies offer significant benefits, they also face barriers to implementation. In the case of blockchain, its effectiveness depends heavily on the quality of input data and good data governance (Powell et al., 2022). Provenance analysis, while useful when there are doubts about declared origin (Melcher et al., 2008), still faces operational limitations and high costs. Artificial fingerprinting systems can complement digital traceability by embedding 3D-printed taggant particles tailored to the specific requirements of the mining and metallurgical industry. Currently, robust methodologies and expanded reference databases are being developed to apply this technique across diverse contexts with higher reliability (Desaulty et al., 2022).

Within this framework, the ongoing European project MaDiTraCe develops the CERA4in1 standard, which aims to cover all minerals and stages of the supply chain; in an integrated approach, it combines analytical and digital technologies, such as mineralogical fingerprinting, artificial tagging, and blockchain, within a unified certification system (Fernández Muñoz et al., 2024b).

7. The EU battery regulation

The EU Battery Regulation (EBR) can contribute significantly to filling the existing data gaps related to the supply chains of batteries. It imposes due diligence obligations on large economic operators in the EU concerning their supply chains associated with four raw materials, i.e., cobalt, natural graphite, lithium and nickel, and the chemical compounds based on them (as listed in Annex X). EBR requires large companies to i) establish a risk management system and ii) implement battery due diligence policies and iii) share information and report it to the market surveillance authorities. The risk management system has to be able to increase the company's associated supply chain transparency through the provision of information on: i) country of origin and suppliers of raw materials; ii) all transactions along the supply chain, from the extraction to the last supplier; iii) implementation of the supply chain transparency system, which includes a traceability system and a chain of custody.

Given the heterogeneity of the current voluntary reporting frameworks and certification schemes, the EBR also aims to establish a minimal due diligence standard for the whole supply chain of the four raw materials ending on the EU battery market.

Traceability of batteries put on the EU market and the information provided via the battery digital passport can emerge as important tools for tracking the data and information throughout their supply chain. First, alongside technical and sustainability-related information, the battery passport can provide detailed data and information on the origin, actors, and all upstream market transactions up to the direct supplier of the EU operator. Second, collection, harmonization, and analysis of the data and information reported by companies to the market surveillance authorities can provide valuable company-level information.

8. Conclusions

The main objective of this paper is to examine the ways to improve the data and transparency of lithium-ion battery supply chains ending in the EU market.

First, we discuss the limitations of capturing real-world supply chains by trade statistics related to i) incomplete coverage of mineral-incorporating commodities along their supply chains, ii) insufficient information provided by country-of-origin reporting, and iii) inconsistent trade data reporting. These existing shortcomings demand identifying complementary data sources. Second, the role of voluntary initiatives and traceability in overcoming the existing data gaps over the battery supply chains is examined. Third, the recent EU Battery Regulation also aims to bridge the existing data gaps along the battery supply chain. The data to be collected from companies reporting on the origin, transactions, and entities involved in the trade flows of mineral-containing commodities used in batteries can also contribute to expanding the knowledge base on the raw material sources, market transactions, and upstream players. Traceability can play a significant role in this context. The EBR sets minimum requirements for the implementation of chain of custody and traceability systems, along with the obligation to document in detail the origin of raw materials, the actors involved in their processing, and the transactions throughout the supply chain. A key element in this framework is the battery digital passport, which consolidates and communicates geographical and transactional information about the materials contained in batteries. This tool can contribute not only to regulatory compliance but also to filling the existing information gaps in supply chain data, enabling better oversight by market authorities and obtaining higher supply chain transparency.

Abbreviations

CAHRAs	Conflict-affected and high-risks areas
CAM	Cathode active materials
CN	Combined Nomenclature
DG TRADE	Directorate General for Trade, European Commission
DRC	Democratic Republic of the Congo
EBR	EU Battery Regulation
ESG	Environmental, Social and Governance
GHG	Greenhouse gas
HS	Harmonized System
IRMA	The Initiative for Responsible Mining Assurance
LFP	Lithium-Iron-Phosphate
LMO	Lithium-Manganese-Oxide
NCA	Nickel-Cobalt-Aluminium
NMC	Nickel-Manganese-Cobalt
RFID	Radio Frequency Identification
RMI	Responsible Minerals Initiative
UNSD	United Nations Statistics Division

References

E. Alonso, A.S. Brioche, R.F. Schulte, L.M. Trimmer, J.-E. Kim, A.L: Gulley and D.G. Pineault (2025): World minerals outlook – Cobalt, gallium, helium, lithium, magnesium, palladium, platinum, and titanium through 2029. Ver. 1.1, March 14, 2025. U.S. Geological Survey Scientific Investigations Report 2025–5021, https://doi.org/10.3133/sir20255021

Amnesty International (2024): The State of the World's Human Rights. Index: POL 10/7200/2024, ISBN: 978-0-86210-509-9, London, April 2024.

R. Bleischwitz, M. Dittrich and Chiara Pierdicca (2012): Coltan from Central Africa. International trade and implications for any certification, Resources Policy, Volume 37, Issue 1, 2012, pages 19-29, ISSN 0301-4207. https://doi.org/10.1016/j.resourpol.2011.12.008

R. Capliez, C. Grekou, E. Hache and V. Mignon (2025): Lithium-Ion Batteries: Dynamic Mapping of the Value Chain and Perspectives. CEPII Working Paper, no. 48, Centre d'études prospectives et d'informations internationales, January 2025.

S. Carrara, S. Bobba, D. Blagoeva, P. Alves Dias, A. Cavalli, K. Georgitzikis, M. Grohol, A. Itul, T. Kuzov, C. Latunussa, L. Lyons, G. Malano, T. Maury, A. Prior Arce, J. Somers, T. Telsnig, C. Veeh, D. Wittmer, C. Black, D. Pennington, D. and M. Christou (2023): Supply chain analysis and material demand forecast in strategic technologies and sectors in the EU – A foresight study. Publications Office of the European Union, Luxembourg, 2023, doi:10.2760/386650, JRC132889.

C. R. Carter, D. S. Rogers and T. Y. Choi (2015): Toward the Theory of the Supply Chain.Journal of Supply Chain Management, 29 January 2015, https://doi.org/10.1111/jscm.12073

P. Cotterlaz and V. Vicard (2024): Why Origin Matters in Trade Data. CEPII Working Paper, Centre d'études prospectives et d'informations internationales, December 2023.

R. Deberdt and P. Le Billon (2021): Conflict minerals and battery materials supply chains: A mapping review of responsible sourcing initiatives. The Extractive Industries and Society, Volume 8, Issue 4, 2021, 100935, ISSN 2214-790X, https://doi.org/10.1016/j.exis.2021.100935.

R. Deberdt and P. Le Billon (2022): The Green Transition in Context – Cobalt Responsible Sourcing for Battery Manufacturing. Society & Natural Resources, 35(7), 784–803. https://doi.org/10.1080/08941920.2022.2049410.

A.M. Desaulty, D. Monfort Climent, G. Lefebvre, A. Cristiano-Tassi, D. Peralta, S. Perret, A. Urban and C. Guerrot, (2022): Tracing the origin of lithium in Li-ion batteries using lithium isotopes. Nature Communications, 13(1), 4172. https://doi.org/10.1038/s41467-022-31850-y

V. Dietrich and F. Melcher (2022): Mineral Raw Material Supply Chain Transparency and Traceability: Does Provenance Matter in the Supply Chain? BHM Berg- Und Hüttenmännische Monatshefte, 167(12), 594–597. https://doi.org/10.1007/s00501-022-01274-8

L. Donnelly, Q. Dehaine, S. Ghosh, I. Corfe, R. Dunn and D. Pop (2023): A Review of Artificial Fingerprinting and 3D Printing for the Potential Tracking of Minerals in Complex Supply Chains. MaDiTraCe project, Deliverable D2.1, December 2023.

Erdmann, M., & Franken, G. (2022): Sustainability Standard Systems for Mineral Resources: A comparative Overview – 2022. https://www.bgr.bund.de/DE/Themen/Min_rohstoffe/Downloads/studie_sustainability_standard_systems_2022.pdf?__blob=publicationFile&v=7

European Commission (2025): Indicative, non-exhaustive list of conflict-affected and high-risks areas under Regulation (EU) 2017/821. DG TRADE, Latest update in March 2025. https://www.cahraslist.net/cahras

European Parliament and The European Council (2023): Regulation (EU) 2023/1542 of The European Parliament and of The Council of 12 July 2023 concerning batteries and waste batteries, amending Directive 2008/98/EC and Regulation (EU) 2019/1020 and repealing Directive 2006/66/EC. Official Journal of the European Union, 28 July 2023.

Eurostat (2023): European business statistics compilers' manual for international trade in goods statistics – detailed data. Luxembourg: Publications Office of the European Union.

P. Fernández Muñoz, M. Tost, V. Dietrich, F. Melcher and W. Kloppmann (2024): Integration von Technologien für mehr Transparenz in Lieferketten. BHM Berg- und Hüttenmännische Monatshefte, 169(4), 192–196. https://doi.org/10.1007/s00501-024-01448-6

P. Fernández Muñoz, M. Tost, M. Eckl, M. Mironovich, C. Nouvel, S. Cunha, G. Aguilar-Hernandez, T. Nowaz (2024a): State of Play and SWOT Analysis. Current interventions for due diligence in the material supply chain. Deliverable D1.3, MaDiTraCe project, https://www.maditrace.eu

P. Fernández Muñoz, M. Tost, V. Dietrich, F. Melcher and W. Kloppmann (2024b): Integration von Technologien für mehr Transparenz in Lieferketten. BHM Berg- und Hüttenmännische Monatshefte, 169(4), 192–196. https://doi.org/10.1007/s00501-024-01448-6

T.A. Gardner, M. Benzie, J. Börner, E. Dawkins, S. Fick, R. Garrett, J. Godar, A. Grimard, S. Lake, R.K. Larsen, N. Mardas, C.L. McDermott, P. Meyfroidt, M. Osbeck, M. Persson, T. Sembres, C. Suavet, B. Strassburg, A. Trevisan, C. West, P. Wolvekamp (2019): Transparency and sustainability in global commodity supply chains. World Development,Volume 121, 2019, Pages 163-177, ISSN 0305-750X, https://doi.org/10.1016/j.worlddev.2018.05.025.

A. González and E. de Haan (2020): The battery paradox. How the electric vehicle boom is draining communities and the planet. The Centre for Research on Multinational Corporations (SOMO), Amsterdam, December 2020.

M. Gustafsson, A. Schilling-Vacaflor and A. Lenschow (2023): The politics of supply chain regulations: Towards foreign corporate accountability in the area of human rights and the environment? Regulation & Governance, 17(4), 853–869. https://doi.org/10.1111/rego.12526

S. Hansen, T. Rüther, M. Mennenga, C. Helbig, G. Ohnemüller, F. Vysoudil, C. Wolf, B. Rosemann, S. Pavón, A. Michaelis, T. Vietor, F. Döpper, C. Herrmann and M. A. Danzer (2024): A structured approach for the compliance analysis of battery systems with regard to the new EU Battery Regulation. Resources, Conservation and Recycling Volume 209, October 2024, 107752.

M. Hiete, P. C. Sauer, S. Drempetic and R. Tröster (2019): The role of voluntary sustainability standards in governing the supply of mineral raw materials. GAIA – Ecological Perspectives for Science and Society, Volume 28, Supplement 1, 2019, pp. 218-225(8), DOI: https://doi.org/10.14512/gaia.28.S1.8

H. Hofmann, M.C. Schleper and C. Blome (2018): Conflict minerals and supply chain due diligence: an exploratory study of multi-tier supply chains. Journal of Business Ethics, 147(1), 115-141. https://doi.org/10.1007/s10551-015-2963-z

C.A. Johnson and J. Khosravani (2024): Greening the global battery chain? Critical reflections on the EU's 2023 battery regulations. The Extractive Industries and Society, Volume 18, 101467, https://doi.org/10.1016/j.exis.2024.101467

I. Kapoor, W. Pratt-Rogers and M. M. Kahraman (2022): The problem of conflict minerals: A review of current approaches and a web 3.0 inspired road ahead. Resources Policy, 79, 103064. https://doi.org/10.1016/j.resourpol.2022.103064

J. F. Kros, Y. Liao, J. F. Kirchoff, and J. E. Zemanek Jr. (2019): Traceability in the Supply Chain. International Journal of Applied Logistics, 9(1), 1–22. https://doi.org/10.4018/IJAL.2019010101

A. Y. Ku, E. Alonso, R. Eggert, T. Graedel, K. Habib, A. Hool, T. Muta, D. Schrijvers, L. Tercero, T. Vakhitova and C. Veeh (2024): Grand challenges in anticipating and responding to critical materials supply risks. Joule 8, 1208–1223, May 15, 2024.

D. Laurance, D. Quentin, G. Shristi, C. Ian, D. Robert, and P. Dan (2024): A Review of Artificial Fingerprinting and 3D Printing for the Potential Tracking of Minerals in Complex Supply Chains. MaDiTraCe project. https://maditrace.eu/results

L. Mancini, N. A. Eslava, M. Traverso and F. Mathieux (2020): Responsible and sustainable sourcing of battery raw materials. EUR 30174 EN, Publications Office of the European Union, Luxembourg, 2020, ISBN 978-92-76-17950-4, doi:10.2760/562951, JRC120422.

N. B. Manjong, S. Marinova, V. Bach, O. S. Burheim, M. Finkbeiner and A. H. Strømman (2024): Approaching battery raw material sourcing through a material criticality lens. Sustainable Production and Consumption, Volume 49, September 2024, pages 289-303.

V. Markhonko (2014): Asymmetries in official international trade statistics and analysis of Globalization. Discussion Paper, International Conference on the Measurement of International Trade and Economic Globalization. Aguascalientes, Mexico, 29 Septembr – 1 October 2014.

McKinsey & Company (2023): Battery 2030: Resilient, sustainable, and circular. January 2023.

McKinsey & Company (2024a): The battery cell component opportunity in Europe and North America, April 2024.

McKinsey & Company (2024b): Toward security in sustainable battery raw material supply, December 2024.

F. Melcher, M. Sitnikova, T. Graupner, N. Martin, T. Oberthür, F. Henjes-Kunst, H.-E. Gäbler, A. Gerdes, H. Brätz, D. W. Davis, and S. Dewaele (2008): Fingerprinting of conflict minerals: columbite-tantalite ("coltan") ores. SGA News 23, 1–13.

S. Mitikj and S. V. Kaushik (2024): Bridging the Gap in Trade Reporting. Insights from the Discrepancy Index. World Bank Group, Development Economics, Development Data Group, June 2024.

G. Mugurusi and E. Ahishakiye (2022): Blockchain technology needs for sustainable mineral supply chains: A framework for responsible sourcing of Cobalt. Procedia Computer Science, 2002, 638–647. https://doi.org/10.1016/j.procs.2022.01.262

D. I. Murguía and A. E. Bastida (2024): The elephant in the mine: Why voluntary sustainability standards are insufficient to ensure responsible mining. The Extractive Industries and Society, 19, 101485. https://doi.org/10.1016/j.exis.2024.101485

OECD. (2019): An introduction to the OECD Due Diligence Guidance for Responsible Mineral Supply Chains for Upstream Actor. https://mneguidelines.oecd.org/An-introduction-to-the-OECD-Due-Diligence-Guidance-for-upstream-actors.pdf

OECD (2023), OECD Guidelines for Multinational Enterprises on Responsible Business Conduct, OECD Publishing, Paris, https://doi.org/10.1787/81f92357-en.

OECD & IEA (2025): The Role of Traceability in Critical Mineral Supply Chains, International Energy Agency, Paris, February 2025, Licence: CC BY 4.0.

M. Onifade, J. A. Adebisi and T. Zvarivadza (2024): Recent advances in blockchain technology: Prospects, applications and constraints in the minerals industry. International Journal of Mining, Reclamation and Environment, 1–37. https://doi.org/10.1080/17480930.2024.2319453

W. Powell, M. Foth, S. Cao and V. Natanelov (2022): Garbage in garbage out: The precarious link between IoT and blockchain in food supply chains. Journal of Industrial Information Integration, 25, 100261. https://doi.org/10.1016/j.jii.2021.100261

L. Rüttinger and G. Corder (2020): KlimRess – Impacts of climate change on mining, related environmental risks and raw material supply. https://www.umweltbundesamt.de/sites/default/files/medien/479/publikationen/texte_106-2020_klimress_ case_study_south_africa.pdf

U. M. Saka, S. Duzgun and M. D. Bazilian (2024): Analysis of world trade data with machine learning to enhance policies of mineral supply chain transparency. Resources Policy, Volume 89, 104671, https://doi.org/10.1016/j.resourpol.2024.104671

B. M. Severiano, S. A. Northey and D. Giurco (2024): Drivers and barriers of voluntary sustainability initiatives in mining raw materials for batteries. The Extractive Industries and Society, Volume 20, 101552, https://doi.org/10.1016/j.exis.2024.101552

S&P Global (2024): Deep Dive: Electric vehicles and batteries, February 21, 2024.

F. Tian (2016): An agri-food supply chain traceability system for China based on RFID & blockchain technology. 2016 13th International Conference on Service Systems and Service Management (ICSSSM), 1–6. https://doi.org/10.1109/ICSSSM.2016.7538424

United Nations Department of Economic and Social Affairs (1998): International Merchandise Trade Statistics: Concepts and Definitions. Studies in Methods Series M, No.52, Rev.2, United Nations, New York, 1998.

United Nations (2011): Guiding Principles on Business and Human Rights. United Nations Human Rights, Office of The High Commissioner.

United Nations Security Council (2024): Midterm report of the Group of Experts on the Democratic Republic of the Congo. S/2024/969, 27 December 2024.

USGS (2025), Lithium Statistics and Information 2025, https://www.usgs.gov/centers/national-minerals-information-center/lithium-statistics-and-information

C. Vallès, M. (2024): Due Diligence and Mineral Supply Chain Mechanisms. In: Mineral Exploitation, Violence and International Law. Global Issues. Palgrave Macmillan, Cham. https://doi.org/10.1007/978-3-031-59439-7_4

W. J.V. Vermeulen (2013): Self-Governance for Sustainable Global Supply Chains: Can it Deliver the Impacts Needed? Business Strategy and the Environment, 24(2), July 2013, DOI: 10.1002/bse.1804

World Bank, World Integrated Trade Solution, https://wits.worldbank.org/

World Resources Institute. Climate Watch, https://www.climatewatchdata.org/

Susanne Roßkogler, Thomas Nigl

Bewertungsmethoden von digitalen Nachhaltigkeitstechnologien

Eine ressourcenseitige Betrachtung

Zusammenfassung: Nachhaltigkeit im industriellen Umfeld ist spätestens seit dem Green Deal weitestgehend bekannt. Mit der Twin Transition und neuen digitalen Technologien kommen weitere Aspekte hinzu. Erwartet wird von der Implementierung der neuen Technologien, dass sie zur Zielerreichung des Green Deals und auch des Clean Industrial Deals maßgeblich beitragen. Die hier vorliegende Arbeit behandelt die Fragestellung, wie die Auswirkungen dieser Technologien auf die Zielerreichung generell aber auch das Auftreten von *Trade-offs* bewertet werden soll. Hierzu wurden bisherige Methoden und neue Ansätze näher beleuchtet und ein Vorschlag zur Weiterentwicklung ausgearbeitet.

Keywords: Zero resource loss, Digital platforms, Key performance indicators.

1. Einleitung

Im Fokus des Projektes ZERO3 ist die Entwicklung einer *Sustainability Monitoring Platform* (kurz SMP). Die Zielsetzung des Projektes umfasst drei wichtige Aspekte der *Green and Digital Transformation* wie auch des Konzeptes Industrie 5.0 (Berndt, 2024). Unter dem Begriff ZERO3 werden drei Losses werden im Projekt als konkrete Potentiale adressiert: Ressourcen, Daten und Datennutzung und Human-Potential. Ziel ist es Ressourcen, Energie wie auch Rohstoffe, zu sparen, Datenlücken zu schließen und vorhandene Daten effizient zu nutzen und die Mitarbeiter:innen und ihr Wissen und Fähigkeiten in den Unternehmen in den Fokus zu stellen. Aufbauend auf dieser Plattform soll eine KI-basierte Engine von Projektpartnern entwickelt werden, welche unternehmensindividuelle ZERO3-Potentiale identifiziert und auf dessen Basis Verbesserungslösungen in Form von Basistechnologien zur Umsetzung empfiehlt. Um die entsprechende Auswirkung der *SMP* zu beurteilen braucht es in der Evaluation eine neue Herangehensweise. Die Aufgabe der Autorin der hier vorliegenden Arbeit ist es die Auswirkung im Bereich *Re-*

source Loss zu bewerten. *Trade-offs* im Bereich der Industrien im Spannungsfeld, Umwelt, Ressourcen und Wirtschaft finden ebenso noch zu wenig Beachtung. Die bisherigen Bewertungsmethoden sind auch noch nicht ausreichend auf neue digitale Technologien ausgelegt und bedürfen einer entsprechenden Neuentwicklung und Definition (Samuel et al. 2022).

1.1. Einfluss der Industrie auf die Umwelt

Die Auswirkungen des vom Menschen verursachten Klimawandels sind in jüngster Zeit verstärkt zu spüren. So haben die Extremwetterereignisse zwischen 1980 und 2020 am europäischen Kontinent, genauer in allen Mitgliedstaaten des Europäischen Wirtschaftsraumes (EWR), wirtschaftliche Schäden in Höhe von 450 – 520 Milliarden Euro (in Euro Wert 2020) verursacht. Meteorologische und hydrologische Ereignisse wie Stürme und Fluten waren für 34 – 44 Prozent der verursachten Schäden verantwortlich, während Hitzewellen zum Beispiel rund 14% verursachten (European Environment Agency, o. D.). Aufgrund technologischer Entwicklungen sind die Treibhausgasemissionen in den letzten 30 Jahren zwar kontinuierlich um in Summe rund 27% gesunken (Directorate General for Communication 2024), eine Senkung der Emissionen ist dennoch weiterhin notwendig und erstrebenswert. Die Industrie ist für rund 20% der CO_{2eq} verantwortlich (Europäisches Parlament, 2024). Eine Transformation hin zu einer Emissionsarmen beziehungsweise Emissionsfreien Industrie, sollte ohne negative Beeinträchtigung der Wirtschaftsleistung erfolgen.

1.2. Beitrag der Industrie zum Wohlstand in der EU

Rund 25% des BIP stammen in Europa aus dem industriellen Sektor (European Central Bank 2022) und über 32 Millionen Arbeitsplätze sind dem Bereich der erzeugenden Industrie zugeordnet (CEDEFOP 2024). Im Bereich der hochwertigen Fertigung gab es in den letzten 14 Jahren ein starkes Wachstum (European Commission o. D). Gut bezahlte Arbeitsplätze der Industrie sichern somit auch den Binnenmarkt. Der Wohlstand auf dem Kontinent ist somit in großen Teilen mit der Industrie verbunden. Die wirtschaftlichen Probleme Europas treten aktuell immer deutlicher Zutage. So zeigen aktuelle Daten zur Industrieproduktion einen Rückgang von 0,2% in der EU zwischen 08/2023 und 08/2024 (Statista 2025). Obwohl hier noch valide Evidenz fehlt, warnen aktuelle Studien aufgrund der Energieabhängigkeit gar vor einer Deindustrialisierung des Kontinentes. (Wandel et al. 2023b).

1.3. Ressourcensituation in Europa

Ein weiterer wichtiger Punkt ist die Frage der Ressourcensicherheit angesichts immer fragilerer Lieferketten. Europas Industrie weist im Bereich von Lieferproblemen eine besonders schlechte Resilienz auf, wie sich während der Covid-19-Pandemie zeigte (Jomthanchai et al. 2021). Generell ist eine unsichere Ressourcenlage, vor allem im Bereich wichtiger Rohstoffe am Europäischen Kontinent zu verzeichnen, welche auch steigende Preise zur Folge hat. Verschiedene Methoden der Ressourcenschonung beziehungsweise des möglichst effizienten Ressourceneinsatzes werden untersucht (Chojnacka et al. 2022).

1.4. Industrie- und Umweltpläne der EU

Innerhalb der Europäischen Union, wie auch in Österreich, gab es in den vergangenen Jahren eine Reihe an Maßnahmen die zum Ziel hatten, unsere Wirtschaft in Richtung Nachhaltigkeit zu transformieren. Dies bedarf zum einen neuen Technologien wie auch einige Änderungen in unserem Wirtschaftsdenken. Im Folgenden werden nur einige der wichtigsten Strategien vorgestellt die auch von dem Projekt ZERO3 adressiert werden.

Twin Transition

Die Europäische Union sieht in der Digitalisierung einen der Hauptantreiber zum Grünen Wandel der Wirtschaft. 2022 wurde hierzu die sogenannte *Twin Transition* vorgestellt. Ein gemeinsamer Übergang zu einer digitalen und grünen Wirtschaft. Die *Twin Transition* sieht Technologien wie *Distributed Ledger*-Technologien wie *Blockchain*, IoT, Robotik, digitale Zwillinge und künstliche Intelligenz, sowie noch zu entwickelnde, neue Technologien als Treiber eines erfolgreichen Übergangs zu einer kreislauforientierten und wettbewerbsfähigen nachhaltigen Wirtschaft die die Langlebigkeit von Produkten steigert und einen ganzen Lebenszyklus mit dem Ziel der Effizienzsteigerung und Verlängerung überwacht. Allerdings kommt die Studie auch zum Schluss das gerade diese Technologien mitunter Energie- und Rohstoffintensiv sind und somit einen hohen (Umwelt-) Fußabdruck haben. Noch gibt es hier keinen einheitlichen Überwachungsrahmen, der Umweltwirkungen und auch eventuelle *Trade-offs* wie Reboundeffekte bewertet (Muench et al. 2022).

Industrie 5.0

Während die vierte industrielle Revolution am Beginn der 2010er Jahre von der Deutschen Bundesregierung angekündigt wurde, definierte die fünfte industrielle Revolution die Europäische Union. I4.0 kennzeichnet sich weitestgehend durch disruptive Technologien, wie das Internet der Dinge (*Internet of Things*, IoT), cyber-physikalische Systeme, *Big Data* oder künstliche Intelligenz und deren Anwendung im industriellen Bereich. Industrie 5.0 definiert sich durch einen Paradigmenwechsel zu einem menschenzentrierten und auf Kollaboration hin ausgerichteten Ansatz. Ressourceneffizienz ist einer der Hauptaspekte der I5.0. Während die I4.0 technologiegetrieben ist, zeichnet sich die I5.0 durch einen systemischen Ansatz aus, der den Schwerpunkt auf den menschlichen Anwender der Technologien legt. Die Senkung des Energieverbrauchs, Abfallaufkommens und der Emissionen ist ein Kernmerkmal der I5.0 (Vogel-Heuser et al. 2023). Die Steigerung der Resilienz gilt als weitere Säule der I5.0 (Zizic et al. 2022). Während die Begrifflichkeiten rund um Industrie 4.0 und Industrie 5.0 diskutiert werden, sollte dies für die Umsetzung des Konzeptes kein Hindernis darstellen.

Clean Industrial Deal

Im Frühjahr 2025 veröffentlichte die Europäische Union den Clean Industrial Deal mit dem Ziel die Wettbewerbsfähigkeit und Klimaneutralität noch stärker in den Mittelpunkt ihrer Handlungen zu stellen. Der Ausstieg aus einer von fossilen Rohstoffen abhängigen Wirtschaftsweise soll als Wachstumsmotor genutzt werden. Leistbare Energie für die Industrie soll durch die Umsetzung ebenso gesichert werden, wie die Produktnachfrage aus nachhaltiger Produktionsweise. Kreislauffähigkeit steht hier einmal mehr im Zentrum des Handelns (European Commission 2025).

2. Methode

Aus dem ZERO3-Projekt und der eingangs beschrieben Situation ergeben sich folgende Forschungsfragen für die hier vorliegende Arbeit:

- Welche Bewertungskriterien müssen bei ressourcenseitiger Betrachtung von *Twin Transition*-Kriterien angewendet werden?
- Welche Methodiken eignen sich und wie sind gängige Methoden anzupassen?
- Welche Rolle spielen *Trade-offs*?

Um eine geeignete Bewertungsmethodik zu finden wurde eine umfassende Literaturrecherche durchgeführt. Hierfür wurden Publikationen ab 2010 nach Bewertungsmethoden die im Kontext mit produzierenden Betrieben und Nachhaltigkeit stehen durchsucht. Des Weiteren wurden auch Bewertungsmethoden für neue digitale Technologien die als nachhaltigkeitsfördernd identifiziert werden gesucht. Die gefunden Methoden wurden anhand der bisherigen Erkenntnisse im Projekt beurteilt und auf Lücken in der Anwendbarkeit hin untersucht.

3. Ergebnisse

Eine erfolgreiche Methode zur Bewertung von Nachhaltigkeitseffekten mit einer großen Bandbreite an Wirkungskategorien ist *Life Cycle Assessment* nach ISO 14040. Um eine größere Bandbreite an wichtigen Anwendungsaspekten, vor allem auch in der Industrie abzudecken, wird sie oft in Kombination mit anderen Methoden angewandt, wie zum Beispiel der techno-ökonomischen Analyse (Mahmud et al. 2021). In der Literatur finden sich ebenso neue, kombinierte Umweltanalysemodelle die Kombinationen mit Energiesystemmodellen und Ökobilanzen vorschlagen um umfassend die Auswirkungen der *Twin Transition* abzubilden (Junne et al. 2020).

Forschungsfrage zwei adressiert das verschiedene Aspekte, um Umsetzungsentscheidungen zu treffen, von diversen Analysemodellen abgedeckt werden müssen, wie der multikriteriellen Analyse (Opon & Henry 2020). Nachhaltigkeits- und Resilienzindikatoren sind in Kombination zur Bewertung von Bedeutung (Grafkos et al. 2016) – ebenso im sozio-technischen Bereich (van Sluisveld et al. 2018).

Trade-offs zeigen sich zum einen im ökonomischen Bereich bei der Umsetzung der *Twin Transition* und den Ambitionen die Zwillingstransformation beiden Hauptmerkmalen entsprechend synchron umzusetzen und auch negative Auswirkungen für eine reale Bewertung in Betracht gezogen werden müssen (Wu et al. 2025). Neben den ökonomischen Aspekten treten in der Analyse zu den Zielkonflikten zu beachtende *Lock-in-Effekte* hervor (Vermeulen & Pyka 2020).

4. Diskussion

Nachhaltige Produktion bedeutet auch die Produktlebensdauer zu verlängern, die Ausschussraten zu senken und den gesamten Ressourceneinsatz, Rohstoffe wie auch Energie, zu optimieren (Worrell et al. 2016). Dies ist eine der Hauptaufgaben der SMP. Um aber eine realistische Bewertung der Umwelt und Resilienz Wirkung abzugeben, bedarf es einer Überarbeitung der bisherigen Bewertungsrahmen. Die bislang verwendeten Bewertungsmethoden haben den Fokus auf eine Technologie und die Auswirkungen ab dem Einsetzen der Technologie. Neue Ansätze analysieren bereits Potentiale im Planungsbereich unter verschiedenen Bewertungspunkten (Kharb et al. 2024). Die Kriterien, welche sich unter anderem rund um das Projekt herauskristallisierten, sind aber breiter gefasst. Es zeigt sich das eine reine Nachhaltigkeitsbetrachtung ohne die Inkludierung weiterer Parameter, ökonomischer und ökologischer Art, nicht den neuen Technologien gerecht wird. Die verbrauchten Ressourcen durch Technologien die der *Twin Transition* zugeordnet werden, sind für eine ganzheitliche Betrachtung notwendig (Munoz de Bustillo Llorente 2024).

5. Ausblick

Die Autoren des Beitrages sehen es als notwendig an, einen erweiterten Bewertungsrahmen zu entwerfen. Dieser soll neben den direkten Umweltauswirkungen von KI getriebenen Analyse- und Nachhaltigkeitstools, ihren positiven Ressourcen- und Umweltbeitrag, im konkreten Anwendungsfall bei Umsetzung der Basistechnologien, ebenso inkludieren, wie auch die Auswirkungen weiterer an der Umsetzung beteiligter Technologien. Um einen entsprechenden Rahmen zu erstellen und diesen zu validieren sind im nächsten Schritt *real case* Anwendungen geplant. Hierzu sollen unter anderem Industriepartner im Projekt zur Anwendung befragt werden und nach einer Überarbeitung diesen auch durchführen. Eine Ausarbeitung des Ressourcenverbrauchs in der Herstellung, Betreibung der Plattform wird ebenso angestrebt. Da der Nutzer die Möglichkeit haben soll, Szenarien der Technologieumsetzung durchzuspielen, dadurch aber noch keine Umsetzung erfolgt, sollen entsprechende Allokationsmodelle entwickelt werden. Ebenso tragen allerdings die Basistechnologien, bei entsprechendem Ressourcenverbrauch, zur Ressourceneffizienz des Unternehmens bei, auch dies muss künftig berücksichtigt werden. Des Weiteren sollte, von Projektpartnern jegliche Bewertung an die weiteren zwei ZEROs, *Human Potential Loss* und *Data Gap* im Projekt angepasst werden, damit eine valide Aussage über die Effekte der *Sustainability Monitoring Platform* getätigt werden können. Um eine möglichst breite Anwendung sicherzustellen gilt es verschiedene Bereiche der Industrie abzudecken, hierzu ist eine Erhebung unumgänglich. Dazu wäre es notwendig möglichst viele Bereiche der Industrie zu clustern um entsprechende Lücken aufzudecken und zu beheben.

Abkürzungsverzeichnis

CO_2eq	CO_2-Äquivalente
IoT	Internet of things
I4.0	Vierte industrielle Revolution
I5.0	Fünfte industrielle Revolution
SMP	Sustainability Monitoring Platform

Literatur

Berndt, R. (2024): A Platform Architecture for Data- and AI-supported human-centred Zero Defect Manufacturing for Sustainable Production. InCom 2024, Vienna, Austria.

CEDEFOP (2024): Sector employment by occupations. URL: https://www.cedefop.europa.eu/en /tools/skills-intelligence/sector-employment-occupations?year=2022&country=EU#1.

Chojnacka K., Skrzypczak, D., Szopa, D., Izydorczyk, G., Moustakas, K., Witek-Krowiak, A. (2022): Management of biological sewage sludge: Fertilizer nitrogen recovery as the solution to fertilizer crisis. Journal Of Environmental Management, Bd. 326, S. 116602, DOI: 10.1016/ j.jenvman.2022.116602.

Directorate General for Communication (2024): Greenhouse gas emissions by country and sector, in: European Parliament, URL: https://www.europarl.europa.eu/pdfs/news/expert/ 2018/3/story/20180301STO98928/20180301STO98928_en.pdf.

European Central Bank (2022): Structure of the euro area economy, European Central Bank, URL: https://www.ecb.europa.eu/mopo/eaec/html/index.en.html.

European Commission (o. D.): Strategic Insights into the EU's Advanced Manufacturing Industry Internal Market, Industry, Entrepreneurship And SMEs, URL: https://single-market-economy.ec.europa.eu/industry/advanced-manufacturing/strategic-insights-eus-advanced-manufacturing-industry_en.

European Commission (2025): Clean Industrial Deal. URL: https://commission.europa.eu/top ics/eu-competitiveness/clean-industrial-deal_en.

European Environment Agency (o. D.): Economic losses and fatalities from weather- and climate-related events in Europe. URL: https://www.eea.europa.eu/publications/economic-losses-and-fatalities-from/economic-losses-and-fatalities-from.

Grafkos, S., Enseñado, E.M., Flamos, A. (2016): Developing an integrated sustainability and resilience framework of indicators for the assessment of low-carbon energy technologies at the local level, in: International Journal Of Sustainable Energy, Bd. 36, Nr. 10, S. 945–971, DOI: 10.1080/14786451.2015.1130709.

Junne, T., Simon, S., Buchgeister, J., Saiger, M., Baumann, M., Haase, M., Wulf, C., Naegler, T. (2020): Environmental Sustainability Assessment of Multi-Sectoral Energy Transformation Pathways: Methodological Approach and Case Study for Germany. Sustainability, Bd. 12, Nr. 19, S. 8225, DOI:10.3390/su12198225.

Jomthanachai, S., Wong, W., Soh, K., Lim, C. (2021): A global trade supply chain vulnerability in COVID-19 pandemic: An assessment metric of risk and resilience-based efficiency of CoDEA method. Research in Transportation Economics, 93, 101166, DOI: 10.1016/j.retrec.2021.101166.

Kharb, R., Shri, C., Saini, N., Kumar, D. (2024): Strategies for environmental sustainability: analyzing the green and digital transitions, in: Sustainability Accounting Management And Policy Journal, DOI:10.1108/sampj-04-2024-0328.

Mahmud, R., Moniruzzaman Sheikh, M., High, K., Carbajales-Dale M. (2021): Integration of techno-economic analysis and life cycle assessment for sustainable process design – A review. Journal Of Cleaner Production, Bd. 317, S. 128247, DOI: 10.1016/j.jclepro.2021.128247.

Muench, S., Stoermer, E., Jensen, K., Asikainen, T., Salvi, M. and Scapolo, F. (2022): Towards a green and digital future. JRC129319, DOI:10.2760/977331.

Munoz de Bustillo Llorente, R. (2024): A critical review of the digital and green twin transitions: Implications, synergies and trade-offs. JRC 140036. https://www.econstor.eu/handle/10419/311129.

Opon, J., Henry, M. (2020): A multicriteria analytical framework for sustainability evaluation under methodological uncertainties in: Environmental Impact Assessment Review, Bd. 83, S. 106403, DOI: 10.1016/j.eiar.2020.106403.

Samuel, G., Lucivero, F., Somavilla, L. (2022): The Environmental Sustainability of Digital Technologies: Stakeholder Practices and Perspectives. Sustainability, Bd. 14, Nr. 7, S. 3791, DOI: 10.3390/su14073791.

Statista (2025): Veränderung der Industrieproduktion in der EU nach Monaten bis Dezember 2024, URL: https://de.statista.com/statistik/daten/studie/5621/umfrage/veraenderungen-der-industrieproduktion-in-der-europaeischen-union/.

van Sluisveld, M.A.E., Hof, A.F., Carrara, S., Geels, F.W., Nilsson, M., Rogge, K., Turnheim, B., van Vuuren, D.P. (2018): Aligning integrated assessment modelling with socio-technical transition insights: An application to low-carbon energy scenario analysis in Europe, in: Technological Forecasting And Social Change, Bd. 151, S. 119177, DOI: 10.1016/j.techfore.2017.10.024.

Vermeulen, B., Pyka, A. (2024): The Twin Digital and Green Transition: Paradigm Shift or Tech Fix? Journal of Innovation Economics & Management, 45(3), 1-29. URL: https://shs.cairn.info/journal-of-innovation-economics-2024-3-page-1?lang=en.

Vogel-Heuser, B., Bengler, K. (2023b): Von Industrie 4.0 zu Industrie 5.0 – Idee, Konzept und Wahrnehmung, in: HMD Praxis der Wirtschaftsinformatik, Bd. 60, Nr. 6, S. 1124–1142, DOI:10.1365/s40702-023-01002-x.

Wandel, J., Bielig, A., Kamińska, K. (2023b): Economic Policy in an Unstable Environment: Dilemmas and Challenges: Polish and German Perspectives.

Worrell, E., Allwood, J., Gutowski, T. (2016): The Role of Material Efficiency in Environmental Stewardship, in: Annual Review Of Environment And Resources, Bd. 41, Nr. 1, S. 575–598, DOI: 10.1146/annurev-environ-110615-085737.

Wu, Y., Ivashkovskaya, I., Besstremyannaya, G., Liu, C. (2025): Unlocking Green Innovation Potential Amidst Digital Transformation Challenges – The Evidence from ESG Transformation in China. Sustainability, DOI: 10.3390/su17010309.

Zizic, M.C., Mladineo, M, Gjeldum, N., Celent, L. (2022): From Industry 4.0 towards Industry 5.0: A Review and Analysis of Paradigm Shift for the People, Organization and Technology. Energies, Bd. 15, Nr. 14, S. 5221, DOI:10.3390/en15145221.

Autorenverzeichnis

Baumüller Josef, Dr.

TU Wien | Institut für Managementwissenschaften

Bouvier-Schwarz Therese, Mag. MEng.

Montanuniversität Leoben | Lehrstuhl für Abfallverwertung und Abfallwirtschaft

Dantine Daniel, Mag.

Decision Advisory Group

Feichtinger Gerald, Mag. Dr.

Montanuniversität Leoben | Lehrstuhl für Wirtschafts- und Betriebswissenschaften

Freiseisen Bernhard, Mag. Dr.

Fronius International

Fernández Paulina, Mag.

Montanuniversität Leoben | Lehrstuhl für Bergbau und Bergbauwirtschaft

Fölser Anna, Dipl.-Ing.

Fronius International

Hofellner Mario, Dipl.-Ing.

Montanuniversität Leoben | Lehrstuhl für Industrielogistik

Katterbauer Gerald

Infranorm Technologies GmbH

Koller David, BSc

Montanuniversität Leoben | Lehrstuhl für Wirtschafts- und Betriebswissenschaften

Kopeinig Clara, Dipl.-Ing.

Montanuniversität Leoben | Lehrstuhl für Wirtschafts- und Betriebswissenschaften

Kopeinig Jacob, Dipl.-Ing.

Montanuniversität Leoben | Lehrstuhl für Industrielogistik

Kriechbaum Kevin Anton

Montanuniversität Leoben | Lehrstuhl für Industrielogistik

Kuballa Patrick, PhD

Infranorm Technologies GmbH

Meltzer Andreas, MSc

Decision Advisory Group

Nigl Thomas, Dipl.-Ing. Dr.

Montanuniversität Leoben | Lehrstuhl für Abfallverwertung und Abfallwirtschaft

Nita Viroel, Dr.

Montanuniversität Leoben | Lehrstuhl für Bergbau und Bergbauwirtschaft

Nusser Heinz, Mag.

Decision Advisory Group

Popowicz Martin, MSc

Universität Graz | Institut für Umweltwissenschaften

Posch Wolfgang, Univ.-Prof. Dipl.-Ing. Dr.

Montanuniversität Leoben | Lehrstuhl für Wirtschafts- und Betriebswissenschaften

Roßkogler Susanne, MSc

Montanuniversität Leoben | Lehrstuhl für Abfallverwertung und Abfallwirtschaft

Schönberg Martin, Mag. M.Sc. MA

VUM Verfahren Umwelt Management GmbH

Schönmayr David, PhD

Fronius International

Schwaiger Walter S. A., Univ.-Prof. Mag. Dr.

TU Wien | Institut für Managementwissenschaften

Tost Michael, Univ.-Prof. Dipl.-Ing. Dr.

Montanuniversität Leoben | Lehrstuhl für Bergbau und Bergbauwirtschaft

Zehetner Andreas

Infranorm Technologies GmbH

Zsifkovits Helmut, Univ.-Prof. Mag. Dr.

Montanuniversität Leoben | Lehrstuhl für Industrielogistik

Index